A SYLLABUS

DECODING

C000131587

Speech in Action
Birmingham, UK

www.speechinaction.com

© Speech in Action 2018

This publication is copyright. Subject to statutory exception
and to the provision of relevant collective licensing agreements,
no reproduction of any part may take place without the written
permission of Speech in Action.

Edited by Sheila Thorn, The Listening Business

Page design and layout by Rosamund Saunders
Printed on demand by Amazon
Cover design by Jane Bromham

First published 2018, 2nd printing June 2018
ISBN 978-0-9543447-7-1

A *Streaming Speech* publication from Speech in Action

While every attempt has been made to do so, it has not always been possible to identify
the sources of all the recordings used, or to contact the rights holders. If any omissions
are brought to our notice, we will be happy to include appropriate acknowledgements in
future editions.

Speech in Action has no responsibility for the continued existence or accuracy of external
websites referred to in this publication. Speech in Action does not guarantee that any
content on such websites will continue to exist, or remain appropriate.

A SYLLABUS FOR LISTENING
DECODING

RICHARD CAULDWELL

A Streaming Speech publication from
Speech in Action

Contents

Part 4 Education, tools and activities **139**

Acknowledgments

Dedicated to the memory of the late David Brazil – scholar, mentor and perpetual inspiration.

Particular thanks to Jane Hadcock, Martin Hewings, Robin Walker, Sheila Thorn, Marina Cantarutti, Sue Sullivan and Olya Sergeeva who read and commented upon early drafts. They have been very influential in helping shape this book. I am solely responsible for any infelicities that may remain.

Thanks also to Richard Chinn, Marie Willoughby and Kezzie Moynihan of IH London, and Shaun Sweeney of IH Barcelona for their comments, conference presentations, and to Melissa Lamb for allowing me to observe her class at IH London.

Huge thanks also go to Alice Henderson and Frédérique Freund of the Université Savoie Mont Blanc for piloting *Jungle Listening* materials.

I am particularly influenced by reading the work of John Field, Linda Shockey, John Wells and Helen Fraser.

Without the support of my wife Estella, this book would not have been possible.

Thanks also goes to:

Heinle ELT for permission to use an audio extract from Hugh Dellar and Andrew Walkley's *Outcomes Upper Intermediate* Class Audio CDs.

Cambridge University Press for permission to use an audio extract from David Brazil's *Pronunciation for Advanced Learners of English*.

Delta Publishing for permission to use an audio extract from Mark Hancock and Annie McDonald's *Authentic Listening Resource Pack*.

Symbols and notation

The symbols for vowels and consonants are shown in the table below.

Vowels					Consonants			
ɪ	pit	iː	bee		p	people	b	boy
e	pet	ɜː	bird		t	tea	d	done
æ	pat	ɑː	bar		k	cat	g	girl
ʌ	putt	ɔː	bore		f	four	v	vat
ɒ	pot	uː	boo		θ	thing	ð	that
ʊ	put				s	sing	z	zoo
eɪ	bay	əʊ	go		ʃ	ship	ʒ	Asia
aɪ	buy	aʊ	now		h	hip	l	light
ɔɪ	boy	i	city		m	man	r	red
ɪə	here	u	thank-<u>you</u>		n	nine	j	yet
eə	fair	ə	<u>a</u>bout		ŋ	sing	w	wet
ʊə	poor				tʃ	church	ʤ	gem

Symbols in the text

The symbols for vowels and consonants in the text are shown between single vertical lines: |æ| |t|. The context should make it clear whether they are to be interpreted as 'phonemic' – broad categories of sounds – or 'phonetic' – fine details of sounds. In *A Syllabus for Listening: Decoding* their main role is to act as a guide to the imprecision and in-between-ness of everyday spontaneous speech.

Word stress and syllable divisions

The stress marks for citation forms are shown thus, using *fundamentally* as an example:

| ˌfʌn.dəˈmen.təl.i |

- the syllable preceded by a superscript stroke |ˈmen| has primary word stress
- the syllable preceded by a subscript stroke |ˌfʌn| has secondary word stress
- the three other syllables, |də| |təl| |i| are unstressed
- the full stop marks other syllable boundaries

Glottal stop

Syllable final |t| and |d| are very often heard as glottal stops |ʔ|: e.g. *a little bit of metal* becomes |ə lɪʔl̩ bɪʔ əv meʔl̩|.

The alveolar tap

Many people who speak American English use what sounds like a |d| instead of a |t| in words such as *writer*, which therefore sounds close to *rider*. The symbol we will use for this sound (an alveolar tap) is |ɾ|.

Diacritics

We occasionally need some smaller symbols – known as diacritics.

- Often when a final consonant |n| is dropped (and even when it isn't) the preceding vowel is nasalised, so that |ten| becomes |tẽ|. The symbol above |e| is a diacritic, called a 'tilde', which means that the vowel is nasalised.

- In Part 4, I refer to 'Irish |t|' – the sound (towards |s|) that many Irish people use for |t|. The symbol for this is |s̞|.

Notation

Double vertical lines || signify a speech unit boundary; uppercase letters show that a syllable is **prominent**; lowercase letters show that a syllable is **non-prominent**.

```
|| i WASn't sure what to DO about it ||
```

In this speech unit there are two prominences: *was* and *do*. The other eight syllables *i –n't sure what to a.bout it* are non-prominent. For the difference between word stress and prominence, cf. Appendix 1.

Introduction

A Syllabus for Listening: Decoding is for teachers, teacher trainers, textbook authors and course book authors in the field of English language teaching (ELT). *A Syllabus for Listening: Decoding* will help you build in a decoding dimension to all your listening activities. Your learners will improve their listening skills so that they are better prepared than they currently are for their real-world encounters with spontaneous speech. If you are teaching students, training teachers, designing a listening course or writing listening exercises for a course book, this book is essential reading.

Decoding is the process of recognising words in the stream of speech as it speeds past your ears, and it is an essential prerequisite for understanding a speaker's meaning. So although *A Syllabus for Listening: Decoding* is not a complete guide to teaching listening, it provides a crucial component (currently much neglected) for bringing learners' listening skills up to the level of their other skills. This is essential because many learners with high levels of competence in the skills of speaking, reading and writing find that their listening skills lag far behind these other skills. As a consequence, they have some unpleasant experiences that could be avoided if we had a systematic approach to decoding.

0.1 A learner's unpleasant experience

Olya from Russia (now a teacher) was appalled to find out that although she did very well in proficiency exams, she could only understand the gist of everyday speech in English. And the gist was not good enough for her, because as an advanced learner she expected to understand far more. She expected her listening ability to match her speaking, reading and writing abilities. Her experience – of listening lagging behind the other skills – is a very common one. This book aims to improve the teaching of listening so that, in future, learners will not find themselves in Olya's situation, and their ability in listening will match their abilities in the other skills.

Listening is often the weakest skill because language teaching typically focuses on an orderly, steady-paced version of speech, whereas the speech that learners encounter in everyday circumstances is wilder, faster and much more disorderly than the speech that they encounter in the typical ELT classroom.

Additionally, the way we teach listening needs to be updated. We have not moved much beyond the point described by another learner, Anna, who was angry with her teacher during a class because, having set 'three silly questions' and received three answers, he moved on to another activity, saying that 'the rest doesn't matter'.

But 'the rest' really does matter when people like Anna want to learn the language. It is 'the rest' that this book is concerned with.

0.2 The realities of the sound substance

Like Anna's teacher, course books conventionally focus on the meanings conveyed by the speaker, but the realities of the sound substance are not dealt with. The purpose of *A Syllabus for Listening: Decoding* is to help learners progress more swiftly to the stage of being expert at decoding and understanding; and it aims to achieve this purpose by providing a description of the realities of the sound substance of spontaneous speech. Let's consider an example which will make clear how this book addresses these realities.

Imagine a listening comprehension class in which the recording features two friends (Andy and David) in a shoe shop, and two of the comprehension questions are 'What type of shoes is David talking about?' and 'What does he think of them?' On the recording David says 'I have a pair of those badminton shoes and they aren't good', so the answers are 'Badminton shoes' and 'He doesn't like them'. If a number of students in the class (probably not all) answer these answers correctly, the teacher may count this as a success in understanding meaning, and therefore (for people like Anna's teacher) the listening lesson is over.

The sound substance of the recording is usually ignored in this type of class. But if we dig down into the recording, we might find that:

1. the four syllables *have a pair of* have become two syllables *haff pairff*

2. the |d| at the end of *and* has been dropped, resulting in *an*

3. the 'th' |ð| at the beginning of *they* has been dropped, resulting in *and they* becoming *annay*

4. the negative component of *aren't* is close to inaudible

5. *badminton* sounds like *bam.ton* where both the consonant |d| and the syllable *in* have been dropped

So crucially, even if students are able to answer the questions correctly, there is still something to be learned about the soundshapes of the words, and the substance which contains these soundshapes.

This shoe-shopping example shows the types of spontaneous speech phenomena that we will deal with in *A Syllabus for Listening: Decoding*:

- the squeezing together of words: *haffpairff*

- the dropping of sounds and syllables: *bamton, annay*

- the lack of clarity around positive and negative meanings: *anayaregood*

In order to decode and understand the speech that they encounter, our students need to become familiar and comfortable with this kind of blurring in the sound substance.

0.3 We're good at top-down processing, but ...

As a profession we are more expert at activating the top-down processes than we are at bottom-up work, which we tend to avoid. In other words, we are good at activities which set the context (e.g. two friends in a shoe shop) and which activate schemas (e.g. the language of choosing and buying shoes), but we are far less expert at teaching the bottom-up process of decoding – recognising the words that occur in the stream of speech.

0.4 Metalanguage

To bring to life the new syllabus presented here, we need terms to refer to the items of the syllabus, and the skill of recognising the items when they occur. These terms will be the metalanguage used in this book, e.g. 'Greenhouse', 'Garden', 'Jungle', 'hiss effect' and so on. The metalanguage is designed to be simple and memorable. It will be defined and illustrated with examples when they occur, and it is gathered into one place in the Glossary at the end of the book. Some of the terms are familiar – or at least have been used by other authors – and some of them are new.

0.5 Recordings and ear-training

The recordings, which are available for download on the Speech in Action website, are a vital part of the publication. Their purpose is to train your ears to hear the mush of the raw sound substance which lies below and behind all the words you perceive. This ear-training is not about exactness and precision, rather it is about training yourself to hear, and be comfortable dealing with, the indeterminate mush of much of the sound substance of speech.

0.6 The structure of this book

A Syllabus for Listening: Decoding consists of this introduction, four parts and appendices. You should read this introduction first, then you can read the other parts in any order. Each of the four parts has its own introduction.

Part 1 *Decoding and perception – Key ideas* consists of ten short chapters which set out in detail the reasons for the approach to listening and decoding in this book. Each chapter introduces a key idea (principle) which acts as a foundation stone for what is to follow in Parts 2–4. Together, the key ideas comprise a framework for understanding the approach to teaching decoding adopted in this book. They are deliberately short so that you can refer back to them (to remind yourself of the relevant principle) as you read the other parts of the book.

1. *Decoding speech and writing – the differences* deals with the fundamental differences between the sound substance (speech) and sight substance (writing) and the different decoding requirements of each.

2. *Styles of speech – Greenhouse, Garden, Jungle* introduces a classroom aid which will make clear the differences between citation forms, the rules of connected speech and the messy realities of spontaneous speech.

3. *Understanding versus decoding* explains how the expert listener's ability to understand meanings deafens them to the realities of spontaneous speech.

4. *The expert listener and the blur gap* explains the problems that expert listeners have hearing the mess and untidiness of spontaneous speech.

5. *The expert listener and the decoding gap* explains the consequences for the classroom when the expert listener cannot hear the mess and untidiness of spontaneous speech.

6. *The land of in-between – mondegreens* explains that the sound substance is much less clear than we think it is, and is capable of being heard – quite justifiably – in different ways.

7. *The unit of perception* explains that the unit of perception is not the word, but the speech unit.

8. *Words are flexible forms* explains that all words are flexiforms, which speakers can mould or crush into different shapes.

9. *Visualising the issues – three zones* presents the issues of the preceding chapters in a visual form.

10. *Diagnosis* uses the key ideas of the preceding chapters to diagnose why decoding is so often neglected in the ELT classroom.

Part 2 *A critique of training, theory and practice* consists of four chapters which together offer a critical analysis of what we teach and why we teach it in the way we do.

11. *Teacher training* describes how our training and early teaching experiences influence the way we teach listening.

12. *Virtuous obstacles* identifies things we do in the classroom which, although useful for other aspects of language learning, are obstacles to effective teaching of listening.

13. *Models of speech* compares the prescriptive Careful Speech Model (CSM) which currently dominates ELT materials with the more descriptive Spontaneous Speech Model (SSM) which we need to cope with the unruliness of spontaneous speech.

14. *The when and what of decoding* looks at conventional approaches to decoding, what activities are recommended and when they should be done.

Part 3 *A syllabus for listening* consists of four chapters which are the central part of the *Syllabus for Listening: Decoding*. These chapters train you to hear the streamlining processes (reductions) that words undergo when they are used in spontaneous speech.

15. *Words* – describes how all words have multiple soundshapes.

16. *Word clusters* – describes how words which commonly occur together are blended into continuous soundshapes which pose decoding problems.

17. *Streamlining I – consonant death* looks at the typical fates that speech sounds undergo (blurring, consonant death) when they are streamlined in fast speech.

18. *Streamlining II – smoothies to teenies* explains ways in which speakers make sounds, syllables and words disappear.

Part 4 *Education, tools and activities* consists of six chapters which explain different ways in which we might set about teaching decoding systematically, using the syllabus presented in Part 3.

19. *Learner education and teacher-mindset* explains how to manage both learners' and teachers' doubts, feelings and frustration.

20. *Teacher tools* describes tools that you can use at any time to demonstrate the different soundshapes that words can have.

21. *Recordings, extracts and activities* describes how to select and use recordings for decoding.

22. *Pen-and-paper activities* describes how decoding activities can start with written prompts.

23. *Visiting the sound substance dimension* describes how to build decoding work into any type of classroom activity.

24. *Internet and digital resources* looks at four different types of software that can help teach decoding.

0.7 Accents, other Englishes, English as a lingua franca

The voices used in the recordings are mostly those of native speakers of British and American English. I believe that streamlining processes happen in Englishes of all types, but they may differ in their nature from accent to accent, or from English to English.

If you work in an English as a Lingua Franca (ELF) environment, you may not need this book. Perhaps you are preparing your learners for situations in which cooperative and sympathetic L2-speakers of English speak to each other in speech styles which are orderly and easy-to-hear. If so, this book is not for you: it contains a description of the messiness and unruliness of spontaneous everyday speech. However, if there is the possibility that your students may encounter circumstances where it is not possible for them to negotiate a more listener-friendly, comfortable speech style, then this book will help you prepare them for such circumstances.

0.8 The relationship to *Phonology for Listening*

A Syllabus for Listening: Decoding is a companion publication of *Phonology for Listening: Teaching the Stream of Speech* (PfL).

PfL is an 'issues' book, which adopts a spontaneous speech stance. It addresses issues such as speed of speech, stress timing and 'hesitation phenomena' (which were reconceptualised as 'drafting phenomena'). It includes chapters on British accents, accents of the USA, and English as a Lingua Franca accents. It provides training in how to transcribe recordings of spontaneous speech so that their properties of spontaneity are respected.

This book, *A Syllabus for Listening: Decoding*, goes into much more descriptive detail about the soundshapes of words and word clusters. It expands greatly on the list of the streamlining processes which were given in Appendix 4 of *Phonology for Listening*.

A Syllabus for Listening: Decoding provides specific items to teach. The overall aim is to make learners familiar and comfortable with the unruliness of everyday spontaneous speech.

Part 1 Decoding and perception – Key ideas

The teaching and learning of listening is very much less effective than it should be. Why is this so? In Part 1 we prepare the ground for answering this question by looking at ten key ideas relating to the teaching of listening.

Chapter 1 *Decoding speech and writing – the differences* explains fundamental differences between speech and writing which require radically different processes of decoding. The implications of these differences are not fully realised in ELT, resulting in the relative neglect of listening and decoding, and leaving learners ill-prepared to cope with the spontaneous speech they will encounter outside the classroom.

Chapter 2 *Styles of speech – Greenhouse, Garden, Jungle* introduces a three-part botanic metaphor for describing styles of speech which helps explain (a) the difficulties of decoding and (b) why important features of the sound substance of speech do not receive adequate treatment in ELT.

Chapter 3 *Understanding versus decoding* explains the importance of distinguishing between the level of understanding and the level of decoding. Our expertise in understanding often deafens us to the true nature of the sound substance.

Chapter 4 *The expert listener and the blur gap* identifies a gap between what expert listeners believe they hear and what is actually present in the sound substance.

Chapter 5 *The expert listener and the decoding gap* identifies another classroom problem that results from the blur gap – teachers and students hear different things.

Chapter 6 *The land of in-between – mondegreens* explains that speech is an inherently indeterminate, in-between substance characterised by a fuzziness that can be heard in different ways.

Chapter 7 *The unit of perception* proposes a minimum unit to work on in decoding and perception – and it is not the phoneme, as might be expected. It is the speech unit.

Chapter 8 *Words are flexible forms* explains that all words are flexible forms and have multiple soundshapes.

Chapter 9 *Visualising the issues – three zones* identifies three zones for the creation, transmission and perception of speech which will enable us to separate work on decoding from work on pronunciation.

Chapter 10 *Diagnosis* uses the key ideas in Chapters 1–9 to summarise why decoding does not receive sufficient attention in the ELT classroom.

1 Decoding speech and writing – the differences

The key idea of this chapter is that the decoding of speech and decoding of writing are radically different in ways that ELT does not yet fully recognise. Indeed, in ELT the written language (which we will refer to as 'the sight substance') dominates and suppresses the realities of the spoken language (which we will refer to as 'the sound substance'). For our learners to become more effective listeners, we need to take active steps to help them become familiar and comfortable with the realities of the sound substance. Among the active steps we need to take is to recognise that the two substances – sight and sound – require different processes of decoding.

1.1 Two substances – sight and sound

In order to become efficient at understanding and creating meanings, you have to have mastery of both the sight substance and the sound substance of language. The term 'sight substance' refers to the visual, graphic shape of words, phrases, sentences and paragraphs in writing that we see, using our eyes. The term 'sound substance' refers to the auditory, acoustic shapes of words, word clusters, speech units and longer stretches of speech that we hear, using our ears.

1.2 The sight substance is visible, and remains in place

The sight substance exists anywhere where print can be presented to the eye: on paper, screens, boards and walls. It hangs around – it doesn't disappear. This means that it can be read, inspected and returned to. And when learners do not know a particular word, they can look it up in a dictionary because (a) the sight substance is easy to perceive – the spelling is generally stable and does not change a great deal from occurrence to occurrence and (b) the word continues to stay in the same location (in the same line, on the same page) while it is being looked up. If you don't know the meaning of a word, you can leave it where you found it, consult a dictionary to find the meaning, then return to the word, and resume the process of meaning building and understanding. You clearly cannot do this with the sound substance of everyday speech.

1.3 The sound substance is invisible, and disappears

Unlike the sight substance, the sound substance does not have a stable existence – it happens and it is gone. In everyday spontaneous speech it happens at speeds that the listener cannot usually control. The sound substance passes through the listener's short-term memory leaving fast-fading traces and is continually replaced by more sound substance which follows quickly. Unless it has been recorded, it cannot be inspected at leisure because it cannot be re-found. And as we will see and hear in the chapters of this book, unlike the sight substance, the words contained in the sound substance have many different soundshapes.

In circumstances where communication is between two willing participants, requests to slow down and for clarification may be happily complied with. However, there are many circumstances (lectures, radio, announcements and so on) where it is not possible to make such requests. There are also circumstances where even willing participants, working under pressure, may have limited patience. They may feel annoyed at having to repeat themselves or rephrase something, and the non-understanding person may themselves feel stupid for not having understood first time (Thorn, personal communication, 2017).

1.4 The sound substance goes at the speed of the speaker

In the sound substance the listener has to go at the speed of the speaker, and there are far fewer occasions when there are gaps (pauses) between words. This differs from the sight substance where, however quickly the writer has written, the readers can go at their own speeds and there are easily discernible gaps between words.

1.5 Recognising forms – easy in the sight substance

In the sight substance, letter recognition is quickly and easily learned so that very soon the fact that you have had to learn it is forgotten.

Different forms of the letters of the alphabet are easily recognised as instances of the same letter. In the lines below, there are ten examples of the first letter of the alphabet, 'A':

a   a   A   a   **a**

a   a   *a*   **a**   **a**

So we can see that letters, the individual components of the sight shape of a word, are easy to recognise by the very fact that they are visible.

1.6 Recognising forms – difficult in the sound substance

However, it is much less easy to identify the individual components of the sound substance. These components – let us refer to them as 'phonemes' for the time being – are very likely to be blurred as a result of being streamed into multi-word rhythmic units. Phonemes change their auditory and acoustic shape – even to the point of vanishing – because of the pressures created by the speaker's choices of speeds and emphasis.

This blurring does not happen in the sight substance. However fast the author wrote, and however fast you read, the written forms stay in place and they retain their ease of recognition.

Also, because sounds occur and are gone (they are transient) and are therefore invisible, it is much more difficult for learners to assign the streamed forms of the sound substance to units of sound and words that they know.

In the sight substance word recognition is generally very easy, even if the actual meaning is not known. But in the sound substance, word recognition is far more challenging.

1.7 Native listeners and learner listeners – the differences

In spontaneous speech, the sound substance is a continuous blur of sound in which an L1 or expert listener easily perceives words and understands meanings, if the accents are familiar. L1 listeners achieve a high level of automaticity in decoding and understanding by having grown up with the language and hearing and using it for most of their waking hours. Expert L2 listeners can also achieve a high level of automaticity due to their years of learning and exposure to the target language.

But in a language we are learning, it is much more difficult to perceive the words that are said and to understand the meanings they convey. Learners can eventually become expert listeners (a term we will explain in Chapters 4 and 5), but it usually requires lengthy exposure to the language in English-speaking environments. Expert-listener abilities are not usually learned during the timeframes of standard language learning at school. This leads us to the situation (cf. Introduction 0.1) where Olya, despite her advanced abilities in reading, writing and speaking can only partially understand the sound substance she encounters.

1.8 What if the sound substance were visible?

If spontaneous speech were able to hang around, and not disappear, it might appear as shown in Figure 1.1. This shows a blurred transcript of a recording (lasting 18 seconds). Being a transcript, and therefore consisting solely of the sight substance, it is a misrepresentation of the sound substance. This is due to the very fact that you can see it, and point to parts of it which (in the sound substance) would have disappeared, leaving no visible trace. The blurring represents some of the messiness and untidiness of spontaneous speech. It is a visual metaphor for how learners experience spontaneous speech.

FIGURE 1.1 EMILY'S JOB AT A SCHOOL

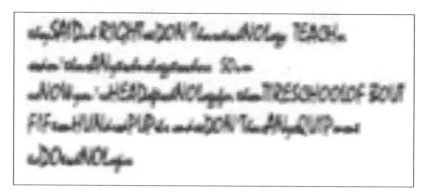

In this transcript there are eleven occurrences of the letter 'a' in the words *said, have (3), a, teachers (2), any (2), head* and *and*. The letter 'a' and the words that contain them are difficult to identify with certainty in this image. Just as you have difficulty picking out letters and words in this image, so learners have difficulty hearing sounds and words in spontaneous speech.

1.9 The sound substance is a radically different form

As we have seen, the sound substance is a radically different form of the language from the sight substance. If the sound substance did leave a permanent trace that we could see, then learners would pester us with 'form' questions such as 'What words are those?' They would then point to them and we would be obliged to answer if we wanted to keep our jobs as teachers.

But the sound substance cannot be pointed at. Although a transcript can be pointed at, it is made of sight substance, and as soon as the sight substance becomes the object of attention, the essential differences between it and the sound substance fade from earshot.

The purpose of this book is to present concepts, activities and classroom-friendly language (metalanguage) which you can use to explain the sound substance. This will enable us to free the sound substance from the domination of the written sight substance.

1.10 Summary and what's next

The key idea in this chapter has been that speech, the sound substance of language, is far more difficult to decode than writing, the sight substance of language.

Chapter 2 will demonstrate further how we can re-think our notion of speech so that we can describe its variability in classroom-friendly terms. To the two substances (sight and sound) of this chapter, we will add a three-part metaphor to describe styles of speech in the domains of the Greenhouse, the Garden and the Jungle.

2 Styles of speech – Greenhouse, Garden, Jungle

In this chapter the key idea is that it is useful to think of the sound substance of speech as existing along a continuum of styles, a continuum which has three domains: the Greenhouse, the Garden and the Jungle.

2.1 The Greenhouse – the domain of citation forms

The citation form of a word is the soundshape spoken in isolation without any contact with other words. It is the form given in the pronunciation key of a dictionary. The word is preceded and followed by a pause and every segment and syllable is carefully articulated. These citation forms of words are like plants in a greenhouse which are kept in separate pots so that they can get strong early growth without any competitive contact with other plants. Greenhouse soundshapes are rare in spontaneous speech. They most commonly occur as answers to the question 'How do I pronounce this word?' and 'What is the correct way to say this word?' Extract 2.1 gives an example of a sentence with each word occurring as a Greenhouse form.

EXTRACT 2.1

```
|| I NEVer DID IT IN COLLege ||
```

Voice: Richard, UK. *It* refers to swimming.

2.2 The Garden – the domain of the rules of connected speech

The Garden domain is home to words-in-phrases-and-sentences and the rules of connected speech, which describe how the edges of words change when they come into contact with other words – for example *did it* becomes *did‿it*. In a garden, plants occur in pleasing arrangements, with agreeable contrasts of plant types, colours and scents. Similarly, there is genteel contact between the soundshapes of words, which are described in the ELT rules of linking, assimilation and elision. The sound substance of the Garden is orderly and describable in terms of rules and it has a faithful relationship with the sight substance of language: units of speech and units of grammar line up alongside each other nicely; pauses occur at phrase and sentence ends; declarative sentences end in falling tones and the nuclear stress occurs on the last lexical item in the sentence. Garden soundshapes are usually found in the acted speech of ELT materials, and may also be found in slow and medium-slow stretches of spontaneous speech.

Extract 2.2 gives the same words as in 1.1, but this time spoken in a Garden style.

EXTRACT 2.2

```
|| i NEVer diditin COLLege ||
```

Voice: Richard, UK.

Note that words that were separate in Extract 2.1, are now linked (as is predictable from the sight substance) particularly the final consonants and initial vowels in *did it in* becomes *did it in*.

2.3 The Jungle – the domain of unruly messy speech

The Jungle is the domain of fast, unruly and messy speech. It is home to the realities of spontaneous speech where words are crushed out of shape. In the sound substance of the Jungle it is difficult, if not impossible to determine where one word starts and another begins. In fact it is often difficult to hear whether a syllable or word has occurred at all. The Jungle is a domain of extreme speeds and huge variations in clarity – a domain which is truly messy and unruly. Pauses can occur anywhere, falling tones occur at non-ends of sentences which may have the nuclear tone anywhere and sentences (if they occur at all) may end with a level or rising tone, whatever their grammar or function. But the biggest issue is that words and groups of words are mushed together into soundshapes which are very different to their Greenhouse and Garden soundshapes. Jungle soundshapes can be found in all spontaneous speech and they can even occur in scripted speech when it is not being spoken at extra-slow, careful speeds.

Extract 2.3 gives the original (Jungle) version of our example sentence, spontaneous speech from Karam from California.

EXTRACT 2.3

```
|| i NEVer diiin COLLege ||
```

Voice: Karam, USA.

Notice that we get something close to |dɪn| in *did it in* where the consonants |d| and |t| are dropped in a process we refer to later as 'consonant death' (cf. Chapter 17).

2.4 ELT is comfortable with the Greenhouse and the Garden

ELT is comfortable with the Greenhouse and Garden domains. Indeed our teaching of the sound substance of English is almost exclusively conducted in these domains. The sound substances of the Greenhouse and the Garden fit well with the major requirements of language learning: that it should be presented in terms of rules and notions of correctness, and that it should be as closely related to the sight substance as possible.

2.5 The Careful Speech Model

Together, the Greenhouse and Garden domains of speech provide the model of speech that we use in ELT – the Careful Speech Model (CSM) – which is described and evaluated in more detail in Chapter 13.

The CSM is ideally suited for the teaching and learning of pronunciation and for promoting clear intelligible speech, and it fulfils this role very well. But those very characteristics which make it suitable for pronunciation purposes (clarity and orderliness) make it unsuitable for listening purposes. This is because what learners have to handle in listening is often very much wilder than anything they have been taught in the CSM classroom.

For listening purposes we need a separate model of speech – a Spontaneous Speech Model (SSM). The SSM needs to be a description of the sound substance of the Jungle which captures the wildness, messiness and unruliness of the sound substance of everyday speech – captures it, tames it and makes it teachable and learnable. And this is the purpose of *A Syllabus for Listening: Decoding*: to present concepts, items and activities that will comprise a Spontaneous Speech Model which will improve the teaching of listening.

2.6 Why spontaneous speech?

Spontaneous speech is the most common speech style, indeed the most common style of language of any kind: the amounts of it in our daily lives far outweigh any kind of scripted or acted speech or writing. It is this type of speech that learners frequently encounter outside the classroom and which shocks learners such as Olya. It poses greater difficulties for language learning and teaching than any other type of language. It is made up, moment by moment by speakers – it is not scripted. And the speakers who shape the sound substance are aiming to communicate their meanings effectively: they are not aiming to obey rules.

So why focus on spontaneous speech, if it is so difficult? Well, it is precisely because it contains stretches which are so difficult, so unruly, so fast and so unclear that makes it suitable as a goal for teaching listening. This is because if learners can perceive and understand the extremes of spontaneous speech, they will be able to perceive and understand any other speech style with ease.

But spontaneous speech is not wholly different from other speech styles. Even scripted speech – which you might expect to be Garden speech – may contain Jungle moments when short sequences of words (particularly word clusters such as *where there were*) may be spoken so fast that they present a perception challenge to learners.

Many of the characteristics of the Jungle are an extension of those characteristics found in Garden, scripted speech. Whereas in the Garden these characteristics may apply singly, and in predictable locations, in the Jungle these characteristics may all apply together in a single randomly chosen location for no obvious linguistic reason, and at much faster speeds.

So when we focus on spontaneous speech, we are preparing students to encounter, and handle successfully, the soundshapes of words that are most different from the Greenhouse (citation) form.

2.7 The syllabus needs to respect the Jungle

The syllabus for listening needs to include the Jungle (wild, messy and unruly) nature of spontaneous speech. Spontaneous speech therefore needs to be handled on its own terms, and not regarded as a degenerate form of the CSM. The CSM is useful for the purpose of promoting clear intelligible pronunciation, but it is not suitable for the purpose of teaching decoding of spontaneous speech. So wherever an expert advises (probably wisely) that a learner should not use 'uncommon reduced forms' in their own speech (e.g. |jə| and |mə| for *your* and *my*) lest they sound 'comically incongruous' (Cruttenden, 2014: 333), such forms must be included in the syllabus for listening. They need to be included because (a) they can occur and (b) they may well be part of a stretch of Jungle speech which poses a decoding challenge.

2.8 Summary and what's next

The key idea of this chapter has been that it is useful to conceive of a continuum of speech styles with three domains: the Greenhouse, the domain of the citation form; the Garden, the domain of connected speech rules; and the Jungle, the domain of messy, unruly, unclear spontaneous speech. The Greenhouse and the Garden together help create the Careful Speech Model (the CSM), which is ideal for teaching and learning clear intelligible pronunciation. But our focus is on listening, so we need to respect and describe the Jungle. And from our description, we need to develop a Spontaneous Speech Model (the SSM) which will facilitate the teaching of decoding.

Chapter 3 describes the two levels of understanding and decoding, and explains how expertise in understanding can deafen us to the precise nature of the sound substance of the language in a recording.

3 Understanding versus decoding

The key idea in this chapter is that expertise in understanding can deafen us to the precise nature of the sound substance of the language of a recording. ELT focuses too much on understanding meanings and not enough on decoding – we do this because we believe that the learner's route to being a successful listener should be the same as that taken by a native L1 listener.

3.1 Two levels

There are two levels to listening: decoding and understanding. Decoding (simply put) involves being able to recognise the words that occur in the sound substance, whereas understanding involves the interpretation of the meanings conveyed by the speaker. Being an L1 or expert listener, we can operate at the level of meaning without (apparently) having to work hard at decoding. In other words we extract meaning with an automaticity that seems not to require much decoding. The main thrust of ELT's approach to listening is to work at the level of understanding, expecting that the requisite expertise in decoding will be acquired as a by-product of successful work on meaning.

3.2 ELT focuses on understanding

Most work in ELT listening classrooms is targeted at the level of understanding. We activate students' expectations of what meanings might be in play in any recording. They then select which meanings they believe were conveyed in the recording. As a profession we have become expert at activating expectations of meaning ('schema activation'), playing recordings and rewarding the capture of meaning.

We are less expert at the level of decoding (bottom-up activities) and, as a consequence, we spend far less time on teaching the nature of the sound substance than we spend on the level of meaning.

3.3 L1 listening bias

For L1 and expert listeners the task of decoding operates below the level of attention – subliminally – so that (it is commonly observed) they do not have to pay attention to every word in order to understand. Additionally, when questioned about this, although expert listeners can accurately report what meanings were communicated, they will not be able to recall precisely what words were used. However, if they do recall accurately, they will be able to identify the words – almost certainly by giving the Greenhouse (citation) form (Cruttenden, 2014: 333).

As we can see, L1 and expert listeners operate at the level of understanding, but they are paradoxically (a) dependent upon the sound substance, and (b) unaware of its precise nature. In ELT our teaching of listening suffers because of this double bias: L1 and expert listeners are both unaware of their dependence on the sound substance and, when they do have to consider it, report it as being like the Greenhouse or Garden.

The view of the relationship between decoding and understanding as portrayed in the preceding paragraphs – although useful – is a very simplified one, as we will see in Chapters 6 and 7. But it is important to recognise that L1 and expert-listener expertise in handling meanings can deafen us to the realities of the sound substance, and therefore to the perceptual challenges that learners face. The next two sections will demonstrate how this happens.

3.4 Meaning deafens us to form – *ton* vs *tan*

This section contains a demonstration of how understanding can deafen us to the forms of the language. Below are five versions of the first letter of the alphabet, which we first saw in Chapter 1.

a   a   *a*   a   a

If you look at the last letter, you will notice that it is close to the form of a different letter, the fifteenth letter of the alphabet 'o' or 'O'. Below are the letters 'a' and 'o' side by side.

a o

They look confusable, and they remain so when we put them into words. The words below are isolated sight shapes of the words 'tan' and 'ton', side by side.

tan ton

If you are like me, you will have to scrutinise each word to determine which is which. But when we add some co-text, it becomes easier to tell what the word is, and consequently what the letter is likely to be. Below, *tan* and *ton* are embedded in a compound noun and an idiom respectively.

suntan lotion   like a ton of bricks

But notice that now we are considering word groups (a compound noun and an idiom) which contain chunks of specific meaning. And because we recognise the chunks of meaning, we know what words must have been intended, and therefore how they are normally spelled. Let's deliberately misspell the syllable 'tan' in 'suntan' (giving us 'sunton') and let's misspell the word 'ton' in 'ton of bricks' (giving us 'tan of bricks'), and put them into sentences.

It's very hot today. Put on some sunton lotion

He collapsed like a tan of bricks

As expert readers we have no trouble in arriving at a perfectly good understanding of the meaning, and if I had not taken you step by step through this procedure, and you had encountered these sentences in the normal course of your daily reading, you would most probably not notice the misspelling. However, learners, going slowly through the sight substance, may notice the misspellings ('ton' for 'tan' and vice versa). They may wonder whether or not these are new words that they have yet to learn. Alternatively, if they are familiar with the words, the unexpected spellings may disrupt their efforts to understand the meaning of the text.

In this way, a person's expertise at making and understanding meaning can blind them to the precise nature of the substance being inspected. (See Walker, 2015 for another example.)

3.5 Meaning deafens us to form – *pupils* vs *peoples*

Having seen a sight-substance version demonstrating how understanding meaning may blind us to perceptual difficulty, here is a sound-substance version. We will go through it step by step as if it were a very short listening comprehension lesson.

The context is that Emily is talking about visiting South Africa as an eighteen-year-old, to help with teaching English in a secondary school. When she got to the school however, she was told that she wasn't going to teach English: she was going to teach something else – despite the fact that she had no previous experience of being a teacher.

So we very clearly have an educational context. Good classroom practice would be to elicit a list of subjects that Emily might be asked teach: perhaps Maths, French, Art and so on. We might also elicit what else we could reasonably expect to hear about the school: perhaps numbers of teachers, numbers of students, how well-equipped it was and so on.

And then we play the recording, Extract 3.1. It lasts 18 seconds.

EXTRACT 3.1

```
They said uh 'Right, we don't have a technology teacher, we don't have
any technology teachers. So um, so now you're head of technology for the
entire school of fifteen hundred pupils.'
```

Voice: Emily, UK.

After playing the recording once or twice, the teacher might elicit the answers from the class: *technology* and *fifteen hundred pupils*. However, a common practice (unfortunately) for what happens next is to leave the recording behind and move on to another activity, such as a discussion or a writing activity.

But if we stay with the recording and do some decoding work, we may discover, as I have done, that my students experienced three 'mishearings':

- *we don't have any* was heard as *we have many*

- *fifteen hundred pupils* was heard as *fifty hundred pupils*

- *pupils* was heard as *peoples*

Note that these 'mishearings' do not fit the meanings of the recording: *we have many* conflicts with the immediately preceding *we don't have a technology teacher; fifty hundred* is not a legitimate number expression in English; and it is clearly impossible for a school to have 1500 *peoples*. So, at the level of meaning, these 'mishearings' are nonsense – literally, they make no sense. But, at the level of decoding, these 'mishearings' are clues to important information about the students' problems with decoding, and about what the sound substance actually contains.

In the case of '*we don't have any/have many*', we have a negative heard as a positive. This is a common phenomenon, even with native listeners, as we will see in Chapter 18. In the case of *fifteen/fifty hundred*, again, the hearing of a -teen number (13–19) as a -ty number (30–90) and vice versa is also very common, as we will also see and hear in Chapter 18. In the case of *pupils/peoples*, there is ample justification in the sound substance for hearing *peoples*, despite the fact that it is contextually very unlikely. Extract 3.2 contains the relevant speech unit, both at normal speed and slowed down. You should hear, fairly clearly, why it can reasonably be heard as *peoples*.

EXTRACT 3.2

```
|| aBOUT FIFteen HUNdred PUPils ||
```

At the level of meaning, we can insist to the class that *peoples* is wrong, and we can insist that they have misheard the clearly intended word *pupils*. At the level of decoding, however, we need to accept that their hearing the word *peoples* is a completely justified, 'reasonable hearing' of the sound substance. Therefore, at the level of decoding, it is NOT a 'mishearing'.

For the effective teaching of listening, we need to recognise that working at the level of decoding and focusing on the sound substance, needs to have a much more significant role than it currently has. We operate far too much at the level of meanings.

In short, our ability as expert listeners to arrive instantaneously at understanding meanings deafens us to the acoustic realities of the sound substance. This deafness results in the blur gap – to which we turn in Chapter 4.

3.6 Summary and what's next.

The key idea in this chapter has been that expertise in understanding meanings can deafen us to the precise nature of the sound substance.

In Chapter 4 we will see that the ELT profession (particularly L1 listeners) suffer from another type of deafness – the blur gap. We treat the sound substance as if it contains words in their Greenhouse and Garden forms, whereas they are very often in Jungle forms.

4 The expert listener and the blur gap

The key idea in this chapter is that the ELT profession suffers from a kind of deafness called 'the blur gap'. This deafness is suffered by L1 and expert listeners (especially L1 listeners), who believe that the sound substance contains words in their Greenhouse and Garden forms, whereas they are very often in Jungle forms.

4.1 The expert listener

Expert listeners are those who understand the meanings conveyed by the speaker, and who can, if asked, (and if they can hear the recording again) report the actual words that were used to convey those meanings. The term 'expert listener' includes both L1 and L2 users of English. Even if you do not regard yourself as an expert listener, you become one in the classroom for the purposes of a listening activity when you have the answers to the comprehension task, and you have a transcript of the recording in front of you.

4.2 A lack of awareness

Almost every book on phonology or phonetics warns that L1 (native) listeners are unaware of the true nature of the sound substance of speech. Shockey (2003: 1) writes:

> Most people speaking their native language do not notice either the sounds that they produce or the sounds that they hear.

Collins & Mees (2013: 120) write of the 'simplification processes' (our Jungle phenomena):

> Most native speakers are totally unaware of such simplification processes and are often surprised (or even shocked!) when these are pointed out to them.

As a consequence of this lack of awareness, L1 listeners are unreliable informants: if you ask how they pronounce words such as *and*, *but* and *of* Cruttenden tells us that they 'will give the rare citation (accented) forms ... rather than the more common ... [weak forms] ...' (2014: 333). In our terms, they will give Greenhouse forms instead of Garden or Jungle forms. Cruttenden goes on to advise caution in asking L1 listeners about speech and suggests that '... it is wiser to listen to the way in which a native speaks rather than to ask his opinion' (Cruttenden 2014: 333).

This is a problem for ELT because it is not simply L1 listeners, but also L1 teachers of English who 'have a very idealistic impression of how English is spoken' (Brown 1990: 2). L2 teachers of English are less likely to have this 'idealistic impression'. This is because, unlike L1 teachers, they will probably have learned English via methods which required them to engage consciously with the nature of the sound substance.

4.3 The blur gap

So 'the blur gap' is the gap between what expert listeners (particularly L1 listeners) believe they hear – typically, whole words in their Greenhouse citation forms – and what the sound substance actually contains – often only rough hints or slight traces of words.

ELT materials encourage teachers to operate at the level of understanding, which is why they rarely pay attention to the soundshapes of the words that were used to convey meanings. When they do focus on the sound substance, they often give inaccurate information because their descriptions will be influenced by their knowledge of how those words should sound as Greenhouse and Garden forms.

This is the reason why the ELT profession suffers from the blur gap.

4.4 The evolution of the blur gap

The blur gap is not part of any malicious plot or wilful misrepresentation of language. It has evolved as the ELT profession has developed its expertise and found success in other areas, such as the teaching of pronunciation (cf. Part 2).

The blur gap is partly a result of natural processes which occur subliminally, below the level of attention, and it requires constant effort to counteract these processes. Even when I know a recording well and have identified its Jungle features, seeing the transcript drags me back towards the Garden and the Greenhouse, and predisposes me to hear the sound substance as tidier than it actually is.

The effects of the blur gap are largely unrecognised in teacher training courses, in textbooks and course books, and in classroom practice. So although we may have been warned about the blur gap, it is not generally recognised that it has had serious consequences for the teaching of listening.

4.5 Summary and what's next

In this chapter the key idea has been that L1 and expert listeners believe that the sound substance that they hear is much tidier and clearer than it is in reality. We believe it to be Greenhouse-like and Garden-like when it is actually Jungle-like.

Chapter 5 explains that the blur gap has consequences for the learners in the classroom. They suffer from 'the decoding gap', meaning that they experience the sound substance very differently from their teachers, who are generally expert listeners.

5 The expert listener and the decoding gap

The key idea in this chapter is that, as a consequence of the blur gap (cf. Chapter 4), there is a decoding gap in the listening classroom. The decoding gap is the gap between what the L1 and expert listeners believe they hear, and what the learners encounter.

5.1 The blur gap causes the decoding gap

The blur gap is when L1 and expert-listener teachers believe they are hearing Greenhouse and Garden forms. In the listening classroom, where decoding is a challenge, our learners encounter the faint traces and rough hints of the Jungle and therefore have a direct experience of the untidy forms in the acoustic blur of speech.

Our learners face the following problems:

1. They hear a mush of a continuous stream of sound substance

2. They cannot reliably match the mush to words they know

3. They consequently do not understand the speaker's meaning

But the biggest problem they face is the fact that – because of the blur gap – teachers, textbook and course book writers cannot share their experience of the mush. This is the problem of the decoding gap (Cauldwell, 2013: 255).

So the decoding gap is the gap between what the expert listener believes they hear (words in their best clothing) and what the learners encounter – raw sound substance (non-word ragged fragments, which are not yet words).

5.2 Learners feel lost

This discrepancy results in the awkwardness and discomfort that often occurs in the classroom when challenging recordings are played: teachers are deceived – by their own expert perception – into believing that the sound substance is more well-dressed than it really is, whereas learners with undeceived ears hear the rags and shreds of words mushed up into an acoustic blur, and feel lost.

5.3 Closing the gap

Our task in *A Syllabus for Listening: Decoding* is to close the decoding gap, so that teachers and learners start in the same place, with a recognition on the teacher's side of what their students are confronting as they encounter the raw sound substance.

The challenge for the teacher (as well as the textbook and course book writer, teacher trainer, and so on) is to develop the capacity to hear the raw sound substance of the Jungle forms and to neutralise the natural processes that tempt them towards the Greenhouse and the Garden. Part 3 consists of ear-training and classroom-friendly terminology to enable the decoding gap to be closed.

5.4 Summary and what's next

The key idea in this chapter has been that there is a gap between what L1 and expert-listener teachers believe they hear in the sound substance (tidy forms) and what their students encounter (untidy and for them, un-decodable forms). This is the decoding gap.

Chapter 6 explores further the properties of the sound substance. It is characterised by indeterminacy, or in-between-ness, and is amenable to alternative hearings such as mondegreens, which will be defined and explained.

6 The land of in-between – mondegreens

The key idea of this chapter is that stretches of the sound substance of speech can be heard to contain different words, for example *for ages* might be heard as *for eight years*.

The sound substance of everyday spontaneous speech is inherently indeterminate. This means that it is characterised by an 'in-between-ness' – a lack of precision in which the speech can be heard by different people to contain different sets of words. Terms that have been used to describe this phenomenon are 'mishearing' and 'mondegreen'. I am going to argue that better terms to use are 'alternative hearings' or 'reasonable hearings', of the sound substance. We'll start with the mondegreen, which is a special case of alternative hearing.

6.1 Mondegreens

The term 'mondegreen' originates from an alternative hearing of a line of poetry. The original appeared as the two lines of poetry 'They have slain the Earl of Moray, **And laid him on the green**', and the alternative hearing was 'They have slain the Earl of Moray, **And Lady Mondegreen**'.

Thus a mondegreen is an alternative hearing of a sequence of words which is different from that intended by the speaker. It is often defined as a 'mishearing' – but we are going to view them as 'reasonable' or 'alternative' hearings of the sound substance, whether they make sense or nonsense in the context.

In the context set by the first line *They have slain ...* the alternative hearing of the second line *And Lady Mondegreen* seems to lead to a contextually plausible meaning. But not all alternative hearings are so plausible as far as meaning is concerned, as we will see and hear later in this chapter.

As teachers of listening, we need to develop a way of listening to speech which enables us to hear the potential for alternative hearings of the raw sound substance.

6.2 Mondegreen: *Completely sober/complete this over*

At the beginning of the 2017 cricket season, I heard a cricket commentator say on the radio – just before allowing another commentator to take his place – 'I'm completely sober'. The commentator probably intended us to hear 'I'll complete this over' (*over* is a unit of play in cricket).

In Table 6.1, the intended wording is shown, syllable by syllable, in Row A. The mondegreen hearing is shown in Row C. Row B represents, in folk spelling, those parts of the syllable structure and prominences which are common to both versions.

TABLE 6.1 EXTRACT 6.1

	1	2	3	4	5	6
A	I'll	com	plete	thi(s)	(s)o	ver
B	i	com	PLEE	iss	SO	er
C	I'm	com	plete	ly	so	ber

For this context, and for this stage in the commentary, my alternative hearing does not make sense. It is not a plausible hearing because it is very unlikely that the speaker intended these words.

But both sides of the mondegreen are valid ways of hearing what the sound substance contains. It happens that the meanings of the words in Row 1 fitted the context better, and so that is what I should have heard them to be. The crucial point, however, is that the sound substance itself can hover between two (and maybe more) possible sets of words.

6.3 Listening for alternative hearings

As teachers, textbook and course book writers, we need to open our ears to the possibility of alternative hearings. One hearing may be correct, in terms of both (a) making sense in the context in which it occurs, and (b) correctly giving the words the speaker intended to say. Alternative hearings can range along a cline from being contextually plausible to being totally implausible.

We will now look at an extreme example of an alternative hearing which results in an implausible alternative hearing.

6.4 Mondegreen – *idle mass*

It sometimes happens that L1 and expert listeners are confused by, and cannot make sense of, the sound substance. If you are a teacher, and it happens to you, you should relish the moment, and try to track what you do to get around your confusion.

This is what happened to me. In preparing for a class using an exercise from Hancock and McDonald's *Authentic Listening Resource Pack* (2014: 27), I had to listen to twelve short extracts of spontaneous speech (from radio broadcasts), and had to fill in the gaps. The focus of the exercise is on the non-prominent ('crowded') syllables which occur between two prominent syllables.

I was working through this exercise and doing very well until I came to the sixth item, shown as Extract 6.2

```
COULD  ................................ haRASSing you [5]
```

There are two prominent syllables (cf. Appendix 1) *COULD* and *-RASS-* and the task is to identify four of the five syllables which occur between them (the first syllable of 'harass' is given to us already). There is no context other than the words given in the transcript. I was surprised that I could not make out what syllables were being spoken. Even on the third or fourth listening, I was still unsure about what to write. And I suddenly realised that this was a wonderful moment because I (an L1 expert listener) found myself in a situation in which learners often find themselves – having to decode a fast-moving mush of sounds.

So I did what my students often do and wrote down what I thought I had heard, even though it resulted in nonsense. And I wrote:

```
COULD be idle mass haRASSing you
```

Clearly, as far as the level of meaning was concerned, this was nonsense – an alternative hearing, but not a plausible one. Even in the context of very few words, this makes no sense. Nevertheless, at the level of decoding, I was happy that this was – at that moment – a good representation of the raw sound substance I had heard.

I then looked up the answer key and found that the sound substance I had decoded as 'idle mass' were in fact the words 'like almost'. The sound substance of this extract was sufficiently mushy – indeterminate – to warrant my non-sense decoding.

Learners are very often in this situation, despite the fact that they have had (in a good listening lesson) a lot of contextualisation, and much more of the recording to listen to, and have had more time to normalise to the speaker's voice and the background acoustic.

6.5 The blur gap returns

As I write, the experience of not being able to make sense of the mush of 'idle mass' lies a year or two in the past. And as I listen back now to the recording, knowing what the answer is, I cannot imagine how I could have been so confused. It seems impossible to me now that I should have perceived the words 'idle mass' – perhaps my brain had an off-day. But what I know intellectually is that my knowledge of the answer primes my perception, and locks me into one interpretation, while simultaneously locking out all others. The blur gap is back in place.

But at the time of doing the exercise, my L1 expert-listener contextualising skills had been neutralised, and I was confronted by a raw mushy sound substance. And this raw mush was sufficiently blurred that I could not make sense of it.

This was an L1 expert listener's struggle with the sound substance/meaning relationship. There was a decoding of the sound substance which was successful to the extent that there was a matching of the mush of the sound substance with recognisably English words, but at the level of meaning, the decoded words resulted in nonsense.

However, it is important to recognise that this is a level of success – rendering the sound substance into words, even though it results in nonsense. It gives us an insight into an important feature of many listening classes – it identifies a decoding gap: the expert listener perceives the correct words, and the learners perceive an alternative hearing. This is a gap which it is not enough simply to be aware of, but it is one that should be bridged with creative activities that get learners to play with the different sides – both 'the wrong' and 'the right', and the intervening stages between them.

We also need to allow for situations where learners can make nothing at all of what they hear – situations where they cannot render the sound substance into anything at all, or at least nothing that is syllable-like or word-like. We will see an example of this in Part 4, Chapter 21 with Sullivan's (2017) gleeps.

6.6 Summary and what's next

The key idea of this chapter has been that the sound substance is amenable to being heard in different ways by different people. It is indeterminate as it often features sounds and words which lie between different alternatives (*October skies* or *Octopus skies*), some of which may be plausible and some of which may not.

As teachers, teacher-trainers, textbook and course book writers we need to help learners with this in-between-ness, and to realise that whereas for the L1 and expert listener it is only rarely confronted, our learners confront it all the time.

So, in short, the expert listener needs to be able to enter the in-between sound world of the stream of speech, and to experience it as a non-expert listener experiences it. The very best way to enter the students' world of decoding the sound substance is to ask learners what they hear, and accept answers which include alternative hearings, both plausible and implausible as far as meaning is concerned.

Chapter 7 explains that the unit of speech that we should use to teach decoding is neither the word, nor the syllable, nor the phoneme, but the speaker-created speech unit – a stretch of speech containing one or more prominent syllables and non-prominent syllables. Prominent syllables are those which the speaker chooses to highlight, and non-prominent syllables are those which speakers downplay (cf. Appendix 1).

7 The unit of perception

The key idea in this chapter is that the unit of speech which we should use to teach decoding is the speech unit.

7.1 Speech units

The speech unit is a quasi-rhythmic stretch of speech containing between one and four prominent syllables, with accompanying non-prominent syllables, but sometimes without any non-prominent syllables. For a full description cf. Cauldwell (2013), but you can also find out more in Chapter 20 and Appendix 2.

For the moment, we can make do with the three examples of speech units shown in Extract 7.1. Speech unit 01 has four prominences, and speech unit 02 has two prominences. Speech unit 03 also has two prominent syllables and seventeen non-prominent syllables.

EXTRACT 7.1

```
01 || aBOUT FIFteen HUNdred PUPils ||
02 || i NEVer did it in COLLege ||
03 || this is ONE i'm going to be looking at in slightly more DEtail in fact ||
```

Voices: Emily, UK; Karam, USA; Geoff, UK.

The prominent syllables are shown in uppercase letters, and the non-prominent syllables are shown in lower-case letters. Note that the first person pronoun, when non-prominent, is shown in lowercase, as it is in 02.

I am going to end this chapter by asserting that in teaching decoding we need to work with speech units like these, rather than working phoneme by phoneme or word by word. But in the next two sections I will briefly describe why other approaches are not appropriate for our goal of improving the teaching of decoding. I make no attempt (not least because space does not allow) to summarise work in the field of speech perception.

7.2 Why not phoneme by phoneme?

Let us consider an approach to the theory of decoding which Magnuson et al. (2013) characterise as the 'phonemic input assumption'.

The phonemic input assumption holds that perception works by matching phonetic events in the sound substance first to phonemes and then to words in the listeners' mental lexicon or dictionary.

So, for example, let's say that a phonetic event occurs and then the phoneme |ɑː| is identified, and the following five words are then activated at that precise moment: *are/art/artist/artistic/ artistically*. They are activated because they all begin with the identified phoneme |ɑː|, and these words are in competition – they are all candidates to be the target word. As each successive phoneme is identified, words either stay in or drop out of the competition depending on whether they possess the next phoneme. So let's say that the next phonetic event leads us to identify the phoneme |t|, giving us |ɑːt|. At this point the word *are* drops out of the competition, and when the third phonetic event occurs |ɑːtɪ| then *art* drops out of the competition as well. This process continues until all but the target word remains. This is a gross simplification of a very complex process, but it will give you an idea of the features of models which exist in this approach. Magnuson et al. (2013: 433) state that this assumption is not a research finding, rather it is a 'temporary simplifying assumption' that has made research possible, but has now become 'a complicating assumption'.

7.3 Do phonemes occur in the sound substance?

Many researchers are of the opinion that it is not helpful to believe that the phoneme, or in fact any sub-phonemic unit, exists in the sound substance of speech. Phonemic symbols are sight-substance aids to the pronunciation of Greenhouse and Garden forms of speech: the citation forms. They are visible, separate symbols which help greatly with the pronunciation of English, where the spelling is a notoriously unreliable guide to the pronunciation.

For some, the use of the phoneme for the analysis of speech is a symptom of the domination by the sight substance over the sound substance. Port (2007: 351) writes that the use of the phoneme is 'a consequence of our lifelong practice of using alphabets and not a necessary psychological fact about speech'.

Port goes on to say that using static graphic symbols (sight substance) is valuable as a form of cognitive scaffolding – an aid to help us understand how speech works – but he argues that we mistake this scaffolding for 'for the inherent structure of the language' (Port, 2007: 358).

Conceiving of the sound substance as a line of phonemes is a fundamental misrepresentation of spontaneous speech. As Brown (1990: 7) writes: 'the stretches of acoustic blur often no longer permit any representation on a segment-by-segment basis'.

Decoding is not about hearing a sequence of small sounds and then matching that sequence with words that have those sounds in the same order. There is increasing evidence that perception is much less orderly and much less sequential than that, as gating experiments (see next section) have demonstrated.

7.4 Fuzzy matching ... then words!

Gating experiments involve a sound file being cut into very small sections which are then played to respondents who write down what they hear. They are given no context. On each play, sections are added one by one, until people hear the full stretch of speech – so on the first play, respondents hear the first section, on the second play the first and second sections, and so on.

Shockey (2003: 103) chose a recording of the sentence *and they arrived on the Friday night*. She divided it into ten sections, and noticed how one of her respondents had several changes of mind over the course of the experiment. The respondent had written *nek, neer, neero, near eye, neerived*, before finally writing *and they arrived on the Friday night*.

Shockey points out two noteworthy moments in this study: first that the respondent moved from the non-word *neero* to having the word *eye* and then back to a non-word *neerive*. But the 'striking change' between *neerived* 'interpretation as gibberish' and *and they arrrived* 'sensible interpretation' demonstrates the sudden jump which is typical of much decoding. So although it may seem to be common sense that the process of decoding operates by gradually accumulating sounds and matching them moment by moment to phonemes and then words, the reality is that decoding proceeds in sudden jumps.

Fraser (2014) describes this process as follows:

> Typically we hear an uninterpretable noise – with no phonemes, syllables words or any other recognisable units – until suddenly we hear an entire sequence of meaningful words (43).

So in *A Syllabus for Listening: Decoding*, we take the view that in order to decode the sound substance **you need to hear more than a word to recognise a word** – you need to hear it in its environment, with the words that occur next to it, and in its larger speech unit surroundings, where nearby prominences may have major effects on its soundshape, as we will see in the next chapter.

7.5 Summary and what's next

In this chapter the key idea has been that the perception of words proceeds in a type of fuzzy matching as increasing amounts of sound substance are processed. We need more than a word to hear the word – we need the rhythmic environment in which the word occurs: the speech unit.

In Chapter 8 the key idea is that all words are flexible forms – flexiforms – with multiple soundshapes which are best dealt with (for teaching purposes) in speech units.

8 Words are flexible forms

The key idea is that all words are flexible forms (flexiforms) with many different soundshapes which are (a) created by the speaker and (b) strongly influenced by the other words which occur around them.

In everyday speech, words exist in a neighbourly relationship with the words that occur next to them. The neighbourly relationship may be viewed either as a friendly one, or as a bullying one.

8.1 Mental representation

People's brains store many different pieces of information about a word. The totality of this information is known as the 'mental representation' of a word.

The mental representation of any word includes its written form, its many soundshapes, its meanings, its most frequent companion words, the social circumstances in which it is used, its power to shock or not, and so on. All of this information is stored in the brain.

As mentioned earlier, formal language teaching and learning is conducted primarily through the lens of the sight substance, and stays close to the domains of the Greenhouse and the Garden. The visible form of the word therefore has a dominating influence on the teacher's and learner's mental representation of the word. The visible form of a word is one that is preceded and followed by gaps on the page, and one that almost always appears whole and complete. So our mental representation of a word is weighted in favour of its whole, complete, separate and written form. This makes it very hard for teachers and learners, in the words of Brown (1990: 2–3) 'to suppose that one has somehow heard *less* than a word'. But in spontaneous speech, in the speech which learners find difficult to decode, we almost always hear 'less than a word', because all words are flexible.

8.2 Words are flexible at their edges

Words are flexible forms – flexiforms – which can be shaped in a wide variety of ways to allow room for other words to sit in blended sharing of the same auditory space.

Part of the way words adapt to each other's presence is described in the linking rules of ELT. These linking rules include consonant-vowel linking where *did it in* becomes *did_it_in*; and where linking |j r w| help join words together, as in *my_eyes, law_and order* and *you_are*. These linking rules are discussed and illustrated in a little more detail in Chapter 13. But these rules are insufficient to describe the full flexibility of words in spontaneous speech. For the purpose of teaching listening, we need to add to these rules. These additions, called 'streamlining processes', will help us recognise and describe what happens to words in the Jungle, and they are presented in Part 3, Chapters 17–18.

8.3 Words are flexible all over

The flexibility of words is not limited to their edges. There are many other ways in which they change their shape. They often blur or drop middle consonants (*little* becomes *liddle* or *lil*), and they may drop initial, medial and final syllables (*cos* for *because*; *accent* for *accident*; *real* for *really*). They drop these elements in order that other words can share the same rhythmic stretch of speech – the speech unit.

The natural state for words is to occur in company with other words in speech units which go at rapidly varying speeds. In speech units, individual words rarely retain their Greenhouse identity. Instead they become part of a multi-word stretch of sound substance which may seem, to learners, to be a continuous mush of non-sense.

8.4 Words as bullying flexiforms

In the previous sections, words were described as if they are polite decision-making entities – sharing space and making room for other words. But we could have taken another – more violent – line, and written that some words punch others into small bits, or even out of existence. Extract 8.1 contains a speech unit which demonstrates this. There are two prominent syllables, shown in upper-case letters and all the remaining syllables, in lowercase, are non-prominent.

EXTRACT 8.1

```
|| this is ONE i'm going to be looking at in slightly more DEtail in fact ||
```

Voice: Geoff, Birmingham UK.

We can consider the two prominences, *one* and *de-* as punches in the ear which forcibly grab the attention of the hearer, while crushing the non-prominent syllables (in lowercase) out of shape and even out of existence – *more* sounds like *moot* and the words *to be* are inaudible.

But although we will use such metaphorical language to describe word-on-word violence, we need to remember that it is, of course, the speakers who are the shapers of the sound substance. It is the speaker's choice, not the language and not the situation, which provides us with this series of soundshapes streamed together.

8.5 Speaker's choice

It is necessary to say a little bit about the use of the words *choose* and *choice*. There is the type of choice which is a slow, time-consuming, careful deliberation of the advantages and disadvantages of taking a certain course of action. There is another type of choice which is the rapid, subliminal choice made below the level of attention. Although spontaneous speech can contain moments of deliberation (pauses, filled pauses, and stepping stones (cf. Cauldwell, 2013) where speakers slow down or stop to choose their words carefully, most words (and the way that they are said) are chosen rapidly in the latter, close-to-subliminal sense.

Because the speaker is the one making the choice, it is the speaker who is the main agent of shaping words and the sound substance. The speaker's choice of words to use, and how to shape these words, will be influenced by the context, their purpose in speaking, the topic, their relationship to their listeners and so on. A change in any one of these components may mean that words will be shaped differently to fit the new circumstances.

With spontaneous speech we cannot predict how words will be said. This is because prediction is not possible, as we do not know what will be said. And if someone provides us with a transcript of spontaneous speech, we cannot predict with accuracy from the transcript what soundshapes occur.

8.6 All words have multiple soundshapes

Both the kindly and violent processes that words undergo result in all words having a variety of soundshapes. It is possible to identify and describe both (a) a range of these soundshapes (cf. Part 3 Chapter 15) and (b) a set of streamlining processes which can apply to words to create an even greater range of soundshapes (cf. Part 3 Chapters 17–18).

Therefore it is not helpful, for the purposes of teaching listening, to hold the view that a word has 'a pronunciation' – they simply do not possess a fixed, correct way of being said. Quite the contrary: it is far more helpful – for listening purposes – to consider words as having a range of possible soundshapes of which the citation form is least likely to occur. Indeed there is increasing academic and research support for the idea that the brain stores not just one, but many soundshapes in its mental representation of each word (cf. Ernestus, 2014).

8.7 Summary and what's next

The key idea in this chapter has been that all words are flexible forms – flexiforms –which can change their shapes to fit into the rhythmic units of speech created by speakers. Because of this flexibility, all words can be streamlined into a wide variety of soundshapes.

Chapter 9 gives a visual explanation of why it is important for the teaching of listening and decoding to distance itself from the approach to teaching pronunciation.

9 Visualising the issues – three zones

In this chapter the key idea is to explain, using a visual aid, that the focus of *A Syllabus for Listening: Decoding* is on describing the nature of the sound substance as it travels to the listener, and on helping the listener to decode it. The focus is not on pronunciation, nor about how sounds are produced, although we will borrow some of the tools of pronunciation teaching to help us.

9.1 Three zones

The three zones shown in Figure 9.1 will help us to conceptualise the differences between (a) teaching pronunciation and clear intelligible speech, and (b) teaching listening where learners have to handle the wildness and messiness of everyday speech, the Jungle.

- Zone 1 is where speech is planned and produced.
- Zone 2 is where the sound substance travels.
- Zone 3 is the space where speech is perceived, decoded and understood.

The sound substance is created in Zone 1, travels in Zone 2 and is perceived and (hopefully) understood in Zone 3.

FIGURE 9.1 THREE ZONES

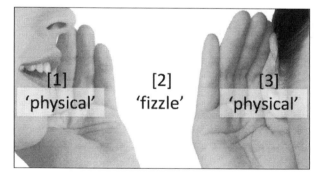

In *A Syllabus for Listening: Decoding* our focus will be on Zones 2 and 3 – providing ear-training and metalanguage to describe the sound substance after it has left the mouth of the speaker, and helping learners to decode and understand this sound substance. We will use some tools from Zone 1 to help us (such as phonemic and phonetic symbols) but our focus is not on pronunciation.

9.2 The fate of *physical*

Let us track the fate of the word *physical* when spoken in a speech unit as it travels across the three zones. Extract 9.1 will act as our sample speech unit.

EXTRACT 9.1

```
|| it was a VEry physical GAME today ||
```

Voice: Richard, UK.

Let's assume a situation where both the speaker and listener are L1 or expert listeners. The Greenhouse form of the word *physical* |fɪz.ɪk.ᵊl| has three syllables, with word stress on the first syllable, and consists of seven segments (counting ᵊl as two segments). But as the speech unit is spoken, the form of the word *physical* that exits Zone 1 is not the same as the Greenhouse form. In the brain of the speaker, it may start with this form, but as the speaker shapes the speech unit, an alternative soundshape emerges – represented in Figure 9.1 as *fizzle*. However, if asked, the L1 speaker will be sure she has said the full word *physical* |fɪzɪkᵊl|.

This *fizzle* travels through Zone 2 and arrives at the ears of the expert listener in Zone 3. The expert listener will be sure that she has heard the full form. But what has actually travelled between the speaker and the listener in Zone 2 is a streamlined form: *fizzle* |fɪzᵊl|.

This is an example of the blur gap, which was introduced in Chapter 4, where expert listeners hear words in their best-dressed forms, when in reality they are much changed and much less clear and tidy.

9.3 Zone 1 – where the sound substance starts

Zone 1 is where speakers decide what to say, and then carry out those decisions using the airflow from the lungs, and using the 'organs of speech' – the lips, teeth, tongue and the roof of the mouth. The processes by which these sounds are made are described by articulatory phonetics, and they are covered in textbooks for teachers such as Roach (2009) and Collins and Mees, (2013). The ELT profession's expertise in answering the questions 'How do I pronounce this word?', 'What is the correct pronunciation of this word?' and 'How can I distinguish between *ship* and *sheep*?' come from such teacher-training textbooks.

The symbols of the IPA are used to describe how sounds are formulated in this zone, and these symbols are helpful in pronunciation activities which aim to teach clear, intelligible speech. However, they are less helpful in describing the mess and unruliness of the Jungle. It has long been recognised that it is difficult to represent the fast transient messiness of the Jungle – Brown's 'obscure acoustic blur' – using these symbols. Brown (1990: 7) writes

> stretches of obscure acoustic blur often no longer permit any representation on a segment-by-segment basis.

Nevertheless, we will use such symbols as aids to help point the way into the fuzziness and the acoustic blur of the sound substance. Therefore, when such symbols are used, they will often be accompanied by text stating 'between this sound and that sound' or 'close to this sound', indicating that they are not to be interpreted as precise descriptors.

9.4 Zone 2 – where the sound substance travels

Zone 2 is where the sound substance of speech travels. In it, the sound substance has a brief existence independent of the speaker and hearer. It has finished being shaped by the speaker, and it has not yet arrived at the ears of the listener. It is travelling through the air, or through a combination of air and electronic medium. We can capture this sound substance and analyse it using recording and sound editing technology.

In fact, the simple act of using a wave editor such as Audacity (Mazzoni & Dannenberg, 2000) to cut up (or at least attempt to cut up) stretches of spontaneous speech into its constituent words reveals a great deal about the true nature of the sound substance. As mentioned above, it is likely that the sound substance created by L1 and expert speakers which is travelling in Zone 2 is more Jungle-like than the speakers and listeners suppose it to be, and on first attempting to cut it up, many L1 listeners are astonished at what they hear.

A major part of the purpose of *A Syllabus for Listening: Decoding* is to provide a classroom-friendly description of what the sound substance consists of in Zone 2; a description which uses phonemic and phonetic symbols while attempting to avoid some of their limitations.

A description of what has happened to the word *physical* in this speech unit goes as follows:

- it is non-prominent in a squeeze zone of a speech unit – it is squeezed between the prominent syllables *VE* of *very* and the word *GAME*

- this squeezing has resulted in the Greenhouse form |fɪz.ɪk.ᵊl| undergoing syllable dropping (a syll-drop cf. Chapter 18.4), to become |fɪz.ᵊl| where the second syllable disappears ...

- ... because of the buzz effect (cf. Chapter 17.11) of the |z| drowning the following weak vowel |ɪ| .

9.5 Zone 3 – where the sound substance arrives

Zone 3 is the space inside the head of the listener where the sound substance is perceived, decoded and processed for meaning. But in the classroom there is a crucial distinction to be made between three types of listener. The first is the learner listener who has difficulties in decoding and understanding. The second is the teacher, an expert listener who knows both what the answers are and what the words are. The third is the author – also an expert listener – who has written the listening tasks contained in the course book.

The decoding gap, described in Chapter 5, resides in this zone. On one side of the gap we have the expert listeners (teacher and author) on the other side of the gap we have the learner listener (students).

Because the expert listeners are likely to hear the recording as more tidy than it actually is, the teacher needs to reach across the decoding gap to find out what students make of the sound substance they are encountering in Zone 3. Techniques for doing this will be described in Part 4.

9.6 Summary and what's next

In ELT, the main tools we have for describing the sound substance are the phonemic symbols of the IPA, which work best in Zone 1, where the goal is to promote clear intelligible pronunciation.

To improve the teaching of listening, we need to take more account of what happens in Zones 2 and 3. The focus of *Syllabus for Listening: Decoding* is to give a more balanced view of speech in which Zones 2 and 3 are given appropriate emphasis.

Chapter 10 uses the key ideas of the chapters in Part 1 to offer a diagnosis of why, in ELT, listening and decoding are rarely given the attention they deserve.

10 Diagnosis

In this chapter we will take the key ideas identified in Chapters 1–9, and use them to identify reasons why, in ELT, the teaching and learning of listening is not very successful, and what needs to change if the situation is going to improve.

10.1 A tale of two substances

Chapter 1 introduced the idea that language exists in two different substances: sight substance (the language as it is written and read) and the sound substance (the language as it is spoken and heard). Language teaching is dominated by the sight substance, and the most common task is the inspection and learning of the printed word or symbol. In addition, descriptions of the sound substance are made to be as sight-substance-like as possible. We invent rules for speech which we can hook to units of sight substance such as phrases and sentences.

The teaching and learning of listening is unsatisfactory because of the profession's attempts to make the sound substance as learner-friendly as possible, and therefore as similar to the sight substance as possible. The trouble is that the two substances are fundamentally different – the crucial point being that the sound substance does not hang around to be studied. It has a momentary existence of rough hints, and it then speeds away, having left fast-fading traces of its passage in the listener's short-term memory.

One way of considering the syllabus for listening is to recognise at all moments in teaching, materials writing, and so on, that there is a sound-substance dimension to everything that we teach and practise. There is an invisible counterpart to all the printed words and rules that appear on the page. The invisible version is made of a fundamentally different substance – streamed, messy, transient.

To improve the teaching of listening, it is vital to treat the sound substance as a parallel, and equally valid, dimension of language. We should be able to switch between dimensions at the drop of a hat to make the properties of the sound substance as familiar and comfortable to learners of the language as the sight substance is.

10.2 Three domains: Greenhouse, Garden and the Jungle

Chapter 2 described three domains of speech, using a botanic metaphor: the Greenhouse, the domain of citation forms; the Garden, the domain of careful intelligible speech, where the genteel rules of words-in-contact are in play; and the Jungle, which is the domain of spontaneous speech, which (when viewed from the other two domains) seems unruly and messy.

The teaching and learning of listening is unsatisfactory because the focus of language description in ELT has been on the domains of the Greenhouse and the Garden. Our teacher-training materials, and our textbooks and course books give guidance on how to create clear speech. At the same time they deprecate, and even demonise, casual speech phenomena. These phenomena are found in spontaneous speech and, rather than being condemned, they need to be embraced and made central to a listening syllabus.

10.3 Understanding and decoding

Chapter 4 identified two levels which are crucial to consider in listening pedagogy: the level of perception and decoding – often thought of as 'the bottom' when we talk about the 'bottom-up' processing of speech; and understanding, or meaning building, – making sense of the speaker's message, which is often talked about as the 'top' level, as in 'top-down' activities.

ELT has a wide range of techniques and activities which work at the level of meaning. But our expertise at teaching at the level of meaning has come at the expense of teaching at the level of decoding, which is why we generally do very little of it. Indeed our expertise as L1 listeners at the level of understanding deafens us to the true nature of the sound substance which our students have to decode. Teachers, textbook authors and course book authors need to become un-deaf to the nature of the sound substance of language, and the decoding challenges that it presents to learners.

To improve the teaching of listening we need to recognise that our students can have a measure of success in hearing sound substance, solely at the level of decoding, even though it results in a stage of the lesson where they have come up with nonsense.

10.4 The expert listener and the blur gap

There is an important gap in our dealings with the sound substance of speech: the blur gap, which L1 and expert listeners suffer from. The blur gap is the difference between what L1 and expert listeners believe they speak and hear (tidy Greenhouse and Garden forms) and what they actually speak and hear (Jungle forms). L1 listeners, through a process known as 'pre-thinking' (Fraser, 2017) organise and tidy up the sound substance without being aware that they are doing so.

This is why, in our teaching, we need to guard against the rapid pre-thinking which creates the blur gap, and which makes us believe that the sound substance is tidier and clearer than it actually is.

10.5 The expert listener and the decoding gap

As a consequence of teachers and course book authors suffering from the blur gap, learners suffer from the decoding gap. Students encounter the raw substance of the Jungle, and are very often unable to decode and understand it. But their materials, having been written by expert listeners, do not take account of the Jungle.

We need to recognise that teachers and students start off by hearing different things, and that we should find out from our students what it is that they hear in the sound substance.

10.6 The land of in-between – Mondegreens

Chapter 6 characterised speech as indeterminate and capable of being heard in different ways: *I'll complete this over* being heard as *I'm completely sober*. These alternative ways of hearing are not 'mishearings' – rather they are 'reasonable' or 'alternative' hearings of the sound substance at the level of decoding. For example, as we saw in Chapter 4, in a school context, the intended word *pupils* was heard as *peoples*. At the level of understanding (because of the educational context), it can only be the word *pupils*: so *peoples* is wrong. But the spelling of *peoples*, and the soundshape that it suggests, is actually a much better representation of the sound substance of the recording. So hearing *peoples* at this point is a partial success – an accurate representation of the sound substance. It is a characteristic of the sound substance of language that it contains many moments where different reasonable hearings are possible.

The teaching and learning of listening is unsatisfactory because it does not recognise that the sound substance is indeterminate: it is in-between, it is mondegreenland. So when students come up with *married* for *made it*, or *peoples* for *pupils* or *big bang* for *I beg your pardon* (all examples from my own teaching), we need to recognise that these are reasonable hearings of the sound substance which happen not to match the intended words and meanings of the speaker. And these reasonable hearings give us a really good place to start teaching – with our students' first perceptions.

10.7 The unit of perception

Chapters 7 and 8 identified the most useful unit of perception to work with for decoding purposes as the speech unit – a multi-word rhythmic stretch of the sound substance. The natural state of a word is to be heard at speed in the company of other words which play a role in giving that word its soundshape.

The teaching and learning of listening and decoding is unsatisfactory because we often succumb to the temptation of thinking that perception is a left-to-right process proceeding incrementally in very small (allophone or phoneme-sized) steps.

So we need to use the word-in-its-rhythmic context (words in speech units) as the unit of perception to work with in class.

10.8 Words are flexible forms

Words have many soundshapes, and are best thought of as flexible forms – flexiforms – which acquire different shapes as they adapt to the pressures that the speaker and the neighbouring words apply to them.

Conventionally, ELT recognises multiple soundshapes for the list of 50 or so weak forms of function words (e.g. *n* for *and*, *cos* for *because*), and allows for streaming effects at word boundaries in the genteel set of connected speech rules (*not at all* becomes *not_at_all*).

The teaching and learning of listening and decoding is unsatisfactory because it does not recognise that all words, regardless of whether they are content words or function words, have multiple soundshapes, even in the speech of one speaker. We can improve the teaching of listening by downgrading the status of the citation form – for the purpose of teaching listening – and, instead, regard it as a brick-like structure which is an extremely rare form in spontaneous speech. We should instead open our minds to the idea that all words have a cloud of possible soundshapes.

10.9 Visualising the issues – three zones

Chapter 9 introduced three zones: Zone 1, where speech is created; Zone 2, the space through which the sound substance travels; and Zone 3, the space where the sound substance is decoded and understood.

The teaching and learning of listening and decoding is unsatisfactory because in the history of language teaching, Zone 1 considerations have dominated work on the sound substance. The focus has been on how the sounds of the Greenhouse and Garden forms of the language are made, and not on the properties that its Jungle forms have in the sound substance that travels through Zone 2. To remedy this we need to provide descriptions of the different soundshapes that words can have, both in isolation and, more importantly, when they are run together in the stream of speech.

In the classroom we need constantly to explore issues of Zone 3, by checking on what students believe they hear. While L1 teachers and expert listeners may be 100 percent successful in arriving at meaning, they may be – indeed they are likely to be – much less successful in recognising what is actually in the sound substance. In fact their students may have more success than they do in perceiving the streamed sounds which occur, even though they may not be able to understand meanings or recognise the words intended by the speaker.

10.10 Summary and what's next

In this chapter we have used the key ideas of Chapters 1–9 to offer a diagnosis of why, in ELT, listening and decoding are rarely given the attention they deserve.

This is the end of Part 1. In Part 2 we will look at in more detail, and give a critical assessment of, current practices in the teaching of listening.

Part 2 A critique of training, theory and practice

Part 2 contains four chapters which offer a diagnosis, from different perspectives, of the problems of conventional approaches to teaching listening/decoding. The diagnosis uses the key ideas of Part 1.

Chapter 11 *Teacher training* identifies elements in early teacher training, and early teaching experiences, which have led to our preferences and biases in the teaching of listening.

Chapter 12 *Virtuous obstacles* explains how some of the things that we do really well in the ELT classroom in pursuit of goals of pronunciation, reading and writing, have negative side effects for the teaching of listening.

Chapter 13 *Models of speech* compares the *Careful Speech Model* (CSM) with the *Spontaneous Speech Model* (SSM). The CSM is the assortment of prescriptive rules about speech that dominate the fields of pronunciation and listening in ELT. For the purposes of teaching listening/decoding, however, we need to develop a classroom-friendly SSM which describes what happens in the Jungle.

Chapter 14 *The when and what of decoding* looks at a variety of approaches to the timing and content of decoding activities, and identifies the assumptions underlying both the timing and content of these activities.

11 Teacher training

Why do we teach listening in the way that we do? This chapter explains how the history of ELT, educational imperatives and teacher preferences have helped shape the way we currently teach listening. We begin by considering how our training as teachers, together with our early experiences, fears and successes in the classroom contribute to shaping our teaching of listening. We will also evaluate the status of 'the knowledge' – the expertise that all trained teachers should possess to count as a 'good colleague and teacher'. Finally, after having dealt with the anger of a student after a traditional listening comprehension class, the chapter ends with a confession.

11.1 Teacher training

When we enter the ELT profession, we enter a world of knowledge, skills and classroom practices that have been established for a long time. We are trained to fit in with the standard practices of the particular ELT environment that we work in, whether this be a publicly funded school system in a country where English is a foreign or second language, or a private language school.

As we receive our initial training, and begin to form our professional identity, we need to develop our confidence in ourselves as teachers and to gain mastery over the key areas of our professional work. These areas include knowledge of the language, knowledge of how to handle classrooms full of students, and knowledge of how language learning happens. A considerable amount of this knowledge is embedded in the textbooks. With our initial and continuing education, together with the repertoire of 'activities which work' that we learn from our colleagues, we become acculturated to the profession. We adopt its norms, beliefs and practices – 'the knowledge' of the profession, which of course includes how to teach listening.

11.2 The knowledge

But what is the status of 'the knowledge'? It has developed from a number of assumptions and starting points, and it has evolved to suit the preferences of the profession: preferences for rules, for respecting tradition, for respecting academic authority and for respecting native-speaker intuition.

11.2.1 Rule dependence

ELT, like most of education, is dependent on rules. It is part of the professional expertise of teachers to have a deep knowledge of rules and exceptions to these rules. It is part of our classroom competence to be able to teach learners to use these rules in tests and examinations.

But the evidence of everyday speech points to a world where all rules are broken, and indeed where it is probably best to regard it as a domain (the Jungle) where there are no rules. We need to move from being rule-dependent, to developing our expertise so that we can embrace types of speech where all rules (if there are any) are both breakable and are often broken.

11.2.2 Tradition, authority and intuition

Our profession has great respect for its traditions and its historical inheritance, which is a praiseworthy thing. But the adherence to tradition, the respect for academic authority, and the veneration of native speaker intuition have a downside.

Tradition provides continuity, but it becomes a problem if it is so fixed and unquestioned that (for example) we justify the inclusion of rules and activities by saying 'because they have been around for ever'. Similarly with academic authority, it becomes a problem if we justify the retention of advice and information from previous decades by saying 'Because Professor X said so', ignoring the fact that more recent research has proven their statements to be wrong. And the veneration of native-speakers' knowledge, and their (questionable) ability to describe this knowledge, is unwarranted, as we have seen in Chapter 4. Thus it is that 'the knowledge' of ELT is dominated by the rules that come from tradition, authority and native-speaker intuition. These rules are seen as sacred, which makes them difficult to challenge. But we need to challenge them if we are going to improve the teaching of listening/decoding.

We need to consider the possibility, for example, that our textbooks and course books might contain misleading statements about everyday speech. There is the possibility that the information and advice of fifty years ago may no longer be valid. For example, this statement from 1967 has now been shown by researchers to be false:

> As far as is known, every language in the world is spoken with one kind of rhythm or with the other ... [syllable-timed ... stress-timed] ... (Abercrombie 1967: 97).

Research by Roach (1982), Dauer (1983) and others (summarised in Cauldwell, 2013: 131) have comprehensively demonstrated that this statement is untrue, but it lives on in the minds of teachers and teacher trainers, as well as textbook and course book writers.

ELT textbooks and course books are written to be commercially successful, and they therefore have to contain what the buyers of such books expect them to contain. The contents have to be seen to fit into the educational circumstances: what teachers can manage and what the examinations require. Their contents therefore evolve slowly, and this may mean that any innovation in one particular area would sit uncomfortably alongside other areas. For example, recent course books increasingly feature 'authentic' recordings. This is a welcome development, but the knowledge, metalanguage, and classroom activities to accompany these recordings remain largely unchanged, resulting in the authentic features of the recording – its Jungle features – being ignored.

11.3 Greatest fear and greatest wish

When I was beginning my career as a teacher, I had a number of fears and wishes. My greatest fear was to run out of material long before the end of the class, and to be faced with filling twenty minutes with nothing to teach. My greatest wish was to be liked by my class – I wanted them to think I was a good teacher, and I would judge whether or not this was the case by the amount of smiling and the level of energy in the classroom.

This fear and this wish led to a warped sense of judgement of what would actually be useful. For me, the criteria for judging the usefulness of an activity were (a) did it use up time and (b) did it get my students smiling and working well together. I realise now, with hindsight, that the alleviation of fear of running out of materials, together with the satisfaction of my wish to be liked, were warping my sense of usefulness.

I quickly developed the habit of allowing activities that were going well to last longer than I had originally planned. As far as listening was concerned, the pre-listening phase – with its enjoyable communicative contextualisations – worked well for me, so I was content to stay in this phase longer than was (as I look back now) useful. This had the wonderful advantage of reducing the amount of time available for the more uncomfortable parts of the listening lesson: the while-listening and post-listening parts. I was not alone in doing this (Field 2008b: 83) notes that there 'is a tendency by practitioners to over-extend' the pre-listening phase. I now realise that spending too much time on the pre-listening phase is just one of many obstacles to the effective teaching of decoding.

When the time came for the while-listening phase, my class suddenly changed from being a happy social group into a group of frowning isolated individuals (cf. Field, 1998b:14) and I did not like this transformation, feeling that it was my fault that they were not looking happy. I was therefore anxious to move on quickly – after checking the answers – to the next activity: a discussion, or a course book-based writing or reading activity. Serious learners who 'want to learn the language' do not always appreciate this use of time and avoidance of difficulty. Anna is one such learner.

11.4 Anna's anger

Anna is now a professor of English. Her first language was not English and so she learned it at school. When she was a student, she hated the approach of one of her teachers to listening lessons. She told me:

> ... I've hated the underuse of the material. I've ... answered three silly questions ... then someone tells me patronisingly (it IS bloody patronising) that the rest doesn't matter. Well it does if I want to learn the language!

It is worth exploring the kind of classroom activity that might have made her angry. Because this is a written book (I am communicating with you in sight substance), I am going to transpose her listening comprehension activity into a reading comprehension exercise on a very short text. It is a text that we have used in Chapters 1 and 3.

11.4.1 Recreating Anna's lesson

We will refer to the teacher as Ben, and this description is an imagined, fictional account of what might have happened in Anna's lesson.

Ben introduces the reading task by saying:

> You will read about an eighteen-year-old British woman, Emily, who was given a teaching job in a school in South Africa. She had gone there to work as a young volunteer. Look at the following questions then scan the text to find the answers.

He then introduces the following questions:

1. What subject was she given to teach? (a) Maths (b) English (c) Technology

2. How many pupils were in the school? (a) 500 (b) 1500 (c) 2000

3. How many times does the word 'teacher' occur? (a) once (b) twice (c) three times

Ben then gives the students the following passage to read (Figure 11.1).

FIGURE 11.1 EMILY'S JOB – THE TRANSCRIPT IS GIVEN IN THE ANSWER KEY

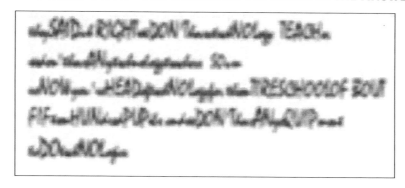

Figure 1 is a blurred version of the sight substance of a written transcription. There are a few differences from normal orthography: uppercase letters are for prominent syllables, and lowercase letters are for non-prominent syllables.

Having given the students time to arrive at answers, Ben then asks the class what they think the answers are, and praises students who answer correctly.

1. What subject …? (c) Technology
2. How many pupils …? (b) 1500
3. How many times … 'teacher'? (b) twice

Ben then moves on to another activity, refusing to answer any other questions, because there is (he believes) nothing else to do. The communicative act of arriving at an understanding of the meaning has been achieved, so Ben believes that his and his students' work is complete as far as this activity is concerned.

Because in this example the language is presented as sight substance, it remains available for inspection. This is completely unlike sound substance, which will have departed the scene, and would therefore be invisible. Out of sight, out of mind – and, unfortunately, ignorable.

However, because (in our imaginary scenario) Anna is looking at sight substance, she and her fellow students can point to the blur and ask: 'What does this mean?' But actually (and this is the point) they are more likely to ask 'What are these words?' Because picking out the words in this blurred sight substance is difficult. And this is the crucial issue about learning to decode in listening: much of the sound substance is experienced as an unanalysable blur. Decoding (recognising words) in the sight substance of normal writing is easy, but it is exponentially more difficult in the sound substance. In the sound substance, decoding requires far more teaching and learning than we currently give it.

Anna's desire to learn the language is not satisfied by having completed the task of answering the questions. For Anna the communicative task is an exercise in coping with language that she has not yet mastered and extracting meanings from it with her current level of resources in the language. For her, answering three comprehension questions does not equate to learning the language – she wants to stay with the recording and try to improve her ability to recognise words in the sound substance.

So rather than walk away from the sound substance, what could Ben have done in the listening lesson? (We now revert to sound substance.) The answer is simple: stay with the sound substance of the recording. Always, always, always allow time for this task:

> Now that you know the answers, listen again, and try and identify the words or sounds that lead to the correct answers.

This is just one way to begin a decoding activity following the use of a recording for comprehension purposes. Part 4 presents more things to do.

11.5 The smiling class imperative

I was trained in the tradition of Communicative Language Teaching (CLT) and, I suspect, so was Anna's teacher. The values of this training are rooted in the ideal sight and sound of an active cheerful class of learners: preferably smiling, but visibly busy doing something. My training predisposed me to obey a communicative imperative which demanded rapid movement from activity to activity in order to provide variety, thereby keeping my students' interest and motivation levels high. I valued the sight of them enjoying social interaction in English.

The problem with this is that decoding speech (of all kinds, not just spontaneous speech) is a private, non-observable mental process. It happens inside the head of the individual. Social elements can be added to the learning of listening in which students co-operate during activities and discuss what they have heard, but essentially the process of listening takes place in a private, unobservable dimension (cf. Vandergrift & Goh, 2012: 82).

So we get into a vicious circle: when students encounter speech which is challenging for them (spontaneous or scripted), they are often horrified (Thorn, 2009: 8), and a happy, active class can be reduced to a silent awkwardness by the isolating effect of needing to work in this private dimension (Field, 1998b: 14).

I wanted to avoid the sight of learners looking uncomfortable or glum as they struggled to perceive and understand the acoustic blur of speech. As mentioned in 11.3, I quickly adopted an avoidance strategy which involved moving on rapidly from the listening activity to the next activity – writing, speaking, reading – which would get the class visibly busy once more.

So one skill (or tolerance) that it is essential for a teacher of listening to have is to be comfortable at the sight of visible discomfort in the learners in the early and middle stages of a listening lesson. It is necessary to allow learners to feel challenged, and it may be necessary for them to feel temporarily frustrated in the face of the learning opportunities presented by the listening task. We return to this issue in Chapter 19.

11.6 My confession

It took me until twelve years into my teaching career before I realised I was deaf to what is really going on in the sound substance of speech. In the terms of Chapter 4, I was deaf to the blur gap. The realisation came when I sat down with a learner (in the early 1990s) in front of a computer screen and edited the sound file of the recording into small sections, each containing a speech unit. The learner looked at the transcript and listened to the sound file and said that he could not hear the words of the transcript. The sound file in question is given as Extract 11.1.

EXTRACT 11.1 WHERE THERE WERE

```
|| where there were STREET LIGHTS ||
```

From Brazil (1994) reproduced with permission.

He acknowledged that he had heard some sound substance, but he could not match it to the words he saw. After a couple of replays he heard the first two words as the single word *weather.* This was astonishing to me. My mental representation of the words *where* and *there* did not include the possibility of their sounding like a single word. My representation probably consisted of a blend of sight and sound substance (which I was wholly unused to separating), and the sound substance component of this representation certainly did not include the possibility of these words being such a fast blur of sound. My mental representation was of the Greenhouse and Garden for the sound dimension, and both sight and sound substance were acting together to prime me into thinking that the reality of the speech in the recording was much slower, clearer and tidier than it was in actuality. I was clearly suffering from the blur gap (cf. Chapter 4).

This realisation awakened memories of my early experiences of teaching, and being trained as a teacher. I believe that like me, many teachers, particularly early in their career, feel that something essential is not being addressed when they are trained to teach listening. But then we become trained in how to teach listening comprehension exercises, and become accustomed to the conventions of what counts as 'a good lesson' in the listening classroom. So accustomed, in fact, that there seems to be no approach to listening that is not a listening comprehension exercise or some version of it. So the initial discomfort fades into the backs of our minds.

As a result we are unable to teach our students how to decode the stream of speech. Not only that – if we follow conventional methodology, we behave as if we do not need to. Fortunately, it seems, some teachers being trained more recently are learning to teach decoding somewhat earlier in their careers than I did (cf. Chinn & Willoughby, 2016).

11.7 Summary and what's next

Students very often feel bad about themselves as listeners. They attribute this to a failing in themselves – a personal failing – when it is, in fact, a weakness in the field of language teaching. Many of their difficulties lie outside themselves. The difficulties lie largely in (a) the poor level of knowledge that the ELT profession in general has about the true nature of the sound substance of speech, (b) our insistence on treating the sound substance of everyday speech as more tidy and rule-governed than it actually is and (c) a tendency to treat the sound substance as if it were just another form of the sight substance.

In Chapter 12 we will continue our analysis of why we teach listening in the way that we do by identifying further obstacles to the effective teaching of listening. Some of these obstacles are 'virtuous' in that they are educationally useful, but happen to have negative side effects for listening; others are obstacles that have come into existence because of the way the ELT profession has evolved.

12 Virtuous obstacles

In this Chapter we will continue our analysis of why we teach listening in the way that we do by identifying further obstacles to the effective teaching of listening. Some of these obstacles are 'virtuous' in that they are educationally useful, but happen to have negative side effects for listening; other obstacles have emerged because of the way the ELT profession has evolved.

We have encountered, in earlier chapters, a number of major obstacles already:

- the attraction of the sight substance

- the preference for the Greenhouse and Garden domains

- the preference for working at the level of understanding

- the avoidance of working at the level of decoding

- the two gaps which expert listeners and learners are victims of – the blur gap and the decoding gap

However, there are additional and significant obstacles to be found in beliefs which are regarded as common knowledge or common sense and 'self-evidently true' in the profession.

12.1 Exposure

The first obstacle is the misplaced reliance on exposure.

There is a very common view that the way to learn to listen in a second or foreign language is through extensive listening, through exposure to large amounts of speech in the target language. This is, after all, how L1 listeners learn. The idea is that we expose learners to large amounts of spoken language without forcing them to try too hard to understand it, instead letting it wash around their ears. The hope is that learners will eventually acclimatise to and internalise the 'rules' of spontaneous speech. This view is articulated by Ridgway:

> Practice is the most important thing. The more listening the better, and the subskills will take care of themselves as they become automatized. (2000: 183)

The view is that by doing lots of listening, and by directing attention to the level of understanding, the problems of decoding will automatically resolve themselves. Buck agrees, writing of the value of practice and the importance of passing 'lots of meaningful language through their language processors in order that natural learning processing can occur' (1995: 123). For Field (2009: 13), however, the idea that 'listening necessarily gets better, the more one hears' is a mistaken one.

Admittedly, 'listening to lots' does eventually work, but it is a very slow process, and usually requires that you live in an English-language environment, often after the end of formal language education.

The reliance on exposure is tantamount to a surrender – a failure to teach when there is something to teach. There is a huge amount of information we can give our students about such things as the soundshapes of words and word clusters, and about Jungle processes, and there are activities which will significantly improve their abilities to catch and decode words in the stream of speech.

12.2 The link to reading

The second obstacle is the link to reading.

We treat listening activities as if they are just another form of reading activity (cf. Field, 2008: 6, 28). The terminology is similar ('for gist', 'for detail') and the exercise and task types are also very similar. On seeing a listening activity that is constructed on the model of a reading activity, the strong temptation is to ignore the fundamental differences which exist between the two skills and the different forms of language involved – sight substance and sound substance. This is a dangerous temptation, because the sight substance of the reading activity presents few, if any, problems of decoding, whereas the sound substance is likely to present many such problems.

And because both activities are mostly focused on comprehension – at the level of understanding meaning – the level of decoding is ignored. Field (2008: 28) describes the effects of treating listening as similar to reading. Such an approach ...

> ... directs the attention of the teacher away from many of the features which make listening distinctive. These features are precisely the ones which cause most difficulty for the learner and the ones that we need to focus on if we wish to promote more effective listening. (Field, 2008: 28)

Thus, because of the (supposed) similarity to the skill of reading, and the similarity of the accompanying activities, the fundamental differences between the skills of reading and listening are ignored, to the detriment of decoding.

12.3 'Just listen to the stresses'

The third obstacle to the effective teaching of listening/decoding is the misplaced trust in the process of catching stressed syllables and then building meanings.

Listening exercises are also characterised by the hope which often appears in the following words of encouragement: 'Just listen to the stresses – they'll be on the most important words – then you'll understand.' Learners are then encouraged to build meaning on the basis of the words that they have caught by listening out for the stresses, and then arrive at a reasonable interpretation of the meaning. Brown (1990, 151) sets out this view:

> It is essential in English to learn to pay attention to the stressed syllable of a word, since this is the best and most stable feature of a word's profile, and to those words in the stream of speech which are stressed, since these mark the richest information-bearing units. (Brown, 1990, 151)

There are three major problems with this widely accepted view: first 'important' words are very often **unstressed**, and so-called 'unimportant' function words such as prepositions and pronouns **are** stressed; second, research indicates that it is difficult to pick out stressed words in a language which is not your own (cf. Roach, 1982); third, the concept of stress is loosely defined and fails to distinguish between word-level stress, and stresses associated with higher order phenomena such as prominences in speech units (cf. Appendix 1 for more on word stress and prominence).

Research by Cutler and Carter (1987) is often quoted in support of this strategy. They found that 85 percent of non-function (lexical) words in English are either monosyllabic, or begin with a stressed syllable, so listening out for stressed syllables would seem to be a good strategy for lexical segmentation – catching and decoding words in the stream of speech. However, their finding came from research into sight-substance versions of the words of the English lexicon, using dictionary and written corpus searches. Thus the Jungle phenomena of everyday speech were not covered.

Learners have a view on this advice. Haga (2017) reports that having given this listen-for-the-stresses advice to her class, one pre-intermediate student told her:

> Yes, it works, but only if you got the words correctly, otherwise you just imagine it's something, when it's something else.

Haga's student is saying two important things here: first that getting 'the words correctly' is a prerequisite for the 'listen for stresses' advice to work. Her second point brings us to the next obstacle, which will expand further on the student's words 'you just imagine it's something, when it's something else.'

12.4 Assigning too much power to context

The fourth obstacle is the over-reliance on guessing meanings from context.

Almost always, looking closely at the contextual factors (situation, topic, preceding conversation) of an utterance will help explain the choices of words, and the meanings expressed. It will enable us to intuit 'what the speaker meant to say' even in cases of extremely streamlined speech in poor listening conditions. So, in L1 listening, contextual clues and the expectations of what someone is likely to say are very powerful aids to understanding. So powerful, in fact, that it may seem to the L1 and expert listener that very little decoding is necessary. But things are different for learner listeners.

For our learners, the use of contextual considerations to guess the meanings is a useful compensatory strategy to use when they cannot decode (Field, 2009: 14). But they cannot simply rely on guessing – they need a threshold level of decoding in order to begin to build meanings: learners need 'to be able to decode a minimum number of words in order to construct that context in the first place' (Field, 2009: 14). So teachers and learners need to be able to focus on, and work with, the raw sound substance to learn how words can be recognised in this substance.

12.4.1 Football

When the process of building meanings involves guesswork, it may go wrong. Imagine two people in a coffee shop in Spain wearing Manchester United and Liverpool football shirts and speaking English. To a learner sitting at a nearby table it will seem from their hand gestures, and the way they are moving cutlery around the table, that they are discussing offside decisions in football. The learner hears the following and believes they are talking about an incident in a recent football game:

> Blah blah blah MAN blah blah blah blah CHEST uh blah blah blah off SIDE blah LIVer blah blah uh blah blah blah off SIDE

But actually it turns out that they are surgeons attending a conference, who are having an evening drink before watching a football match on television. In fact they happen to be talking about the topic of the conference, the use of anaesthetics:

> There was this **man** who came for a **chest**-wall uh operation and we used nitrous o**xide** and then we had a **liver** procedure when we also used nitrous o**xide**.

Seeing a Manchester United shirt and hearing *chest uh* and then taking *oxide* to be *offside,* and then hearing *liver procedure* as *Liverpool,* the keen learner wrongly guesses, from the context suggested by the football shirts and the hand movements that this is a conversation about football. In short, guessing is not a reliable aid to comprehension – it will help sometimes, but it is not dependable. Indeed, research (see next section) has shown that an adequate level of decoding skills is required to cope with the huge number of situations in which the conversation, or a turn in a conversation, does not match the observables in the context.

12.4.2 Research

Tsui and Fullilove (1998) investigated learners' answers in L2 listening exams. They state that the use, by 'less-skilled L2 listeners', of compensatory guessing made possible by 'plenty of contextual support' is insufficient to allow them to cope with listening test recordings which set up a predictable situation and then deviate from it. This is because their bottom-up processing is so weak that 'they need plenty of contextual support to compensate for the lack of automatized linguistic decoding skill' (ibid: 448–9).

So, to become more skilled L2 listeners, Tsui and Fullilove say that learners 'need to learn to become less reliant on guessing from contextual or prior knowledge and more reliant on rapid and accurate decoding of the linguistic input' (ibid).

The use of context, and guessing strategies, are helpful as strategies for coping in the absence of the ability to decode. But they are not in themselves activities which teach learners how to decode the sound substance.

12.5 Second mention

The fifth obstacle is a reliance on the power of a clear first mention of a word to help in the catching and decoding of subsequent Jungle-form versions of that word.

Another optimistic view of speech is the belief that words, the first time they occur in a discourse, will be spoken clearly and that only in subsequent mentions will they occur in streamlined Jungle forms. The view is that any Jungle form will not be a problem for learners because it will be easy for them to relate the Jungle soundshape to the Greenhouse/Garden form, and thus be able to decode the word.

I have described this view of repeated words as 'optimistic' because it assumes a situation in which speakers are considerate of the listener's needs, and that they do what they are supposed to do (clear form first, then less clear forms are allowed). It also assumes that the listeners have been listening from the very beginning, when the words concerned were mentioned for the very first time. It further assumes that words can be identified when they are merged or streamed with neighbouring words and when they are spoken non-prominently in the squeeze zone of a speech unit (cf. Chapter 9.4).

However, research by Bard et al. (2000) suggests that speakers may not be so listener-considerate in their behaviour. And Wilson (2003), in the lesson described in Chapter 14.7, reports that his students could not hear the second mention of the word 'construction' in the noun group 'construction projects' even though…

> … they had successfully recognized 'construction' at the beginning of the text, and knew the word 'projects' (Wilson 2003: 340)

My experience is that words in their reduced forms can suffer such extreme streamlining (e.g. *student* becomes *stewn*; *actually* becomes *ashy*) that learners cannot catch or decode them in the stream of speech, even if they have been mentioned earlier and successfully decoded at that point.

12.6 Success in comprehension means success in decoding

The sixth obstacle is an over-reliance on the idea that success in listening comprehension automatically means that there has been success in decoding.

Because of the preference for dealing with listening at the level of understanding (and the non-preference for decoding), it is tempting to regard success in the listening comprehension task as a sign that decoding has been successful. Unfortunately, comprehension success is not a reliable indicator of success in decoding. In fact it is possible for students to answer the comprehension questions correctly, without having successfully decoded much of the sound substance. Indeed Field (2008 :81) suggests the possibility that two different learners may have arrived at the correct answer, with one of them having a 90 percent decoding success, and the other only 10 percent, the latter succeeding only because she 'relied upon contextual information for support'.

It is possible that even someone with very low decoding ability can use contextual considerations, world knowledge and astute analysis of the listening comprehension questions to arrive at the correct answers from the way the activity is set up, both by the materials and the teacher. As Field warns us:

> L2 listeners manage to identify much less of the word-by-word input which is presented to them than we tend to suppose. (Field, 1998a: 24)

12.7 The limitations of the transcript

The seventh obstacle is that offered by the temptations of the transcript.

Let's be clear here: the transcript is not the recording. It is something else entirely: it is a translation into a sight-substance version of the sound substance. It may represent accurately the words and meanings the speaker intended to say and convey, but it does so in a way that misrepresents the sound substance. In the sight substance all words have equal realisations – they are preceded and followed by spaces, and they are experienced at the speed of the reader. The extent to which they are reduced in the sound substance, and the relative speed of different sections, can only be guessed at. The decoding problems associated with the sound substance are obscured from view by the certainty, concreteness and stick-around-ability of the sight substance.

As teachers and materials writers prepare lessons and course books, the transcript also provides a strong temptation to ignore the properties of the sound substance. After all, it already provides a rich source of new vocabulary, structures and idiomatic usages. All of these things are useful but they can easily be an excuse for ignoring work on decoding.

I would argue that the transcript should be used as a discovery tool which leads to the identification of problems, either by teachers before the class, or by learners as a preparation for future work, as we will see in Part 4.

12.8 Goal-mimicking activities

The eighth obstacle is the tendency to try to teach listening through an unchanging diet of goal-mimicking activities based on findings from research into L1 listening.

One of the pieces of advice given to learner listeners is 'Don't try to listen to every word.' This advice is often justified by research into L1 listening: 'We don't listen to every word when we are listening in our first language, so you don't need to listen to every word in listening in your second language'.

This advice is unhelpful because it confuses goal and pedagogy. We would like our learners to acquire the expert-listener ability to be able to decode automatically without apparent effort – this is the goal. But achieving this goal is not best done by getting learners to replicate goal behaviour on repeated occasions.

We need to think of the journey to the goal as consisting of baby steps of learning that start where the learners are, and which take them item-by-item towards the goal of becoming an expert listener.

12.9 Goal-mimicking – one listening only

The ninth obstacle is the view that listening comprehension lessons should only consist of one play of the recording.

The justification for this is that in most situations in the real world, you only get one chance to listen: you can ask the speaker to repeat what they say, but you cannot do this all the time because the speaker may lose patience with you.

There is value in the single play if you are preparing learners to cope in the real world with their current linguistic and decoding abilities. But it is training in coping – it is not in itself a teaching or learning activity. Even in listening tests, this single-play option is unfair. As Field (2015) points out, a single listen places demands on a listener which are greater than the real world presents – they have to normalise the speaker's voice and tune in to it, while simultaneously completing the tasks of the test – all on the basis of a single listen. This is in contrast to the real world where normalisation is already likely to have happened over a period of time prior to any particular three-minute stretch of speech.

12.10 The lure of authenticity

The tenth obstacle is the reliance on the very presence of authentic recordings as the solution to the problems of L2 listening.

Authentic recordings come in many different types: they may be recordings that were not originally created for language learning or recordings of ordinary people speaking spontaneously about their daily lives (cf. Thorn's 'Real Life, Real Listening' series, 2013). The arrival of authentic recordings on the ELT scene has been a great step forward in materials design.

However, in order to cope with what happens in these recordings we need to upgrade our capacity both to hear what the sound substance contains, and to describe it in classroom-friendly terms. Our current methods of describing speech phenomena are very much Greenhouse- and Garden-based, and comprise a Careful Speech Model which does not have the conceptual tools to deal with the untidiness and unruliness of the Jungle.

Part 3 of *A Syllabus for Listening: Decoding* will present the descriptive language (metalanguage) and ear-training to help develop a Spontaneous Speech Model (SSM) to cope with the sound substance of authentic recordings.

12.11 Important information is not in the training chain

The eleventh obstacle is that we don't receive (possibly because we don't want to, or it is thought that we can't cope with) the truth about speech from the academic sources that should be providing it.

One way of viewing the method by which the ELT profession obtains its knowledge is that there is a chain of transmission from phoneticians and phonologists, to teacher trainers, and then to teachers. The problem is that the knowledge of the realities of spontaneous speech which exists at the start of this chain does not travel along the chain – it remains at the top. This is partly because ELT demands information and material which fits well with its Greenhouse/Garden paradigm of rules, predictability, notions of correctness and the imperative of being a good fit with the written language.

When phoneticians write for the ELT market, their focus is heavily weighted towards pronunciation (cf. Cauldwell, 2017). They are writing for teachers of pronunciation, and although they may occasionally mention rapid or casual speech phenomena, it is often with a warning along the lines of 'it's rare – and you shouldn't speak like this … avoid it'. This may be excellent advice for pronunciation, but we need a different kind of advice for teaching decoding – advice which tells us what can happen in the Jungle.

12.12 The role of strategies

The twelfth obstacle is an over-reliance, and an inappropriate use, of strategies.

The use of compensatory strategies such as 'prediction' and 'monitoring' are primarily tools for learners to use when their knowledge of the language (grammar, vocabulary and sound substance) is insufficiently expert to decode and understand what they are listening to. These strategies are not in themselves language-learning tools.

The overreliance on strategies, coupled with the lack of a decoding syllabus for listening, results in the contents of course book sections titled 'Understanding fast speech' containing the following recommendations:

- Make predictions

- Look for visual clues

- Enjoy listening

- Ask questions about what you have heard

(Dummet et al. 2017: 31)

In this list, as well as the strategy of predicting, there is advice about enjoying listening and asking questions. These pieces of advice are virtuous in themselves, but they are obstacles to progress in decoding.

Prediction and other strategies tend to occupy course book space to the exclusion of something that would be equally, if not far more useful – activities which build up learners' capacity to decode. There is more on strategies in Chapter 14.

12.13 'We've done it in pronunciation'

The thirteenth obstacle is the belief that if something is good for pronunciation, then it is also good for listening.

Sometimes, in teacher-training workshops, experienced teachers – when Jungle ideas are being introduced to them – respond 'Yeah yeah, we know all that, we've done it in pronunciation.' But what they actually mean is that they already know about the Garden – the rules of connected speech, such as linking, assimilation, elision and so on.

These rules are extremely useful for the goals of pronunciation – creating a clear, fluent stream of understandable and listenable-to speech – but they are not appropriate for the teaching of listening. Indeed it is vital to separate the notions of pronunciation and decoding. The term 'pronunciation' has very strong connotations of correctness, and equally strong associations with the Greenhouse and Garden forms of words. The reason we are using the terms 'soundshapes', 'sound substance', and 'vocal gymnastics' (cf. Part 4) rather than 'receptive pronunciation' is to avoid these connotations and associations.

12.14 Summary and what's next

Current listening methodology is dominated by strategies, prediction, schema activation and an adherence to an inappropriate model of speech – the Careful Speech Model (CSM) – to which we turn our attention in the next chapter.

Top-down activities take up too much time in the listening classroom and leave little space for the huge prerequisite for understanding speech: the perception and decoding of speech.

Strategy training, prediction, schema activation and so on comprise a peripheral syllabus that distract us from the heart of the matter. It is like going to a dance class where the instruction is all about the correct clothes and shoes to wear; biographical information about the composers of songs that you dance to; and about how to sit correctly while watching others dance. But all you do is sit and watch.

Language teaching is dominated by a model of clear intelligible speech which has been devised for the purpose of teaching of pronunciation. This is the Careful Speech Model, to which we now turn our attention.

13 Models of speech

Chapter 12 identified thirteen obstacles to the effective teaching of decoding. However, perhaps the biggest obstacle is the dominance of the Careful Speech Model (CSM). In this chapter we contrast the assumptions and rules of the CSM with statements from the Spontaneous Speech Model (SSM), which we need to help us improve the teaching of listening/decoding.

As a profession, I believe that we have been very successful in using the CSM for the purpose for which it has evolved – pronunciation. But for the purposes of improving the teaching of listening, and doing more decoding in the classroom, we need another model to sit alongside it – the Spontaneous Speech Model (SSM).

As you read through this chapter, you may get the sense that *A Syllabus for Listening: Decoding* is anti-CSM and that I want to get rid of the CSM. There are four reasons why this is not so. First, it is not possible to abandon the CSM – it is simply too entrenched in the fabric of 'the knowledge' of ELT to be abandoned. Second, it is useful for the goals of pronunciation: it promotes clarity and intelligibility. Third, it is as closely related as it is possible to be to the other components of language teaching and learning: words, sentences, questions and statements, and so on. Fourth, it enables the construction of items for tests about teachers' knowledge of the language. It is a (relatively) safe, pedagogically-friendly model, and is a good starting point for dealing with the real world of everyday speech. However, as soon as learners walk out of the classroom into the real world they find that this model, as delivered by ELT, has failed them. They discover that they are underperforming on an essential component of proficiency – listening. So for all its strengths, it has one major weakness: it does not prepare learners for real-life encounters with everyday speech.

In the sections which follow, we will look at some of the features of the CSM and then give a contrasting view of each feature from the point of view of the Spontaneous Speech Model.

13.1 Careful speech model (CSM)

The CSM is the assortment of statements, rules and guidelines about the soundshapes of words and soundscapes (to be defined below) of sentences that are used in ELT. The CSM is a means of mapping the sound substance on to the sight substance of the written language so that it provides answers to questions such as 'What is the correct way to pronounce this word?' and 'What is the correct way to say this sentence?' It is valued because it can be referred to as a set of rules or guidelines for learners to make their speech clear, intelligible and easy to listen to.

The CSM is a prescriptive model which has evolved to suit the preferences of ELT. It is taught on teacher-training courses and it informs the rules of speech which are found in textbooks. It includes both Greenhouse and Garden forms of the soundshapes of words and descriptions of what happens to words in sentences. Examples of the latter are 'rules' including 'pauses occur at the end of a sentence', 'English is stress-timed', 'nuclear stress goes on the last lexical item in a sentence' and 'falling tone means certainty'. In the sections which follow we will cover some of the reasons why these rules are not true of the Jungle, but for a fuller account, cf. Cauldwell (2013).

Before we go on, I need to define the term mentioned earlier, 'soundscape'. This term is derived from the word 'landscape' which refers to a long-distance view of a flat plain, or rolling hills, or mountains and valleys. We will use 'soundscape' to mean something larger than a speech unit: a stretch of speech which has a distinctive soundshape – from monotone to mountainous and from slow to fast. The soundscape is not about words themselves, but about the overall shaping of the sound substance into which the soundshapes of words fit.

13.2 First approximation

The statements and rules of the CSM are best thought of as first approximations to the truth. A first approximation is an idea that you start with to help you begin to understand a certain issue. It is a simple statement, and only partially true: a first step on a path of explanation and investigation which – if pursued – reveals levels of increasing complexity, increased understanding and, eventually, expert knowledge. As a profession, our knowledge has tended to stay close to first approximations – 'English is stress-timed' and 'Questions have rising intonation' are examples of this. Expert knowledge exists, but it does not have a foothold in language teaching.

In essence, the route to expert knowledge starts with something simple but not wholly true, and as further steps are taken on the route to expert knowledge, the not-wholly-true elements are discarded along the way and replaced by items of expert knowledge.

13.3 The Careful and Spontaneous Speech Models

The sense in which we are using the word 'model' is 'the set of statements which prescribe, or advise, how speech ought to be spoken' (the CSM) or 'the set of statements which describe how speech is spoken in reality' (the SSM). The word 'model' is not used here to denote a system or a process in the sense of an ordered sequence of events.

13.3.1 The Careful Speech Model (CSM) – easy to find

Components of the CSM can be found in the contents pages of many ELT course books and in teacher-training textbooks. Recent accounts of the CSM can be found in publications such as Wells (2006), Celce-Murcia et al (2010) Roach (2009) and Cruttenden (2014).

13.3.2 The Spontaneous Speech Model (SSM) – hard to find

Partial descriptions of the SSM can be found in most of our teacher-training textbooks. But you have to look hard, and read carefully past the first-approximation statements. You need also to be aware that where the focus is on pronunciation (as it most often is), we will be warned not to teach the phenomena of spontaneous speech. Cruttenden (2014), the 8th edition *Gimson's Pronunciation of English* gives us an example:

> … there are some **uncommon** reduced forms which are heard **only in rapid speech** … and **these should not be imitated by foreign learners**. The use of |jə| or |mə| in such phrases as *your mother, my father* will sound slangy and, if employed inappropriately by a learner, could appear comically incongruous (p. 333 – emphasis added).

The key words in this quotation are given in bold: two of them are statements of frequency ('uncommon' and 'only in') and the other is a piece of advice to avoid these examples ('these should not … ').

From the Jungle perspective of the SSM, statements of frequency such as 'uncommon' and 'only' need to be taken to mean 'can happen at any time', and 'are very likely to happen in spontaneous speech' (cf. Cauldwell, 2017). We need to embrace, rather than avoid, these phenomena because our goal is the teaching of listening.

The fact that our current teacher training of the sound substance focuses almost entirely on pronunciation means that spontaneous speech phenomena are largely excluded from consideration. And this exclusion contributes hugely to the situation where listening lags behind the other skills.

13.4 The shaping of speech

Speech is shaped. Words and word clusters (cf. Chapter 16) have many different soundshapes, and together they make up a stream of multi-word sound substance which has its own soundscape: it has a rhythm and an intonational shape which varies from the mountainous to the monotonous. Who or what creates this shaping?

13.4.1 CSM – The English language shapes speech

In the CSM, it is the English language which shapes speech. Words have a structure of consonants, vowels and syllables in their Greenhouse form. In the Garden, words are assembled into sentences where the nature of the sentence (statement or question) dictates the intonation; and the nature of the words (content or functional) dictates where the most important stresses go.

13.4.2 SSM – Speakers shape speech

In the SSM, it is the speakers who shape the sound substance of spontaneous speech. The words that they speak come out as a stream to which they – the speakers – give shape. What they say, and how they say it, is appropriate – in their eyes – to the context in which they are speaking. They shape the soundscape in any way they like, provided it is consistent with their communicative purposes.

Speakers' attention is on effective communication under real-time pressures, not on creating accurate sentences by applying rules. They shape the sound substance, pausing where they like, assigning prominences where they feel they need to and using intonation in ways which defy any attempts to set rules. The speakers – not the language, not the vocabulary, nor the grammar – shape the sound substance (cf. Chapter 8.5).

13.5 Greenhouse, Garden and Jungle

Chapter 2 introduced the three domains of speech: the Greenhouse (domain of the citation form), the Garden (domain of connected speech rules) and the Jungle (domain of the unruly messiness of spontaneous speech). The CSM and the SSM inhabit different domains.

13.5.1 CSM is content with Greenhouse and Garden

The domains of the CSM are the Greenhouse and the Garden. The CSM has evolved for, and is ideal for, teaching pronunciation. It is a tidy model, featuring rules which are suitable for answering questions such as 'How do I pronounce this word?' and 'How do I say this sentence?' or 'How can I use my voice more effectively in giving presentations?' Behind all such questions is the desire to be clear and intelligible – the goal of pronunciation teaching and learning. And this is the key point – the CSM is extremely well suited to the task of giving advice to learners on pronunciation.

13.5.2 SSM and the Jungle – focus on listening

The domain of the SSM is the Jungle, where words are crushed into shapes of all kinds and may occur in a huge variety of flavours (accents) and in a wide variety of colours (emotionally-loaded). Speech will vary in speed moment-by-moment, and will feature long patches of lack of clarity. Patches of Greenhouse and Garden speech may occur, but it is not helpful to treat them as if they are the norm.

13.6 Units of speech

The CSM and SSM have different views of the units of speech.

13.6.1 CSM – People speak in clauses

The CSM is a snug fit for sentence grammar, and this makes it sit comfortably in a teaching environment that is dominated by study of pages of sight substance. It is rule-governed and tidy. The CSM rests on the assumption that there is a pre-existing sentence, which is being read aloud, and as we have seen, it provides advice and rules which are answers to the question 'How do I say this sentence?' Both the learner asking the question and the teacher answering it can look at the sentence, analyse it phrase by phrase, and make judgements about which rules to apply. This is essentially work on 'sounding out' the sight substance of language.

The CSM promotes the view that there is a close relationship between the intonation group and the clause, or another grammatical component of a clause such as noun groups or verb groups (cf. Roach 2009: 155). In the CSM, pauses come at boundaries of grammatical units. They do not occur inside noun groups or verb groups.

Because the object of attention is the pre-existing written sentence, the CSM believes that it is possible to make predictions about how a speaker would normally say the sentence. This is often done by conceiving of a situation where an utterance comes 'out-of-the-blue' with no preceding co-text or context, or that it occurs as an answer to the question 'What happened?' In such cases, the rule is that '… the nucleus falls on the relevant syllable of the last lexical item' (Cruttenden, 2014: 286).

The logic of the concept of 'out-of-the-blue' seems to depend on the view that the English language is the main determinant of the shape of speech. But as we have seen in 13.4.2, the agent of nuclear stress placement is not the language, nor the situation, but the speaker for whom there is always a preceding psychological context, and not necessarily one that is shared with the listener.

13.6.2 SSM – People speak in rhythmic bursts

In the SSM, speakers create speech step-by-step in real time. They speak in multi-word rhythmic rushes, bursts, torrents, flows, trickles and seeps. They create an acoustic flow whose physical attributes (the pauses, undulations and ups and downs of the soundscape) are an emergent feature of (a) higher-order choices at the level of meaning/understanding and (b) their desire to communicate effectively in real time.

Extract 13.1 shows an example from Dan (Cauldwell, 2013: 82) who breaks up the noun group *the main stuff* with a long pause.

EXTRACT 13.1
```
01 || and then I'D sing the || 5 sps
02 || the MAIN || 4 sps
[pause 0.8  seconds]
03 || STUFF || 2 sps
```
Voice: Dan, UK. The figures at the end of each line give the speed of each unit in syllables per second.

Thus because speech is created step-by-step in real time, predictions about the sound substance of what will be said, and how it will be said, are unlikely to be accurate, useful, or even possible. Pauses can occur anywhere, even interrupting noun groups and verb groups – something that would be strongly deprecated in the CSM.

13.7 Disfluencies and drafting phenomena

The sight substance of language as used in ELT is carefully edited for accuracy and is largely intolerant of errors and mistakes, or indeed anything which disrupts the smooth flow of the perfect sentence. The term 'disfluency' (also 'dysfluency') is a pejorative term widely used to refer to spontaneous speech phenomena such as pauses, hesitations and restarts.

13.7.1 CSM – Disfluencies

The CSM has the view that the normal form of the language is a more-or-less perfect sentence, with no disfluencies. When we look at the sentences which make up our textbook examples, we are looking at text in its final version which has been through an editing process. This final version contains no trace of the history of the creation of the text. No trace of writers pausing mid-sentence to choose the best word, deleting phrases and sentences that are no longer wanted, taking a sip of coffee and correcting spelling. The CSM predisposes us, therefore, to regard language which contains drafting phenomena such as *um*, *er*, and restarts (cf. Cauldwell 2013: 81ff.) as deviant in that they contain disfluencies.

13.7.2 SSM – Drafting phenomena

Spontaneous speech does not have a pre-existing life as edited sight substance. It is created at the time of utterance, and added to piece-by-piece in real time. And because it is 'online', in that it occurs in real time, all acts of editing are audible. They are present in the sound substance, and – unless you are dealing with a recording – cannot be excised after the event, because they have already occurred. They form an integral part of the sound substance.

So if we take the following written sentence, we can see that it is tidy and fluent, and therefore worthy of a place in the CSM:

```
He ran all the way to the station.
```

A version loaded with drafting phenomena would look more like this (the basic sentence is shown in bold and everything else is part of the drafting process):

```
Well, um, I mean, it was like he kind of like ran pretty much all um the
way to, you know the, bus-stop, sorry not the bus stop, I meant to say
the station.
```

The SSM recognises that the sound substance of spontaneous speech contains drafting phenomena rather than disfluencies.

13.8 Soundshapes

The word 'soundshape' refers to the sound-substance version of a word, how it sounds to a listener. In this book we are deliberately avoiding the use of the term 'pronunciation' because it has very strong connotations of correctness.

13.8.1 CSM – Citation form preference

The CSM holds the view that all words other than 'weak forms' (see below) have a single soundshape, the citation form, which may be modified slightly, according to a limited set of connected speech rules (cf. Chapter 13.12 below).

13.8.2 SSM – Multiple soundshapes

In the SSM, all words of all types have multiple soundshapes and accents. This is because, as Brown (1990: 62) tells us, every consonant and vowel (and not just those found in the most frequent words) 'will be affected by its neighbouring consonants and vowels and by the rhythmic structure in which it occurs'.

Indeed the really small words (such as articles and prepositions) may have a zero soundshape. Although they may be perceived to be present by L1 and expert listeners, they may not in fact exist in the sound substance. There will be more on this in Part 3.

But it is not simply these small words which undergo changes in their soundshapes. Research shows that all words, including long lexical words, are subject to processes which give a wide variety of soundshapes (cf. Johnson, 2004; Ernestus, 2014: 28).

13.9 Weak forms

The CSM recognises, to a certain extent, the variability of soundshapes through the list of 'weak forms'.

13.9.1 CSM – Weak forms an exclusive list

In the CSM, the list of weak forms in Cruttenden (2014) is regarded by many, erroneously, as a complete list. There are approximately fifty function words in the list. Examples include *and*, *because*, *could*, *than*, etc. A careful reading of the accompanying text reveals that the list of weak forms is not intended to be complete – it merely consists of just 'the most common' forms of such words, but many people seem to think that this is a complete list (cf. Cauldwell 2013: 106).

13.9.2 SSM – Weak forms not an exclusive list

For the SSM, the CSM's list of weak forms does not cover all possible words that have weak forms, and the words that are covered have many more soundshapes than are listed (cf. Cauldwell, 2013: 108).

13.9.3 SSM – Not weak forms, but word clusters

For the purposes of teaching listening, it is best not to focus on individual soundshapes of such short function words. They very often occur in clusters made up of other weak forms and they are blended into bursts of sound substance in which it is difficult, and misleading, to attempt to isolate individual words. We will look at this issue in much more detail in Part 3, Chapter 16, but Extract 13.2 illustrates the issue.

Extract 13.2 shows a speech unit with a pair of word clusters: *that's gonna be* and *one of the*. In the extract you will hear the entire speech unit, followed by that portion of the speech unit which corresponds to *one of the*.

EXTRACT 13.2
```
|| that's gonna be one of the MAIN reasons i THINK || 6.3
```

Voice: Emily, UK.

As an L1 listener, I hear *one of the* in the full extract, but when it is cut out, all I hear is a single syllable close to *wun* |wʊn| or |wʊm|. It is because this kind of extreme squeezing happens frequently, and so destructively, that it is better to deal with clusters of weak forms (word clusters) rather than the individual words.

13.10 Speed

Speed of speech is a major issue for language learners. First, the faster someone speaks the more likely they are to squeeze words into unfamiliar soundshapes by streamlining them – such as *one of the* becoming *wun*, that we heard in Extract 13.2. Second, because even if words occurred in their full forms in high-speed speech, the learners encounter the problem of transience – they have to decode and understand as the words stream past them, rapidly followed by other words.

13.10.1 CSM – Speed: moderate and constant

The CSM assumes that speech occurs at moderate speeds which remain relatively constant. Cauldwell (2013) surveyed the research literature on NES speed of speech in order to derive a set of benchmarks about what constitutes 'slow', 'average' and 'fast' speech. The consensus is that speech is fast when it goes at 5.3 syllables per second, or 240 words per minute. And, for reference, as reported by Rodero (2012), the BBC World Service bulletins are spoken at 170 words per minute, roughly 3.8 syllables per second.

It should be noted that the values one gets for speed of speech depend very much on the size of the units of analysis. An average speed of a minute's speech will hide a lot of variation in speed that happens at the level of the speech unit. The research that informs the CSM's view of speed typically uses minute-length measures.

13.10.2 SSM – Speed: neither moderate nor constant

In the SSM speeds of speech can reach 400 words per minute, or 11.0 syllables per second, and beyond.

Speech units typically have durations of two seconds or less, and have a great variety of speeds, including extreme variations between neighbouring units (very slow, followed by very fast). This is important for decoding purposes because it is vital to focus on what happens to those short sections of speech which have to be held and processed in the listener's short-term memory. It is necessary to deal with the extreme speeds and accelerations that happen second-by-second, rather than minute-by-minute.

These kinds of sudden bursts of speed cause real perceptual difficulties for learners, even when the words captured in the speech sample are 'known' by the listener, and are (supposedly) part of their active vocabulary. They also demonstrate that momentary flashes of Jungle phenomena can intrude even within CSM/Garden conditions. Therefore, another feature of the SSM is that speeds of speech (when measured moment-by-moment) are considerably more extreme than those typically depicted in the CSM, or contained in ELT textbooks.

13.11 Rhythms of speech

All languages have their very own distinctive rhythmic feel, and many people believe that it must be easy to classify languages into different rhythmic categories. A common classification is to view languages as either stress-timed or syllable-timed.

13.11.1 CSM – English is stress-timed

The CSM continues to claim that English as a stress-timed language. Despite it being a fully refuted hypothesis (cf. Roach, 1982; Dauer, 1983; Cauldwell, 2000), many phonology textbooks for the ELT teacher describe it in full, and then end the description by saying the equivalent of 'It ain't necessarily so.' As a profession, it seems, we are happy to live with the contradiction: on the one hand we operate as if the terms and concepts of stress-timing are true, and then when reminded of the evidence, we say: 'Well we know they're not really true, but heck, it's still a useful concept.'

People mean different things by the term 'stress timing', and some of them are more true than others. It can mean:

1. Languages can be divided into those that are stress-timed and those that are syllable-timed.

2. English stresses occur at equal intervals of time, and syllables vary in length in order to allow stresses to occur on time.

3. English has its own distinctive rhythm, which is different from languages such as French and Spanish.

4. English, like many other languages, features the alternation of prominent (stressed) and non-prominent syllables.

Statements one and two are false; statements three and four are true.

13.11.2 SSM – English is not stress-timed

In the SSM, the rhythm of English is functionally irrhythmic (cf. Cauldwell, 2000). It contains sequences of short bursts of sound substance of varying lengths, with rhythmic patterns which change all the time. Occasionally, short stretches of speech (typically speech units with three or four prominences, which are rare) may sound sufficiently rhythmic that they may be judged to be stress-timed. But this rhythm does not last. And that's a good thing, because if it did, the rhythm would draw attention to itself (as in certain styles of reciting poetry) and would distract listeners from the meanings being conveyed (cf. Bolinger, 1986).

Another way of thinking of the rhythm of English is that it is speaker-timed. The rhythms that emerge are a by-product of the choices that speakers make in constructing their speech – the rhythm is an emergent property.

13.12 Connected speech rules

The natural state of words is to occur in the company of other words at speed. When words come into contact, they no longer retain their citation-form soundshapes. A set of genteel connected speech rules have been identified which describe how the edges of words change when they come into contact with other words.

13.12.1 CSM – Connected speech rules are Garden-friendly

The CSM defines connected speech as 'non-mechanical' speech (Roach, 2009: 107ff.) or speech which is 'run together' (Celce-Murcia et al., 2010: 163). In the ELT literature the rules of connected speech are rooted in the Garden. Such rules are useful for teaching pronunciation because they promote the production of intelligible, clear speech and ensure that learners' speech is non-mechanical. However they are not so useful when it comes to teaching listening/decoding.

Typical presentations of CSM rules focus on the genteel contact between the phonological edges of words: for example, the separate words *East* and *End* when occurring next to each other become *East_end* – where the final |t| of *East* attaches to *End* in a process known variously as 'linking', 'resyllabification' or 'catenation'. These rules are usually demonstrated by teachers speaking very slowly. Such demonstrations serve a useful purpose in leading teacher trainees and L2 learners along the path from the Greenhouse to the Garden. However, such 'rules' are not in fact rules, they are rather an indication of a range of things that may or may not happen – there may be 'a rainbow of intermediate stages' (Shockey, 2003: 77; Alameen & Levis, 2015).

The CSM believes that the six categories of connected speech rules, or processes, (both Celce-Murcia et al. and Alameen and Levis give six categories) can adequately explain what happens when word meets word. In the next two sub-sections, we will explore whether this is in fact the case.

13.12.2 'n' before 'p' becomes 'm': *then people, them people*

Connected speech rules predict that |n| before |p| becomes |m|, in a process known as 'assimilation'. According to this rule, *then people* should become *them people*. To my ears, in Extract 13.3, the |m| is just about audible, but there are many other streamlining processes at work in this extract, some of which are much more likely to dominate perception.

EXTRACT 13.3

```
01 || and then PEOple had to be RUSHED down the MOUNtain because ||
```

Voice: Arun, UK.

It is worth explaining the context of this extract. Arun is describing what happens on Mount Kilimanjaro in Tanzania (5,895 metres high) when tourists get altitude sickness: they become disoriented and are not able to walk on their own. The remedy is to have two guides, each taking an arm and walking the tourist rapidly down to the bottom. Below is a partial list of what is going on in the sound substance. Each item on the list ends with a technical term that will be explained in later chapters:

- *and then* becomes *anen* – an example of d'eth-drop (cf. Chapter 17.3)

- *people* loses its final syllable and becomes a single syllable *peep* – an example of tail-clip (cf. Chapter 18.4.4)

- *had to be rushed* becomes very close to *had to rush* – an example of a blurring which makes grammatical distinctions (here, active vs. passive) unclear

- *rushed down* has only one |d|, and therefore becomes *rush down* – an example of a D.R.Y. ('Don't Repeat Yourself', cf. Chapter 18.5)

- *down* sounds close to *dan* |dan|, an example of a smoothie (cf. Chapter 18.1)

- *mount-* sounds close to *mahn* |mɑːn|, an example of a smoothie (cf. Chapter 18.1)

- *mountain* loses *-tain* and becomes *mount* – an example of a tail-clip (cf. Chapter 18.4.4)

To my ears, these streamlining processes dominate the experience of the sound substance here, and not the predicted assimilation.

13.12.3 't' before 'b' becomes 'p' or glottal stop: *not big, nop big*

The connected speech rules predict that |t| before |b| may become |p| or a glottal stop. So *not big* may sound closer to *nop big.* In Extract 13.4 Emily is talking about her group of close friends, and she explains that they do not regularly go out drinking and dancing in clubs. Notice that *big* here means something close to *enthusiastic.*

EXTRACT 13.4
```
00 || not big ||
01 || we're NOT BIG kind of like CLUBBers ||
```

Voice: Emily, UK.

To my ears, we do not get *nop* here, but we do get a glottal stop (also predicted) at the end of *not* where there is no audible release of the |t|; then, during the glottal closure, the lips come together for the first consonant of *big* It is hearable as |nɒʔ bɪg|. But again, the main decoding challenge here lies elsewhere, in the non-prominent *kind of like* for which there is an alternative hearing, a mondegreen, *carnal like* |kɑ:nəlaɪʔ|.

13.12.4 SSM – we need more 'connected speech rules' for the Jungle

Over a quarter of a century ago, Nolan and Kerswill (1990: 295) defined connected speech as 'the fluent continuous speech performance of everyday life'. ELT's conventional lists of connected speech rules and processes need to be expanded to match this definition. Standard demonstrations of the rules and processes are useful for the transition from the Greenhouse to the Garden, but inadequate to cope with the wildness of the Jungle forms found in spontaneous speech.

In sum, the CSM linking rules are best thought of as being on the path between the domains of the Greenhouse and the Garden, and are best used to promote clear intelligible pronunciation. But as they stand, their power to describe what happens in spontaneous speech for listening purposes is very limited. They need to be augmented to cope with the Jungle. In Part 3, an extended list of connected speech rules (called 'streamlining processes') will be presented to help describe what happens to spontaneous speech in the 'fluent continuous speech performance of everyday life'.

13.13 The meaning of intonation

One of the most noticeable features of the soundscape of speech is that it goes up and down – it has intonation. There have been many attempts to link intonation with grammatical, discoursal and attitudinal meanings (cf. Cauldwell, 2013: 223ff.)

13.13.1 CSM – Tones have meaning

In the CSM, the following statements are held to be true of the relationship between intonation and meaning.

- Yes/No-questions have rising intonation
- *Wh-* questions have falling intonation
- Falling intonation means finality, the speaker has finished
- Rising intonation means the speaker is going to continue
- High falling tone means surprise

But interestingly, a close reading of the major authors of teacher-training books shows that they disagree. Wells (2006: 15) begins his chapter on the relationship between sentence type and tone:

> In English ... statements may have a fall – but they may also have a non-falling tone ... In general there is no simple predictable relationship between sentence type and tone choice.

This seems to be a direct rebuttal of the CSM view of statement and question (cf. also Cruttenden, 2014: 335). But it is not – it is simply a statement about the SSM. For users of the CSM, Wells posits the existence of a 'default tone', as follows: 'Nevertheless, it is useful to apply the notion of a **default** tone (= unmarked tone, neutral tone) for each sentence type ... ' (Wells, 2006: 15; emphasis in original). For him, the 'default' tone: 'is at the very least pedagogically useful' (ibid: 91–92).

The CSM is pedagogically useful, in that it gives rules – and therefore something to teach – about the relationship between intonation and meaning. But, as we shall see, it is not true of everyday spontaneous speech.

13.13.2 SSM – Tones have no generalisable meaning

In the SSM, any tone can be used with any question type and any statement type. There is a random relationship between tones and attitudinal meanings. An SSM version of the list given in the previous section would go as follows:

- Yes/No questions can have any intonation
- *Wh-* questions can have any intonation
- Falling intonation can mean anything, or nothing
- Rising intonation can mean anything, or nothing
- High falling tone can mean anything, or nothing

There is ample academic justification for these statements. Here is Cruttenden, (2014: 335).

> Learners should note that, despite what is often stated in textbooks on English language teaching, both rises (usually low rise) and falls (usually high fall) occur frequently on yes/no interrogatives and wh-interrogatives.

13.14 Summary and what's next

The CSM is a prescriptive model, a set of guidelines for people to work with to make their pronunciation clear and intelligible. It is a useful model of speech for teaching pronunciation, but it is not the descriptive model of spontaneous speech that we need to teach listening/decoding. It is therefore not an appropriate model for the teaching of listening.

The model of speech needed for listening has to be descriptive of language in the Jungle, because that is the language that learners encounter, and have to deal with, when they engage in spontaneous speech. The very strengths and advantages that the CSM has for intelligible pronunciation are weaknesses when it comes to teaching listening.

The CSM is very powerful because it has been (and continues to be) the only model of speech in use. It is cemented firmly in place as part of the historical tradition of what is included in course books – people who commission, write and buy ELT course books expect it to be present.

The CSM occupies all of the conceptual space available in ELT for speech models. For many people, the CSM is the whole story. This needs to change, not by eliminating it, but by getting it to move over and allow an appropriate amount of conceptual space for the SSM to help us with teaching listening.

As far as the CSM and SSM are concerned, we need to accept that the two models have separate areas of operation (pronunciation and listening) and not worry too much about the incompatibilities between the two, unless issues of 'truth' are in play. In this case you need to make a decision for yourself whether or not to side with the cultural inheritance of 'the knowledge', or whether you prefer to side with the information that emerges from the study of everyday spontaneous speech.

In Chapter 14 we will conclude Part 2 by surveying the different suggestions that are made in ELT about when to do decoding activities, and what to do in these activities. We will then propose an alternative view of both (a) what decoding involves and (b) when to do it.

14 The when and what of decoding

This Chapter has two tasks. The first task (Sections 14.1–7) is to survey conventional practice in decoding – what authors and teacher trainers expect us to do, and when they expect us to do it. The second task (Section 14.8) is to suggest an alternative view of what decoding involves (teaching the sound substance) and when to do it (any time) for which the tools are described in Parts 3 and 4.

14.1 The 'when-question' and the 'what-question'

We will seek to answer two questions: 'When should we do decoding activities' and 'What decoding activities are recommended?' We will refer to these questions as the 'when-question' and the 'what-question'.

As far as the when-question is concerned, the conventional answers range from 'never', to 'at the end of the activity', or 'throughout the listening activity'.

As far as the what-question is concerned, the activities include: listen again to short extracts, dictation, gap-fills and listening while following the transcript.

14.2 Not at all – Anna's lesson

We begin by revisiting Anna's lesson which we relived in Chapter 11, where the answer to both questions is 'not at all'.

Anna was angry at one of her teachers for getting her to answer three 'silly' listening comprehension questions and then telling her that 'the rest doesn't matter' (cf. Chapter 11.4). She complained that she 'wanted to learn the language', and that the teacher was simply abandoning the recording and moving on to something else.

Her lesson is a good starting point for looking at the basic structure of a listening comprehension lesson. Its probable structure had four phases:

1. pre-listening – teacher sets questions

2. while-listening – learners listen and select their answers

3. post-listening – teacher checks answers

4. something else – [very quickly move to doing something else]

You will at once notice that phase 4 'Something else' is not properly part of a listening lesson, but I include it because it was the transition from the giving of answers to this phase that provoked Anna's anger.

The teacher's attitude is well described by Field (2008b: 1)

> … there is a tendency for teachers to work through well-worn routines without entire conviction… a hasty topic-driven session wedged between reading and writing, which tend to be regarded as more manageable skills.

In Anna's lesson, there is no decoding work. Over recent decades, the structure of the listening comprehension lesson (henceforth L/C lesson) has evolved. The three-phase structure (Pre-, Post-, and While-listening) is still used, but now the ideal listening lesson has many more discernible elements, and teaching methodology for each part has become more sophisticated.

14.3 The phases – pre-, while- and post-listening

The pre-listening phase is now likely to include a detailed description of the context and the people involved in the recording, as well as the topic and purpose of what they talk about. It may also involve schema activation in which the learners are asked to awaken and bring to the forefront of their minds ('brainstorm') their knowledge of similar interactions in similar contexts. Learners are then asked to predict what they will hear and to guess what the outcomes are likely to be. In this phase there will also be a close look at the questions that the learners have to answer, or at the task that they are expected to do (e.g. complete a schedule, find the time of a train). There may also be pre-teaching of new vocabulary.

The while-listening phase is now likely to involve at least two listens to the recording. The purpose of the first listen – extensive listening – is to allow learners to 'tune in' to the voices contained in the recording (a process known as 'normalisation'), and to tune in to the recording level, quality of the recording and to any background noise which it might contain. In addition there might be a general question on the 'context and attitude of the speakers' (Field, 2008b: 17). The purpose of the second listen – intensive listening – is for learners to answer the pre-set questions, or complete a task.

The post-listening phase involves checking the answers with students, and may involve focusing on and replaying parts of the recording that have caused learners problems.

For some authors, the checking of answers is regarded as a component of while-listening; for others it is thought of as belonging to post-listening. The labels do not really matter, and skilled teachers may use a series of re-listening, discovery and discussion activities which will blur the differences between the two parts.

If it happens at all, decoding happens in the post-listening phase, and involves the teacher replaying sections of the recording.

14.4 Strategy training

Perhaps the most sophisticated version of the three-phase structure is given by Vandergrift and Goh (2012), who are foremost among scholars who advocate the use of cognitive and metacognitive strategies (e.g. inferencing, planning, monitoring and evaluation) in listening. Their focus on strategies is aimed at training learners to cope with language that is beyond their current, non-expert level. In their 'pedagogical sequence' there are three listening phases, preceded by a contextualisation phase.

According to Vandergrift and Goh, work on decoding ('perception activities') needs to come no earlier than the post-listening stage (at the 'third listen'), because

> At this stage learners no longer feel the pressure that often occurs during real-time listening, when they are mainly concerned with understanding meaning. (Vandergrift & Goh, 2012: 132)

They suggest the following as techniques to help learners: careful text selection, reducing the speech rate, and repeated listening to short extracts. They also suggest a procedure which 'can be particularly helpful in making learners aware of the variations and irregularities of spoken language' by using an extract of the recording to do a dictation in five stages:

1. Select a segment – identify language features

2. Play a relevant segment of the recording and get learners to transcribe it

3. Show a copy of the original transcript … [and repeat 2]

4. Discuss how the features may have contributed to listening difficulties …

5. Listen to the text again without any support (ibid: 158)

However, these suggestions are accompanied by a warning against fostering 'a word-for-word translation approach to L2' otherwise the lesson might 'fall into a simple focus on form with little attention to meaning' (ibid: 163). Clearly, they are wary of working on form (our sound substance) and they have a preference for working at the level of meaning. Indeed they repeatedly assert that context is the most powerful aid in word-recognition:

> Many segmentation challenges (e.g. "ice cream"/"I scream") are easily resolved by the larger context within the oral text, the co-text … or the context in which the utterance is spoken. (ibid: 150).

For Vandergrift and Goh, decoding activities should happen in the post-listening phase, after issues of understanding have been dealt with, using repeated listenings and dictation.

14.5 Expanding the post-listening phase

Many teachers are most expert, and therefore most confident, when doing the pre-listening activities. But as we have seen, the pre-listening typically takes up too much time. Field (1998a: 24) argues that we need to reduce the length of the pre-listening phase and lengthen the post-listening phase:

> Instead of the over-long pre-listening session adopted by many teachers, we need to provide an extended *post-listening* session.

In this extended post-listening, Field (2009: 12) argues that we need to avoid the temptations (a) to be teacher-centred, and (b) of assuming that students who have answered the questions correctly, have 'recognised every word'.

He suggests that teachers should be 'non-interventionist', and not rush to give answers; he argues for learners to work together in pairs and, crucially, that the teacher should ask learners how they arrived at their answers.

In Field's opinion, the teacher's role is not to give out answers directly after the while-listening phase, but to reveal them slowly as part of a process of exploration and discovery. And the exploration happens by getting students to justify their choice of answers by asking them what words they heard that led them to choose their answers. Even those students who have got the correct answers will have 'misheard' some of the words in the recording, and the mishearings will probably include words which are the evidence for those correct answers.

So for Field, decoding work should be done as part of an expanded post-listening phase in which students justify their choice of answers by answering the question 'What words did you hear that led you to this answer?'

Up to this point we have covered decoding activities recommended (and not) for use with any published L/C materials. We now turn to look at materials which are themselves specifically designed to teach decoding.

14.6 Materials design

Thorn (2009) presents what she terms a 'prognostic approach' to the creation of teaching materials and the teaching of listening. She uses authentic recordings of unscripted, informal conversations. Although she sets conventional-looking comprehension questions, they are designed not so much to test understanding, but to be 'easily achievable' so that the teacher can then embark on decoding/perception work very quickly. For Thorn, the priority 'should be on enabling students to make sense of what they hear by training them to identify and recognise individual words in a stream of speech', thereby helping learners focus on 'the *process of listening* i.e. *how things were said.*' She suggests using gap-fills or dictations which 'focus on words that were not articulated clearly … Rather than to focus on key content words' (Thorn, 2009: 9).

She believes that 'students need training in identifying the, often important, words in-between the stressed syllables'. For Thorn, the answer to the when-question is that decoding is built into the very structure of the materials and is a goal of the lesson; and the answer to the what-question is gap-fills and dictations.

Thorn created a series of authentic listening practice books (Thorn, 2013) embodying these ideas, but of course teachers themselves often create their own materials, and it is to one of these that we turn now.

14.7 Discovery listening

Wilson (2003) describes a type of listening lesson where the purpose, from the very beginning, is to do decoding. His approach is a conscious reaction against what he sees to be an over-emphasis on top-down processing in teaching listening. He calls his approach 'discovery listening'. Wilson uses an adaptation of a dictogloss activity which is itself a derivative of a dictation exercise in which learners note down key words and then reconstruct the text in pairs or groups. He aims to remedy what he sees as '… an excessive focus on meaning' which comes about 'either through extra vocabulary learning or additional listening practice' which he believes 'will not necessarily solve the listening comprehension problems of many students' (Wilson 2003: 336).

Wilson believes that 'Bottom-up approaches that focus on word recognition… have been comparatively undervalued.' (ibid: 335):

> Word recognition has generally been neglected in favour of using the context to work out meanings (ibid: 335).

In Wilson's approach to the dictogloss there are three main phases: 1. Listening three times to a short text; 2. Reconstructing the text into written form in small groups; 3. Discovering the differences between the original and their reconstructed versions. (Wilson's version is more sophisticated than this, but these are the essentials.)

The key phase is phase 3, where teacher and students identify and assess the importance of the decoding gaps. In his example, most of the class identified their greatest decoding problem as being with the words 'the unemployment'. These words were heard variously as 'the employment', 'employment', 'an employment' or 'some employment'. The negative prefix 'un-' was not decoded accurately.

The activity ends with each student having a list of their own decoding problems:

> … the hope is that in subsequent listening activities they will improve their awareness and therefore their perceptual processing. Of course until properly tested, it remains just a hope. (ibid: 340).

Thus, for Wilson, the answer to the when-question is 'throughout the lesson' which is designed to focus on decoding, and the answer to the what-question involves a dictogloss activity using the teacher's voice.

14.8 Summary and what's next

In the conventional L/C lesson, decoding work is typically done (or recommended to be done) towards the end of a listening activity. But in the cases of Thorn and Wilson, the goal of the entire listening activity may be a decoding one – in which case the answer to the when-question might be 'at any time'.

14.8.1 The future of the when-question

In Part 4 we will expand on the idea of 'at any time', and demonstrate that decoding activities can be (a) an ever-present possibility which you can move into and out of very quickly at any moment or (b) a stand-alone activity which can precede or follow or even replace a conventional L/C lesson.

Decoding work can be 'first up' in a lesson prior to, or even in the absence of, work on a recording. The syllabus presented in Part 3, together with the activities suggested in Part 4, make it possible to choose items to teach, and to have a separate decoding component to a lesson which may not feature a conventional listening activity at all.

14.8.2 The future of the what-question – teaching the sound substance

In Sections 14.1–7 we saw that the answers to the what-question included gap-fill, dictation, dictogloss, repeated listening and giving responses to 'What words did you hear that led you to your answer?'

This answer to the what-question needs to be expanded in two ways: first, it should include teaching the forms of the sound substance of the language; and second, it should include getting learners to 'embody' the flexiforms of the sound substance.

The training and tools needed to teach the forms of the sound substance of the language are presented in Part 3 (Chapters 15–19). These chapters present items and processes of the sound substance of speech which will enable us to construct a syllabus for listening. The guiding principle is that **the sound substance is a code that needs to be taught.**

The chapters of Part 3 will give you (the teacher, the course book writer) the ability to hear and describe what happens when words are used in spontaneous speech. The central components of the syllabus are word clusters (Chapter 16) and streamlining processes (Chapters 17–18). Word clusters are groups of words of between two and six words in length which very frequently occur together (e.g. *a bit of a, where there were*) across a wide range of topics and styles of speech; they are often spoken much faster than the words around them, and are therefore difficult for learners to hear. Streamlining processes are those processes which result in words having different soundshapes. They include 'syll-drop' where words lose a syllable (e.g. the three syllables of *physical* become the two syllables of *fiscal* or *fizzle*, cf. Chapter 9.1), and 't-drop' where consonants are dropped (e.g. *little* becomes *lil*, cf. Chapter 17.5).

14.8.3 The future of the what-question – the need to embody

The items of Part 3 need to be brought to life in the classroom. Learners need to become familiar and comfortable with the sound substance of speech, and the best way to do this is through activities which give them a physical feel of what it is like to handle the sound substance with their own voices. We need our learners to play with the sound substance in vocal gymnastic exercises, where they (at one extreme – the Greenhouse) exaggerate the clarity and (at the other extreme – the Jungle) exaggerate the messy possibilities of the words concerned. This, remember, is in pursuit of the goal of listening, not pronunciation. In doing this, we would be following a suggestion of Field's who suggests that target words should be 'practised orally as items of vocabulary' (2008b: 155) so that learners are 'internalising recurrent chunks'.

14.8.4 Expand our comfort zone

If you have had training experiences similar to mine, you will be comfortable with teaching the pre-listening phase of an L/C lesson, and with working at the level of meaning. You will probably be less comfortable with decoding work.

We can do much better in teaching decoding by systematically teaching the streamlining processes which happen to words in their natural environment.

We need to expand our comfort zone to include decoding work, which we will now think of as 'teaching and learning the sound substance'. We need to have the confidence and skills to switch rapidly between the level of understanding and the level of decoding, and not be shy of bottom-up activities which focus on forms – not least because, as mentioned in Chapter 1, the learning of the forms of the sound substance (forms we have to listen to) is a far more onerous task than it is for the sight substance.

Part 3 A syllabus for listening

Part 3 contains four chapters, each of which contains elements of the syllabus for listening. Chapters 16–18 contain the heart of the syllabus – word clusters and streamlining processes.

THE FOUR CHAPTERS

Chapter 15 *Words* considers whether words and their soundshapes are the best candidates for items on a syllabus for listening. The answer is 'no', but important dimensions of the syllabus are revealed as we consider their potential role. Then a sample of one class of words – adverbs – is examined, and this examination provides a useful entry point to identify elements of the syllabus to be introduced in subsequent chapters.

Chapter 16 *Word clusters* identifies word clusters as the best candidates for items on a syllabus for listening (indeed they have been used as a structuring device for *Jungle Listening* Cauldwell, 2016). Word clusters are frequently-occurring groups of words of varying lengths (*you know; it's gonna be one of the*) which occur across a wide range of speech styles. Because we say them so often, they are typically spoken faster than other words in their speech units, and even advanced learners find them difficult to decode.

Chapter 17 *Streamlining I – consonant death* looks at the variety of streamlining processes that happen to consonants in spontaneous speech. They may be dropped entirely (and not just at word boundaries), or blurred in such a way that they create other sounds.

Chapter 18 *Streamlining II – smoothies to teenies* continues the work of the previous chapter, and begins by focusing on the fates of vowels. We then look at a number of processes, including those in which syllables are blended and dropped, and those where it is difficult to determine whether statements are positive or negative. The chapter ends with a presentation of the 'teeny' process.

RECORDINGS

The recorded extracts are essential listening. You should listen to them carefully. They are there to give you ear-training in hearing the variability that occurs in the Jungle: we need to be able to hear the raw sound substance, the rough hints in the acoustic blur of speech, which the learners have to match up with words. We need to train ourselves to hear the raw sound substance beneath and behind the words that we may 'know' are present, or were intended by the speaker. In other words, it is a training in hearing the imprecision and in-between-ness of the sound substance. Our focus should not be on 'What speakers meant to say', but rather on 'What it sounds like they said' or 'How many different ways can this be heard?'

A key concept is that of 'alternative hearing' (also 'reasonable hearing'), by which I mean 'the sincere attempt to describe or mimic the raw sound substance with the focus on form (how it sounds) rather than the words and the meaning'. Knowing what the words are, and knowing what meanings were intended, will deafen us to the true nature of the raw sound substance.

TO MY EARS

As we go through the examples, you will find I use the expression 'to my ears' when referring to what I believe to be perceptible in the recorded extracts. You may hear differently from me, and your students may hear even more differently. I do not want to impose a way of hearing on you; I simply want to open your ears to the characteristics of the sound substance at a pre-lexical level, before we have locked on to what words were said and meant.

THE USE OF SYMBOLS

We will use those symbols which are likely to be familiar to experienced teachers – the symbols which are used in dictionaries and pronunciation keys of textbooks. These are shown in the Symbols and Notation section of the Introductory matter to this book. The symbols for vowels and consonants in the text are shown between single vertical lines: |t|. The symbols are used where folk spelling representations of sound would be misleading, because of the problem of the lack of reliable sound-spelling correspondence in English. Their use will be supplemented by accompanying text which will indicate that the symbols are used as a guide to the in-between-ness of the sound substance. The aim is to be as clear as possible in explanation, and to use just as many symbols as are needed, and no more.

NEW TERMINOLOGY

In Part 3, some new terminology is introduced – a metalanguage to help you describe for yourself and your colleagues (and your intermediate and advanced students) the phenomena that occurs in the Jungle. This is not to say that you cannot use the ideas and activities of this book at beginner and elementary levels, you can. The aim is to make the terminology easy to remember and classroom-friendly. 'Classroom-friendly' does not necessarily mean that you would use the terms in the classroom with all levels of learners. 'Classroom-friendly' means 'helpful for teachers who want to teach their students to be familiar and comfortable with the mess and unruliness of fast spontaneous speech'. Intermediate and advanced students may find the terms useful, but for lower levels, you would have to use your judgement about whether or not to use the terms in class – and (of course) you can always devise your own terms.

Some of the terms are derived from ideas about what the speaker had to do to create the soundshape (e.g. 'syll-drop' where a speaker omits a syllable) and some terms are derived from the perceptual difficulties that learners might have (e.g. 'polarisk' where a listener may have difficulty determining whether the speaker is using a negative or not).

The purpose is to open your ears to the world of the learners who have difficulty recognising the soundshapes which are caused by these streamlining processes. The processes identified here do not claim to be a coherent phonetic or phonological theory. The categories overlap, and there may be relationships between them, which I have not written about, which in an academic treatise would be given fuller treatment. It would be a mistake to try to match too closely the processes that are described here with those of phonetics or phonology textbooks.

Part 3 of *A Syllabus for Listening: Decoding* can best be thought of as a 'data-driven' (Johns, 2002) presentation, rather than a theory-driven presentation. The presentation comes from more than three decades of enthusiastic investigation of spontaneous speech, not from a perspective of phonological or phonetic theory.

ACCENTS AND OTHER ENGLISHES

The voices used in the recordings in Part 3 are mostly those of native speakers of British and American English. I believe that streamlining processes happen in Englishes of all types, and that many of the processes listed below will occur in these other Englishes. However, I would expect that other streamlining processes may well be more salient.

DON'T TRY TO BE CERTAIN

We will also see that it is not always possible to be certain how many sounds, syllables and words have occurred in a speech unit. Although it is very tempting to try to achieve certainty – to try to decide 'what is **really** going on' – it is important to recognise that the sound substance is often indeterminate, and open to different interpretations about what is, and is not, present. It is also important to be cautious about the effects of listening in different ways (adding gaps to the recording; slowing it down) because you will hear different things each time, none of which may be 'right'.

15 Words

What items should be in a *Syllabus for Listening: Decoding*? One answer might be 'all the soundshapes of all the words of the language'. The hope would be, once learners have mastered all the soundshapes that a word can have, they can then decode it accurately every time it occurs. There are a number of problems with this idea. Four of these problems have to do with:

- our concept of the mental representation of a word
- the numbers problem
- the 'other words' problem
- the speed problem

In the first four sections of this chapter I will explain why it is best not to focus on the individual word as the key item in a syllabus for listening. There is some repetition of the contents of Chapter 8. I will then contradict myself by focusing on adverbs ending in –*ly*. The contradiction is apparent rather than real, because each adverb will be presented in a speech unit – and you will hear that the immediate co-text, and the soundscape that the speaker gives the speech unit are key influences on the resultant soundshapes of the adverbs.

15.1 Mental representation of a word

The brain stores a lot of information about a word: its meanings (denotation and connotation), its likely neighbours (collocations) and its likely grammatical contexts. But our focus (because we are primarily interested in decoding) will be on what the brain stores of the forms of a word: its written shape in the sight substance of language and its soundshapes in the sound substance of the language. As we have seen earlier (Chapter 1, Chapter 10.7), for people who learned to read and write very early in life, the sight substance of a word dominates their mental representation of it – we have a clear mental picture of how the word looks in the sight substance.

The sight substance characterises the word as a separate entity, preceded and followed either by a space or a punctuation mark. The soundshape that most resembles this separate written entity is the citation form because it has pauses where the spaces would be. Thus there is a strong bond of association between the spelling and the citation-form soundshape. Our mental representation, or rather the mental representation that we think we have, of the forms of a word, and the one that we call up and use in ELT is heavily weighted towards this isolated – Greenhouse – form.

We have a poor sense of how words actually sound in everyday speech (cf. Chapter 4.2). Of course expert listeners can decode the rough hints and the mush of acoustic blur – but they do this below the level of awareness, without knowing that they are hearing less than a word.

A syllabus which focuses on the word as the unit of teaching would need to accommodate very many more soundshapes for each word than just the citation form. This is because part of expert knowledge of a word is the ability to recognise it in all its soundshapes. But that brings us to the numbers problem.

15.2 The numbers problem

All words have a very large number of soundshapes, even in the speech of one speaker. Listen to Extract 15.1 where there are six occurrences of *and* from Jess from the USA.

15.2.1 *and*

EXTRACT 15.1

|| and | and | and | and | and | and ||

Voice: Jess, USA.

To my ears, Jess gives us five different soundshapes in these six versions of *and*, which is a lot of soundshapes from a single speaker. It would be a great deal many more with more speakers of different accents. In fact Greenberg and Fosler-Lussier (2000), found eighty different soundshapes of *and*.

As you will hear below, it is not just function words such as *and* that have multiple soundshapes. Words of all kinds do. Extract 15.2 contains six versions of *able/be able to/able to*: four from the USA, and two from the UK.

15.2.2 *able to*

EXTRACT 15.2

|| able | be able to | able to | able | be able to | able to ||

Voices: Jess (x 2) Karam (x 2) (USA); Richard junior, Joey (UK).

To my ears, they sound close to (in folk spelling) *awol, baybull, eb bluh, evil, be-ell tuh,* and *abba to.* But, as you can hear in these examples of *able*, it is not simply a question of what the individual word sounds like. There are other words that occur in the same speech unit, and the priority assigned to them by the speaker has a major effect on the soundshapes of words. We return to *able to* in Chapter 18.7.

15.3 The 'other words' problem

In everyday speech, words exist in a neighbourly relationship with the words that occur next to them. As we saw in Chapter 8, this neighbourly relationship may be viewed either as a friendly one, or as a bullying one.

15.3.1 Words as neighbourly flexiforms

All sizes of sound substance, from 'individual sounds' to syllables and words, have the property of being flexible. Words are thus flexible forms – flexiforms – which can be shaped in a wide variety of ways to allow room for other words to sit in a blended sharing of the same sound-substance space.

Part of the way they allow room for each other is familiar to many teachers in the form of the linking rules – a genteel coming together of the edges of words. These linking rules (e.g. linking |j r w| in *my eyes, law and, you are*) together with rules of elision (dropping of sounds) and assimilation (blending and blurring sounds) comprise the 'connected speech rules' of ELT. However, these rules are too genteel and sight-substance friendly to cope with the variety and messiness of the sound substance of everyday speech, in which there are many more processes at work (cf. Chapter 13.12).

15.3.2 Words can lose their middles

The generosity of words as flexiforms is not limited to their edges. There are many ways in which they change their personal shape and space to fit in (they are 'streamlined') with the rhythms of speech. They often blur or drop middle consonants (*little* becomes *lil*); they may drop initial medial and final syllables (*because* becomes '*cos*; *accident* becomes *accent*; *really* becomes *real*). Words drop or blur parts of themselves in order to allow room for the other words with which they are sharing a speech unit to fit into the rhythmic pattern created by the speaker during a short burst of speech.

15.3.3 Words as bully-boy flexiforms

I've been writing about flexiforms as if words themselves are kind-hearted, decision-making entities. I could have taken another – more violent – line: that some words bash other words into cowering submission and pulverise them into small pieces, or even out of existence. For an example, look at the speech unit below which we saw earlier in Chapter 8. There are two prominences, shown in uppercase letters, and seventeen non-prominent syllables in lowercase.

EXTRACT 15.3

`|| this is ONE i'm going to be looking at in slightly more DEtail in fact ||`

Voice: Geoff, Birmingham, UK.

We can consider the two prominences, *ONE* and *DE-* as punches in the ear which forcibly grab the attention of the hearer, while crushing the non-prominent syllables violently out of shape (*more* sounds like *moot*) and even out of existence (*to be*). (This speech unit is discussed extensively in Cauldwell, 2013: 113.)

But although we will use such metaphorical language to describe word-on-word violence, it is of course the speakers who are the shapers of the sound substance. It is the speaker's choice, not the language and not the situation, which provides us with this series of soundshapes streamed together (cf. Chapter 8.5).

15.4 Words occur in speech units

Speakers communicate by constructing a series of quasi-rhythmic units of sound substance called 'speech units'. And as we have seen in 15.3.3 above, it is in the shaping that the speaker applies to the speech unit that gives each component word its soundshape. So the ideal unit for presentation and inspection of the soundshape of a word is the speech unit within which it occurs.

In Parts 3 and 4 of *A Syllabus for Listening: Decoding* we will use two modes of presentation of a speech unit: transcripts and tables. We have seen, in previous chapters, transcripts such as that shown for Extract 15.4.

EXTRACT 15.4

```
|| and kind of BUILD up the SNOW mounds ||
```

Voice: Ellen, USA.

But another useful mode of presentation is in the tables which form part of 'the window on speech' (Cauldwell, 2013: 26–59), which we will briefly explain again here. Table 15.1 has five columns, numbered in reverse order from 5 to 1, for reasons which will become clear but which are also explained in Cauldwell (ibid).

TABLE 15.1 THE WINDOW ON SPEECH

		5	4	3	2	1
Transcript	01	and kind of	BUILD	up the	SNOW	mounds
Rhythm	02	ba ba ba	BAM	ba ba	BAM	ba
Instructions	03	(crush)	BANG!	(crush)	BANG!	(relax)

Row 02 (ba ba ba BAM, etc.) gives the rhythmic pattern of the syllables in this particular speech unit, with the prominent syllables represented by *BAM* and the non-prominent syllables by *ba*. The bottom row gives instructions (in the form of stage directions) on how to say each part, for anyone who wants to create this speech unit at a fast speed: Columns 5 and 3 have the instruction *[crush]* and Column 1 has the instruction *[relax]* to instruct the speaker to slow down before a pause.

Columns 4 and 2 are shaded, and the syllables in them *BUILD* and *SNOW* are shown in uppercase letters – these are prominent syllables, syllables that the speaker has made more noticeable (longer, louder, a different pitch) than the neighbouring syllables. The prominent syllable in Column 2 is also known as the tonic prominence – it is the location for the start of the tone (fall, rise, etc.) which continues over the syllables in Column 1, if there are any. The reason for the reverse numbering of columns is that we can say for speech units of any size (there can be up to nine columns, with a maximum of four prominences) that the tonic prominence always occurs in Column 2. (For further explanation, see Appendices 1 and 2.)

For decoding purposes, the parts of the table that are most important are Columns 5, 3 and 1 where the syllables are non-prominent – they are often much less clear than the prominent syllables. The syllables in the last column, Column 1, when they occur before a pause, are likely to be soft but clear as the speaker slows down as he or she approaches the pause. In speech units such as that shown in Table 15.1 (two prominences, with non-prominent syllables preceding and following each of them) the syllables in Columns 5 and 3 are particularly vulnerable to being crushed into new soundshapes.

15.5 Observing adverbs

Although taking a word approach to a syllabus for listening is impractical, focusing on one set of words – adverbs ending in -*ly* or -*lly* |li| – will provide a useful entry point to the key elements of the syllabus which will be presented in Chapters 16–18. Such adverbs are particularly useful to focus on, as they are often reduced (we will use the term 'streamlined' from now on) in ways which are easy to notice, which is probably why they have received attention in popular culture, and in scholarly publications. Cruttenden (2014: 315) tells us that they are 'liable to reduction in casual speech' and Laver (1994: 63) shows many soundshapes for *actually*. Indeed, adverbs of all lengths, from the two-syllable *really* to the five-syllable *unfortunately*, are a fruitful source of evidence for the different streamlining processes that single words undergo. This is why we will spend the rest of this chapter looking at the soundshapes of some adverbs ending –*ly*, and observe how their soundshapes are influenced by their position in speech units, and by the words which are their neighbours.

Sports commentaries, and pundits' comments after sporting events are fruitful sources of a wide variety of soundshapes of adverbs. Unfortunately I do not have the permissions to use such recordings, so the selection below will be based around those adverbs for which I do have recordings. A fuller list of adverbs and their ranges of soundshapes – but with no recordings – can be found in Appendix 4.

As we observe these soundshapes, we will be alert to their mondegreen potential, the potential for 'alternative hearings' as other soundshapes, and reference will be made to streamlining processes that are covered in later chapters.

15.5.1 *really* – UK

Pronunciation dictionaries list versions of *really* both with and without a diphthong, and – when without a diphthong – a choice of simple vowel. Roach et al (2011) gives us these three soundshapes |rɪə.li| |riːə.li| and |riː.li| and Wells (2008) gives these and adds two more, the first of which is archaic (these days, not even the Queen would use it) |reə.li| and |rɪ.li|.

In this section we will listen to both British and US versions of *really* in different speech units. These speakers are nineteen and twenty years old and, as Wells says, younger people are beginning to favour *really* as rhyming with *freely*. In Extract 15.5, Laura gives us a non-prominent *really*.

EXTRACT 15.5
```
|| so THAT was really nice ||
```

Voice: Laura, UK. You will hear the original, and then a gapped version.

The first syllable of Laura's non-prominent *really* has a vowel close to |i|. And at one time I thought (I now think I was wrong) that as the |l| goes so fast, and the |n| of *nice* is so quiet, that an alternative hearing of the words *really nice* would be *re-ee-ice*. This would have been an example of consonant death, where |l| drops below the threshold of audibility.

But when I came back to this extract after a month, I heard it differently. I could hear both the |l| and the |n|. This was interesting. So I tried to settle the issue by inserting a 0.2 second-pause between the words, a task that I found difficult. I ended up with an alternative hearing: I heard *really* as *brilliant*.

There are several points to make about this experience.

- It is a fact of life that you hear different things in the same sound file on different occasions.
- When you cut up a sound file, it will be difficult to isolate specific words without including fragments of other words.
- You may hear things in the cut-up sound file that are inaudible in the original continuous sound file.
- The very act of cutting up a sound file may introduce sounds where the cuts were made.
- Alternative hearings are often available, even for an L1 listener.
- Students may well hear other alternative hearings – it is important to respect these hearings.

15.5.2 *really* – USA

We now turn to an example from a speaker of American English (AmE). Wells reports in his survey of AmE speakers (Wells, 2008: 671) that for 60 percent *really* is rhymed with *freely* and for 30 percent it is rhymed with *frilly*. Extract 15.6 has an example from Kennon who is in his early twenties.

EXTRACT 15.6

```
|| the MOUNtains are REAlly SCRAGgly ||
```

Voice: Kennon, US. You will hear the original, and then a gapped version.

To my ears, Kennon's *really* sounds closer to |rɪ.li| than |ri.li|, but the most interesting feature of this speech unit is what can be heard when we isolate the words *are really*. They sound more like the single word *early* – an alternative hearing. Therefore, if students report hearing *early*, they are actually doing well in their perceptions of the raw sound substance.

15.5.3 *really really*

In everyday speech, *really* is often repeated, and this what we hear from Olivia in Extract 15.7.

EXTRACT 15.7

```
|| and THEY were REAlly really NICE ||
```

Voice: Olivia, UK. You will hear the original, and then a gapped version.

Olivia's *really really* also has |i| and sounds close to *really ree* because the |l| of the second *really* is dropped, giving us a single syllable in which Olivia's second *ree* is close to |rɪiː|.

The dropping of |l| is a streamlining process which we will refer to later as 'consonant death' (specifically 'ell-drop') which results in a 'syll-drop' (cf. Chapter 18.4) – where the number of syllables is reduced. This results in the two syllables of *really* becoming the single syllable *ree*.

In the gapped version the first three words *and they were* can be alternatively heard as *I know.*

15.5.4 *particularly – perticky*

Wells (2008: 590) gives three British English soundshapes for *particularly*: a five-syllable soundshape |pɔ.tɪk.jʊl.ɔ.li| and 'in casual speech sometimes also' a four-syllable version |pɔ.tɪk.jɔl.i|, and a three-syllable version |pɔ.tɪk.li|. Emily gives a 'casual speech' version in Extract 15.8. You will hear the original first, and then a version in which gaps are placed between the syllables.

EXTRACT 15.8

```
01 || and parTIcularly ||
```

Voice: Emily, UK. You will hear the original, and then a gapped version.

To my ears, Emily, in the original speech unit, gives us a three-syllable version but omits |l|, so I believe that I hear something close to |pɔ tɪ ki|. But two people whose judgement I trust disagree with me – they both hear the |l| of the final syllable, and one of them hears four syllables |pɔ tɪ kɪ li|. This is another example of the fact that different people will hear different things in the sound file. That said, in the gapped version, I do hear something where the |l| should be – perversely it is a |b| thus giving (to my ears) something like |pɔ tɪk bi|.

15.5.5 *actually*

I mentioned earlier that awareness of what can happen to the soundshapes of adverbs exists in popular culture. An example of this is with the word *actually*. The English author and actor Stephen Fry tells of his early days as a student at Cambridge University when he kept on hearing the word *Ashley*, which – he jokes – he thought was the name of a college in the university (it isn't).

Many scholars list multiple soundshapes for *actually*. Laver (1994: 63) lists seven, Wells (2008: 9) lists six and Roach et al. (2011: 6) list eight. The first one in Wells's list is the four-syllable citation form: |æk.tʃu.ə.li| which rarely occurs. More commonly used is the three-syllable version |æk.tʃu.li|, but more common still are three two-syllable versions |æk.ʃli| |æ.ʃli| and |æk.ʃi|. Extract 15.9 illustrates, respectively, the four-syllable, three-syllable and then three two-syllable versions. These were recorded for the purposes of demonstration; they are not from recordings of spontaneous speech.

EXTRACT 15.9
|| ACTually .. ACTually .. ACKshlee .. ASHlee .. ACKshee ||

Voice: Richard (the author), UK.

Notice that in all versions of *actually* in this extract, the word stress is on the first syllable. Word stress is the property of the Greenhouse or citation form of a word; it refers to the syllable which is most noticeable when the word is spoken in isolation. But in speech units in the Jungle, the syllables of words that would be stressed in the Greenhouse do not necessarily become prominent syllables (cf. Appendix 1). In Extract 15.10, Toby gives us a single prominence speech unit, with *actually* as part of the non-prominent tail of a falling tone that starts on the first syllable of *badminton*.

EXTRACT 15.10
|| who i used to play BADminton with actually ||

Voice: Toby, UK. You will hear the original, and then a gapped version.

To my ears, Toby's *actually* is the two-syllable version |æk.ʃi|. And in both the ungapped and gapped part of the sound file you will be able to hear the word stress on the first syllable. But in the context of the speech unit, it is non-prominent compared to the prominence of the first syllable of *badminton* (for more, see Cauldwell 2013, and Appendix 1). Notice that an alternative hearing is available for *actually* – to my ears we have *that she*, because the final segment of *with* is blended with the initial vowel of *actually*.

Our next example features a soundshape for *actually* which is not predicted by any of the scholars mentioned above. In Extract 15.11, Dan produces a three-syllable version with (to my ears) a prominence and rising tone on the final syllable.

EXTRACT 15.11

```
|| something FUNny happened actualLY ||
```

Voice: Dan, UK. You will hear the original, and then 'naturally' (-n actually).

Occasionally, speakers do create new soundshapes by making the stressed syllable of the Greenhouse form non-prominent, and by making a syllable which is normally unstressed in the Greenhouse form prominent (cf. Cauldwell, 2013: 120). In this case the final syllable of *actually* has a strong vowel and although in the Greenhouse it is an unstressed syllable, Dan exploits the long vowel to give a rising tone.

As is often the case, this speech unit offers us an alternative hearing. If we were inspecting the written transcript, with no recording available, we might predict that the final |d| of *happened* would link to the initial vowel |æ| of *actually* to give us *happened_actually*. But in fact the final |d| of *happened* is dropped ('d-drop' cf. Chapter 17.6) and the |n| of *happen* is linked to *actually*. This gives us an alternative hearing, and a mondegreen, of *naturally*.

15.5.6 *absolutely*

An adverb that is more likely than *actually* to occur in its maximal four-syllable form is *absolutely*, the Greenhouse form of which is |æb.sɔ.luːt.li|. In Extract 15.12 Catherine is speaking quite slowly and emphatically, giving us this four-syllable version, followed by Joey who gives us a two-syllable version.

EXTRACT 15.12

```
01 || ABsolutely FABulous || 3.8
02 || can be ABsolutely ANywhere and just || 10.2/8.3
```

Voices: Catherine, USA; Joey, UK.

Catherine speaks her version slowly – at 3.8 syllables per second (sps) – whereas Joey speaks extremely fast, at 10.2 sps if we count *absolutely* as having four syllables, or 8.3 sps if we regard it as having two syllables.

It is also worth noting that in both speech units, the soundshape of *absolutely* is stress-shifted (cf. Cauldwell, 2013: 117ff). Its first syllable is the location of the first prominence in a double-prominence speech unit.

Joey gives us a two-syllable soundshape *absi*, which is somewhere between |æbsi| and |æbsju|. So we have a double syll-drop (two syllables are dropped, cf. Chapter 18.4). Many words which have three or more syllables in the citation or Greenhouse form have soundshapes which are at least one syllable fewer than the maximum.

15.6 Summary and what's next

In the early parts of this chapter (15.1–4) I argued that the word is not the best choice of item for *A Syllabus for Listening: Decoding* – the large number of soundshapes for each word, their varying contact (neighbourly or bullying) with other words, and the speed they go at, militate against their being the best unit to focus on.

In the latter part of the chapter (15.5) I contradicted myself, and used individual adverbs to act as an introduction to what is to follow. We saw and heard how they blend with the words around them, and mentioned some of the streamlining processes which are to be introduced in the chapters which follow, including d-drop, syll-drop and the hiss effect. At several points, the analysis revealed that listening in different ways led to different ideas about what was actually present in the sound substance. In particular, the insertion of gaps between syllables and words revealed sounds which were not audible in the original ungapped extract. Adding gaps also revealed the possibility of alternative hearings and mondegreens of an implausible wording that does not fit the context, but could be reasonable hearings of the sound substance (*really* was heard as *brilliant* (cf.15.5.1); *naturally* was heard in part of *happened actually* (cf. Chapter 15.5.5).

Because we hear different things with different modes of listening, it is tempting to ask: What is really going on? Which is the best description of this sound file? These questions are tempting because they arise from a desire to be certain and to give a definite answer.

It is important in the face of the evidence of spontaneous speech, to allow that different interpretations and descriptions are valid. And in teaching decoding it is necessary to work with what is audible (a) to you as a teacher and (b) to your students in the classroom, and to allow for the fact that if you analyse or treat the sound file in different ways, or even simply listen repeatedly, you will probably hear different things.

In Chapter 16 we will look at word clusters, groups of words which commonly occur together and which are often run together into a continuous blur. Word clusters, viewed at work in speech units, are the central component of the syllabus.

16 Word clusters

The more frequent the word, and the smaller it is, the less likely it is to have an independent, clear identity. This is because a frequent word is very likely to exist as part of a blur of several words blended together. You might think that these small frequent words – function words – are so well known to the learner listener that they can decode them easily. However, this is not the case, as Field points out:

> At most levels of proficiency ... [learners] ... have much more trouble identifying function words accurately than they do content words ... (Field, 2008b: 146)

The key point about Field's research is that learners at both advanced and lower levels of proficiency had difficulties identifying function words. Field (2008b: 155) recommends that learners 'listen out for familiar chunks rather than attempting word-by-word processing'. He goes on to say that it 'is useful, from quite an early stage, to draw ...[learners'] ... attention to the role that chunks play in everyday speech'. So in this chapter, we are going to focus on very common chunks, which we will refer to as 'word clusters'.

A word cluster (Carter & McCarthy 2006: 828ff) is a group of words from two to six in length which occurs frequently across a wide range of speech styles and topics. They vary in length from the two-word *you know* and *I mean* to the six-word *do you know what I mean?* (although you can make them longer, as we will see, by adding them together). As well as prepositions, articles, personal pronouns and conjunctions, verbs such as *know, think, want, can* and *have* occur in such word clusters. These words are quite likely to occur between prominences, in the squeeze/crush zones of speech units.

They are therefore part of the sound substance that learners should supposedly ignore, when they follow the advice 'just listen to the stresses' and 'don't listen to every word'. However, if learners 'want to learn the language' and become efficient decoders (and not just copers) they need to learn to decode these clusters. Not least because they include words which – although not topic- and context-specific – are extremely important for the purposes of building meaning. For example *don't* occurs nine times in the Carter and McCarthy lists, *know* occurs 21 times and *want* occurs seven times.

So, word clusters are groups of words that commonly occur together, and in this chapter we are going to look at and listen to a sample of them. We will begin with the two-word clusters, *you know* and *I mean.*

16.1 *you know, I mean, do you know what I mean?*

Spontaneous speech contains many references to the here-and-now of real-time communication. Speakers constantly refer to their own and their listeners' roles in building meaning through the use of the word clusters *you know*, and *I mean* and *do you know what I mean?* which I have termed drafting phenomena (cf. Cauldwell, 2013: 81ff). These clusters are often spoken very fast, with multiple differences between the Garden forms and Jungle forms. Field (2003: 331) mentions *narp meme* as a two-syllable version of the six-syllable *do you know what I mean*. We will hear some streamlined versions below, but first we need to note that this cluster can contain four prominent syllables as in Extract 16.1.

EXTRACT 16.1

`|| do YOU KNOW || what I MEAN ||`

Voice: Richard (the author), UK.

This might occur in a context where the speaker is trying to establish the level of understanding in a group of people. However, far more often we hear streamlined versions. Two are given in Extract 16.2.

EXTRACT 16.2

`|| do you know what i mean ||`

Voice: Laura, UK – there are two different versions.

Note that there are response tokens from a listener (*mm, mhhm*). To my ears, these clusters sound close to *gin ower ta mean* |ʤɪn ɔʊə tmiːn| and *jurr tuh meme* |ʤɜː tmiːm|. But as we noted in Chapter 15, it is possible to hear different things each time you listen, and so these folk spellings and phonemic symbols should be viewed as provisional and approximate – as guides to the mush of sound rather than an accurate representation.

There is a variant of this phrase which begins with *if* rather than *do* (*if you know what I mean*) and in Extract 16.3 we will hear a two-syllable version of it. The transcription – even more than is usually the case – misrepresents the sound substance: we can see six separate syllables, but the sound substance (to my ears) has just two.

EXTRACT 16.3

`|| if you KNOW what I MEAN ||`

Voice: Joey, UK.

The six syllables of the Greenhouse/Garden version become just two syllables – the first syllable takes the place of the first four – *if you know what* becomes *fnot* |fnɒt| and *I mean* becomes |miːn|. There is a mondegreen hearing available here: *it's not me*.

Table 16.1 shows the degree of streamlining at work here.

TABLE 16.1 STREAMLINING OF SEGMENTS IN *IF YOU KNOW WHAT I MEAN*

Greenhouse	ɪ	f	j	uː	n	əʊ	w	ɒ	t	aɪ	m	iː	n
Jungle		f			n			ɒ	t		m	iː	n

The top row shows the thirteen segments of the Greenhouse version of *if you know what I mean* and the bottom row shows the seven segments which survive in the sound substance. The seven segments are the mush of speech that learners encounter as they try to decode everyday speech. They are an example of the rough hints, the rags and shreds of words, which we need to be aware of in order to help learners handle everyday speech.

16.2 *then* and *the* – d'eth-drop

Some of the most interesting sets of word clusters are those which feature the consonant |ð| in words such as *the*, *then* and *then*. The symbol |ð| is known as 'eth'. We will first hear the two-word cluster *and then* followed by the three-word clusters *and then I* and *and then they*.

16.2.1 *and then*

As with all word clusters, they normally occur as a fast blend of sound, but occasionally you will hear clear versions, as in Extract 16.4, where the speaker uses the two words *and then* as stepping stones (cf. Cauldwell, 2013: 81ff).

EXTRACT 16.4
|| AND THEN ||

Voice: Emily, Birmingham, UK.

You can hear that the words are spoken with a level tone (typical of stepping stones) and that their segments are all pretty much complete as in the citation forms |ænd ðen|. However, in Extract 16.5 you will hear three instances of *and then* from Dan which are dramatically different from Extract 16.4.

EXTRACT 16.5
|| and THEN | and THEN | and THEN ||

Voices: Dan, UK (3 times).

You will notice that the final consonant |d| of *and* and the first consonant |ð| of *then* are almost entirely inaudible – giving us soundshapes close to *annen* |ænen| or |ɔnen|. Similar processes happen to word clusters *in the* (*innuh*) *on their* (*onair*) – where |ð| is very likely to become unhearable. This is a type of consonant death that I term d'eth-drop (cf. Chapter 17.3). In Extract 16.6 we can hear two further examples of d'eth-drop.

16.2.2 *and then I*

We now add the first person pronoun to the cluster giving us *and then I*. Extract 16.6 gives five versions of this: a combination of US and UK voices in approximate order of speed. Notice how the individual words of the cluster become less clear as they get faster.

EXTRACT 16.6

```
|| and THEN i | and then i | and then i | and then i | and then i ||
```

Voices: Ashley (USA) Travis (USA), Olivia (UK, twice), and Dan (UK).

Notice also that although it possible to hear traces of |ð| at the beginning of this list, by the end it becomes inaudible. (See Shockey, 2003: 43 and Collins and Mees, 2013: 126 for further explanation.)

For many teachers and learners of English, the ability to produce an accurate clear |ð| is one of the goals of pronunciation. But to pursue the goal of listening, teachers and learners need to be able to decode fast speech where the consonant |ð| is dropped, or blurred into neighbouring sounds. So although eth-dropping or blurring would be frowned upon in the pronunciation lesson, it is essential to acknowledge that this kind of thing happens, and to deal with it in the listening/ decoding lesson.

16.2.3 *and then they*

Extract 16.7 contains three examples of *and then they*. We hear two versions from Jess from the USA and one from Emily from the UK.

EXTRACT 16.7

```
|| and then they || and then they || and then they ||
```

Voices: Jess (USA, first and third versions), Emily (UK, the second version).

In the first version, the initial consonants of *then* and *they* are close-ish to |ð|, but in the second version, they are closer to *anenay* |ɔnenei|. To my ears, the third version can be heard as only two syllables *nenay* |nenei|.

Reminder: the sight substance folk spellings (e.g. *anenay*) and the version in symbols (e.g. |nenei|) are not meant to represent precise characterisations of the sound substance. Their purpose is to act as guides to the mushiness of the sound files, so that you can hear them as learners are likely to hear them.

From this three-word cluster, we move to a very frequent two-word cluster.

16.2.4 *in the*

The cluster *in the* is the fourth most frequent two-word cluster, according to Carter and McCarthy (2006: 829). The consonant |ð| is very frequently missing (it suffers from d'eth-drop) and therefore *in the* often sounds very close to *in a* |mə|. In Extract 16.8 there are three occurrences of *in the* in three speech units 01–03. In row 00 in the extract, I have placed the three versions of *in the* from 01–03 side by side.

EXTRACT 16.8
```
00 || in the ... in the .. in the ||
01 || in the VEry CENtre || 7.1 (11.4)
02 || in the GARden || 4.4 (8.3)
03 || in the MIDdle of a WILDlife conSERVency || 5.6 (11.9)
```

Voices: Jess (US) and Dan (UK) twice.

To my ears, *in the* sounds close to *in a* in all three versions.

The transcriptions in Extract 16.8 introduce a new feature in our exploration of the Jungle. There are two sets of numbers at the end of each line. The first number in each case (e.g. for speech unit 01 it is 7.1) represents the speed of each speech unit in syllables per second. The second number in parentheses (for 01 it is (11.4)) gives the speed of the cluster within the speech unit. You will notice that the speed of the cluster is much faster than the speed of the speech unit overall – in 01 the cluster goes 60 percent faster than the unit overall, in 02 the cluster is 90 percent faster, and in 03 it is more than 100 percent faster. As mentioned previously, it is often the case that word clusters are spoken faster than the words around them. These speeds, and the streamlining of *in the* to *innuh* |mə|, makes it a very likely candidate for decoding problems, especially as a potentially crucial grammatical distinction, that between the definite article and the indefinite article, is neutralised here. A mondegreen hearing is also made possible by this streamlining: *in the middle* could be heard as *inner middle*.

16.3 *a lot of – a lot of people*

The second most common three-word cluster in Carter and McCarthy's list is *a lot of*. We will look at the fate of this cluster, and of the four-word cluster *a lot of people*, and see what challenges these clusters may present to learners.

16.3.1 *a lot of*

In the sight substance, *a lot of* is clearly three words and three syllables. For learners, however, it can often be difficult to hear the first and last syllables *a* and *of.* In Extract 16.9 you will hear three soundshapes for *a lot of* (line 00) followed by the speech units from which they were taken. The speed of the speech unit and the speed of the cluster are given at the end of each line.

EXTRACT 16.9

```
00 || a LOT of || a lot of || it's a lot of ||
01 || a LOT of time TRAvelling || 4.7 (6.6)
02 || a LOT of LAND || 5.0 (7.5)
03 || it's a lot of FUN || 5.6 (8.1)
```

Voices: Emily (UK), Jess and Karam (USA).

In 01, the British soundshape has a glottal stop at the end of *lot*, giving us |əlɒʔə| and the US versions in 02 and 03 feature a flap at the end of *lot*, giving us something close to *lada* |lɑɾə|. The third *a lot of* is preceded by the |s| of *it's.* I wanted to remove this hiss, but in editing I found it impossible to separate the |s| sound from the beginning of *a lot of.* Also, the vowel and consonant |ɪt| of *it's* are drowned by this same |s| so that in this speech unit *-s a lot of* sounds close to *slodda* |slɑdə|. In Chapter 17.9 we will term this the 'hiss effect'.

As explained in 16.2 above, the figures at the end of each line show that the speeds of the clusters are much faster than the overall speeds of the speech units in which they occur. Unit 03 is particularly notable for the extreme speed of *slodda* at 8.1 syllables per second – the calculation was made based on a syllable count of two (*slo.dda*), not the four of *it's a lot of.* If we made the calculation using a syllable count of four, the respective speeds would have been 9.3 sps for the speech unit, and 16.4 for the cluster! Even if the words were clearly articulated at this speed (they are not – they are extremely streamlined) learners would have great difficulty catching them as they flew past.

And this highlights once again the decoding difficulties that our learners face: the two sound-substance syllables *slo.dda* are the rough hints that remain after four words (*it's a lot of*) have been streamed together.

16.3.2 *a lot of people*

One of the many words that can follow *a lot of* is the word *people.* In Extract 16.10 you will hear three examples of *people, a lot of people,* and then you will hear the speech units which they come from.

EXTRACT 16.10

```
00 || people .. people .. people ||
00 || a lot of people .. a lot of people .. a lot of people ||
01 || there's a LOT of people from my HIGH school || 7.6 (9.0)
02 || a LOT of people RANCH || 5.3 (7.1)
03 || what QUITE a lot of people DO || 5.9 (8.8)
```

Voices: Jacklyn, Jess, (US) and Jack (UK).

The word *lot* is prominent in 01 and 02, but non-prominent in 03. At the end of each speech unit, you can see the speed of the entire speech unit, and in parentheses the speed of the cluster *a lot of people*. Notice again that the speed of these clusters is faster than the overall speeds of their respective speech units.

Three things are particularly noteworthy.

- Unit 01 begins with something close to *thuzlahd* |ðəzlɑːd| with the first and third words of our cluster (*a, of*) being almost entirely inaudible. However there are alternative hearings of these words with a schwa after *there's* and after *lot* which gives us |ðəzəlɑːdə|. The occurrence of schwa in such circumstances is often subject to doubt and disagreement.

- In unit 03, the second syllable of *people* seems to begin with a blurred |p| which sounds close to |f|. So if students report hearing *peefu* then this is a hearing success.

- In unit 03 Jack's *quite a lot of* offers a mondegreen hearing (to my ears) of *choir loff*.

We now turn to another common three-word cluster, *and it was*.

16.4 *and it was*

The three-word cluster *and it was* is ranked 17th in Carter and McCarthy's (2006) list. It can occur before noun groups (e.g. *and it was a wonderful sight*), and as part of verb groups (e.g. *and it was going to rain*), but in Extract 16.11 we will look at examples in which it is followed by an adjective. The extract begins with three soundshapes of *and it was* – from the US, the UK and Canada – and then you will hear the speech units in which they occurred.

EXTRACT 16.11

```
00 || and it was ... and it was ... and it was ||
01 || and it was BEAUtiful || 5.6 (8.8)
02 || and it was REAlly GOOD || 7.3 (10.5)
03 || and it was INTeresting || 7.4 (16.5)
```

Voices: Jacklyn (US), Olivia (UK) and Omira (Canada).

Notice again that the speeds of the three-word clusters are faster than the overall speeds of the speech units in which they occur. We also have some mondegreen hearings available here, but you have to turn off your knowledge that the three words *and it was* are meant, and move instead to consideration of the sound substance alone. Then perhaps you might hear:

- in 01 *earners* |ɜːnəz| for *and it was*
- in 02 *Annie was* |æni wɔz| for *and it was*
- in 03 *a news* |ɔnjuːz| for *and it was*

If you can do this, (remember you have to put the level of understanding meaning to one side) then you have successfully entered the world of your students' decoding problems.

16.5 *I think*

The words *I think* frequently occur in word clusters of two, three and four words. *(I think, I think it's, I think it was.)* Here we will focus first on the two-word cluster *I think*, and then on the three-word cluster *I think it's*.

16.5.1 *I think*

Extract 16.12 features five different versions of *I think*, all of them with a clear final consonant |k|.

EXTRACT 16.12
```
|| i think | i think | i think | i think | i think ||
```
Voices: Ashley (US), Emily (UK, three times) and Jack (UK) are the speakers.

The first version is from Ashley, and it occurs at the end of a clause, before a pause. She is very low in her vocal range and you will hear a lot of creak. The next three versions are from Emily, and her first person pronoun is close to schwa each time, although in her third version (the fourth in the extract) a trace of |æ| can be heard. The final version is from Jack, who makes the first person pronoun prominent so that we can clearly hear the diphthong |aɪ|.

We now move to consideration of the three-word cluster *I think it's*.

16.5.2 *I think it's*

In Extract 16.13 you will first hear two versions of the three-word cluster *I think it's* and then the speech units which they come from.

EXTRACT 16.13
```
00 || i think it's | (and) i think it's ||
01 || i THINK it's PRObably || 4.4 (4.1)
02 || and i THINK it's a BIT more MEDical || 8.8 (8.8)
```
Voices: Emily and Jack (UK).

From the linking rules of the CSM, we might expect *I think it's* to feature consonant-vowel linking, with the final |k| of *think* linking with the vowel of *it's* to give us *I think‿ it's*. But that is not quite what we get. To my ears, in 01 *think it's* sounds close to |θɪŋʔɪz| with a glottal stop instead of |k|. There is an alternative hearing of a |g|, resulting in something close to *thing* |θɪŋgɪz| in both units. Notice that the measured speed of the clusters is pretty much the same as their respective speech units. But I perceive the speed of the cluster in 02 to be much faster than the rest of the unit. It is worth noting that perceived speed can be different from measured speed.

There are three other points to notice about speech unit 02.

- The word *and* is streamlined almost out of existence – it survives as the nasalised (nosey) sounds of *I think*.

- We have two clusters occurring one after the other: *and I think it's* is followed by *a bit more*.

- This super cluster goes at 11.1 sps compared to the 8.8 sps of the speech unit – it is 25 percent faster.

16.6 *it was just*

The word *just* ends with an |st| cluster and is therefore likely to lose the final |t| (cf. Brown, 1990: 66; Field, 2008b:150), but not necessarily. Listen to Extract 16.14, where Catherine is explaining the extreme enjoyment she got from travelling to the Antarctic, and places *and it was just* in a speech unit of its own, choosing to pause between *just* and *absolutely*.

EXTRACT 16.14
```
01 || it was JUST || 2.3 [pause 0.3 secs]
02 || ABsolutely FABulous || 3.3
```

Voice: Catherine, USA.

The final cluster of *just* is very clear as it occurs before a pause and because Catherine assigns great importance to the choice of this word – it is prominent and tonic with a level tone.

Catherine's *it was just* goes at 2.3 sps, which is slow. We will next listen to two other speakers whose *it was just* clusters go three and four times faster.

EXTRACT 16.15
```
00 || it was just .. it was just ||
01 || and it was just SO frusTRAting || 4.6 (8.4)
02 || it was just MOSTly ADmin work || 5.6 (10.6)
```

Voices: Sylvia (Romania) and Arun (UK).

In 01 Sylvia gives us a four-word cluster *and it was just* which goes at 8.4 sps – more than three times faster than Catherine's – whereas Arun's three-word version goes more than four times faster, at 10.6 sps.

Sylvia's four-word cluster *and it was just* sounds close to *enniwasjuss* |enɪwɔzdʒəs|. Arun's version is difficult to distinguish from the two-word cluster *it was*, but I hear an extra pulse to the buzz at the end of *was* giving us something between |ɪwɔzz| and |ɪwɒʒə| and which to my ears counts as an extreme streamlining of *just*. But the evidence for this is not absolutely clear, so *it was mostly* would be a reasonable hearing of this stretch of sound substance.

As I mentioned earlier, when we encounter such streamlining in recordings in the classroom, it is important not to insist on a right-answer approach to issues of decoding, and instead recognise that alternative hearings are legitimate.

16.7 *kind of – and that kind of thing*

The two-word cluster *kind of* can act as a marker of imprecision and also as a component of a larger cluster *and that kind of thing* meaning 'et cetera'.

16.7.1 *kind of*

The two-word cluster *kind of* is very commonly used as a marker of imprecision. As Carter and McCarthy state, it is one of those clusters which 'softens expressions so that they do not appear too direct or unduly authoritative and assertive' (2006: 202).

In Extract 16.16 you will hear three different soundshapes of *kind of*, with the first two having two syllables, and the third one having one syllable only. In none of the soundshapes is the |d| of *kind* audible, despite the fact that conventional connected speech rules predict a consonant vowel linking: *kind‿of.*

EXTRACT 16.16
```
00 || kind of || kind of || kind of ||
01 || and like wanted to be aNONymous KIND of || 7.1 (4.5)
02 || kind of DON'T LIKE it || 8.3 (9.1)
03 || and so it was kind of HARD to find FRIENDS || 5.8 (10.0)
     (7.8 for 'and so it was')
```

Voices: Jacklyn (New Jersey, USA – twice); Jess (New Mexico, USA).

The first soundshape has the diphthong $|aɪ|$ and the second and third have vowels close to $|æ|$ and schwa respectively. The third soundshape, from Jess, has only one syllable, and features a lot of breathiness as she makes the speedy transition between the initial consonant $|k|$ of *kind* and the first consonant of *hard* while briefly visiting the vowel $|æ|$. As is often the case, the preposition *of* is omitted.

The temptation may be to ignore any decoding problems presented by *kind of* and words like it because their meaning load is not very heavy – almost everyone would agree that the word *anonymous* in 01, and the words *don't like* and *hard to find* in 02 and 03, are more important for meaning than *kind of*. But remember, our goal is decoding and teaching the sound substance of language, and with this goal even clusters with light meanings (such as 'this is imprecise') occur frequently in the sound substance of everyday speech, and therefore need to be recognised.

Let's now turn our attention to clusters of increasing size which feature *kind of*.

16.7.2 *and all that kind of thing*

In Extract 16.17 you can hear three UK speakers saying *kind of* in clusters of four, five and six words in length. The first, by Richard, is the fastest of the three at 10 syllables per second. The recording begins with the three soundshapes of *kind of* extracted from these speech units.

EXTRACT 16.17
```
00 || ..kind of .. kind of .. kind of .. ||
01 || that kind of thing || 10 sps
02 || all that kind of thing || 5.6 sps
03 || and all that kind of thing || 8.3 sps
```
Voices: Richard, Olivia and Laura (UK).

In all three speech units, the final consonant $|d|$ in *kind* is dropped. In 01, to my ears, *kind of* becomes one syllable $|kən|$ with schwa, but there is an alternative hearing with two syllables $|kənə|$. The versions in units 02 and 03 have two syllables, and in unit 02 *kind of* has a vowel flavoured with $|ɑː|$, whereas in 03 it is flavoured with something between $|æ|$ and $|ʌ|$. Note also that the two words *all that* in 02 and 03 sounds close to *all at* $|ɔːlæʔt|$, where the initial consonant of *that* is inaudible (once again, d'eth-drop).

We have seen and heard how a word cluster can become larger by the addition of one, and then two words. We now turn to clusters which occur with other clusters.

16.8 *one of the*

We end this series of examples of word clusters by looking at *one of the* (ranked seventh in Carter and McCarthy's list) as a three-word cluster on its own, and then in its role in larger clusters, ending with a six-word cluster.

16.8.1 *One of the*

We begin with the *one of the* cluster in a speech unit of its own preceding the words *wonderful memories* (unit 02). It occurs in a speech unit on its own because it is followed by a slight pause, and the unit which follows has a different rhythm (cf. Appendix 2).

EXTRACT 16.18
```
01 || ONE of the most || 6.5 (11.0)
02 || WONderful MEMories || 5.4
```

Voice: Jess (New Mexico, USA).

To my ears we have an alternative hearing available for the last two words in 01 – *the most*. Jess's *most* has no final |t| and the vowel quality of *most* is close to schwa. This results in *the most* becoming hearable either as *them was* or *them as*.

We will end this chapter on word clusters by looking at four- and six-word clusters.

16.8.2 *and one of the – that's gonna be one of the*

In Extract 16.19 we hear two British voices: in 01 Laura adds the word *and* to the *one of the*, and in 02 she adds another cluster, the five-word cluster *was a bit of a*. In 03 Emily precedes the cluster *one of the* with another cluster *that's gonna be*, giving us a cluster combination of seven syllables: *that's gonna be one of the*.

EXTRACT 16.19
```
00 || ... one of the ... one of the ... ||
01 || and one of the BLOKES || 7.1 (10.0)
02 || was a bit of a GOTH || 7.5 (10.6)
03 || that's gonna be one of the MAIN reasons i THINK || 6.3 (11.0)
```

Voices: Laura and Emily (UK). A goth is someone who follows the fashion of wearing black clothes and pale make-up.

Consistent with what we have observed before, the speeds of the clusters are faster than the overall speeds of the speech units which contain them. In 01, the speed of *and one of the* is 40 percent faster (10.0 sps compared to 7.1 sps); in 02 the speed of *was a bit of a* is again 40 percent faster and in 03, *one of the* is 70 percent faster (11.00 sps compared to 6.3 sps).

Again we get a mondegreen feature in unit 02. To my ears, Emily's *one of the* sounds close to the monosyllabic *were*, but of course it is difficult to hear anything other than *one of the* when you have the words as sight substance in front of you.

16.9 Summary and what's next

Word clusters comprise a very large component of the sound substance of speech. They are made up of very frequent words, often spoken very fast. In fact we have seen that they are often the fastest parts of the speech units that contain them. The component words of clusters are crushed together, making blended stretches of sound substance that are likely to present decoding difficulties for learners at all levels. They are typically non-prominent, or have significant non-prominent sections. They should not be ignored. Even if their meaning-bearing load is light, they form a significant part of the sound substance of the language and, because many, if not most of our learners want to 'learn the language' rather than just cope, these are things that we should teach.

Word clusters appear in speech of many different kinds, on many different topics. Therefore mastering the variety of soundshapes that these clusters have will help make learners able to decode speech much more successfully, and will make them feel more comfortable about coping with listening as a whole.

They are a good starting point for a teaching syllabus. I have written pilot materials (Cauldwell, 2016) which demonstrate how this can be done (see the Speech in Action website). These materials use a highly conventional methodology to do what I term 'first-up' teaching of decoding: ten units of presentation, practice and free production based around word clusters which undergo severe streamlining.

Additionally, any ELT course book recording is likely to contain a fair range of clusters, any one of which can form the basis of decoding work. It is vital, however, that – for any cluster – work is done on the multiple soundshapes that the cluster can have. There is more on this in Part 4.

Field (2008b: 155–156) also recommends a focus on word clusters (he refers to them as 'formulaic chunks') in 'exercises which move from awareness raising to the practising and internalising of recurrent chunks' and he suggests that the 'Teacher plays them; learners report what they hear. Learners then practise producing them'.

So word clusters are going to be an important component of the listening activities of Part 4. For lists of clusters of different sizes, see Appendix 5.

In this chapter we have made reference to streamlining processes such as 'd'eth-drop' and the 'hiss effect'. Chapters 17 and 18 introduce these streamlining processes and describe them in more detail.

17 Streamlining I – Consonant death

In this and the following chapter we will identify, describe and give examples of a number of streamlining processes that speakers apply to words as they seek to achieve their communicative purposes. The speaker's application of these streamlining processes results in the wide variety of soundshapes that we hear in the Jungle. We have already encountered examples of some of these processes in our description of the soundshapes of word clusters in Chapter 16 ('consonant death', and the 'hiss effect').

In this chapter we focus on the processes of blurring and dropping of consonants, which we investigate under the general heading 'consonant death'. There is insufficient room to demonstrate all the possibilities for all consonants, so in this chapter we will focus on a few key consonants.

In the literature, of which Johnson (2004) and Shockey (2003) are key publications, streamlining processes are referred to as 'reduction processes' and terms for these processes which are common in our teacher-training materials include 'elision' and 'assimilation'. In what follows, I have suggested some new, more teacher- and classroom-friendly terminology whenever I believe an easy-to-remember term suggests itself.

It is essential to know about these processes, and to be able to apply them and mimic them in operation, whenever you demonstrate the relationship between Greenhouse, Garden and Jungle forms in the classroom activities introduced in Part 4.

We begin with two reminders.

17.1 Reminders: streamlining, practical not theoretical

REMINDER NUMBER 1

By 'streamlining process', I mean the way speakers re-shape words in order to fit them smoothly, or force them roughly, into the quasi-rhythmic units of the stream of speech. Many of these processes apply to a range of clusters, words, syllables and speech sounds, and so they are generalisable to a wide range of circumstances. They are therefore useful items in a syllabus for listening. Being able to hear them in recordings is an important skill for a teacher of listening/decoding.

REMINDER NUMBER 2

The purpose is a practical one: it is to open your ears to the world of the learners who have difficulty recognising the soundshapes which are caused by streamlining processes. The processes identified here do not claim to be a coherent phonetic or phonological theory. The categories overlap, and there may be causal relationships between them which I have not written about, and which would be given fuller treatment in an academic treatise. It would be a mistake to try to find an exact match between the processes that are described here with those of phonetics or phonology textbooks.

17.2 Consonant death

The term 'consonant death' refers to the fate of consonants which are either bullied out of existence by neighbouring sounds (actually by the speaker) or are partly on the way out of existence. For the former case we will use terms such as 't-drop' (elision of |t|), and for the latter case, we will use the term 't-blur' to refer to a blurring of |t| which takes it towards sounding like an |s|, |d|, |r| and so on. Our task in this chapter is therefore to observe and describe examples where consonants disappear or where they become blurred versions of themselves, or where they blend into neighbouring sounds.

It is well known that consonants tend to disappear at the ends of words, but – as we will see and hear in this section – they also frequently disappear in the middle of words. We begin by listening to Kaili and Jacklyn in Extract 17.1. In unit 01 Kaili produces a beautifully clear |t| at the end of *might*, but listen to what she does at the end of *thought*:

EXTRACT 17.1
```
01 || i THOUGHT i MIGHT ||
02 || get OUT on my OWN ||
```
Voices: Kaili, Jacklyn, USA.

In unit 01, to my ears, *thought* has no final |t|, even though we might expect it to participate in consonant-vowel linking, with the diphthong of the first-person pronoun – *thought I* becoming *thought_I*. Kaili says something close to *thaw* |ðɔː|. In 02, from Jacklyn, neither *get* nor *out* has |t|. She gives us something close to |geaʊɑmaɪoʊn|.

17.3 D'eth-drop

One of the most practised and most challenging-to-learn speech sounds in English is the *th*-sound which begins words such as *the*, *this* and *then*. It has the symbol |ð|, known as 'eth'. Paradoxically, it seems to be one of the sounds which is most often discarded, as we have already heard in our word clusters chapter (cf. Chapter 16.2.1). We will refer to this process as 'd'eth-drop'. In Extract 17.2 we hear Olivia beginning a speech unit with *and then* as *anen* |ænen|.

EXTRACT 17.2
```
01 || and then AFTer that i did inTErior deSIGN || 7.1
02 || ... and then ... AFter that ... that i ... ||
```
Voice: Olivia, UK. The second row of the extract contains pairs of words extracted from the full unit.

It is a noticeable feature of spontaneous speech that very often multiple streamlining processes are operating at the same time in any given extract. It is therefore useful to note when other streamlining processes are at work in the extracts we use.

With Extract 17.2, when I am looking at the words of the transcript, I hear all the syllables of all the words reasonably clearly. But as I delve into the recording, and listen bit-by-bit, I realise that alternative hearings are available:

- the second syllable of *after* blends with *that* (lots of creak) giving *affthat* – a 'tail-clip' (cf. Chapter 18.4.4)

- the words *that* and *I* blend together to sound close to *thy* – a 'syllablend' (cf. Chapter 18.4.1).

It is therefore important, when designing decoding activities, to avoid the danger of the sight substance of the transcript making you believe that words are spoken more clearly than they actually are.

We should note here that, although I have no recorded examples of it, when $|ð|$ occurs in the middle or at the end of words such as *smooth* or *father*, it can blur towards $|v|$, giving us something close to *smoover* $|smuːvə|$ and *faaver* $|fɑːvə|$. For more on this cf. Cruttenden (2014: 199) and Collins and Mees (2013: 126).

We end this section with a list of other examples of possible d'eth-drop events:

- *all this* can be heard as or *all lis* $|ɔːl lɪs|$ or *alliss* $|ɔːlɪs|$

- *in the* can be heard as *in na* $|ɪn nə|$ or *in a* $|ɪnə|$

- *and this* can be heard as *an niss* $|æn nɪs|$ or *aniss* $|ænɪs|$

- *and they were all* can be heard as *n neyrall* $|n neɪrɔːl|$ or *neyrall* $|neɪrɔːl|$

17.4 Theta blur – *I think*

The *th* spelling is also associated with another 'pronunciation problem' – the sound that begins words such as *three*, *thick* or *think*. The symbol is $|θ|$, known as 'theta'. It is problematic for a number of reasons, a major one being that it does not transmit well in radio-telephony (RT) communications between pilots and air traffic control. This is why the recommended RT pronunciation for the number three (3) is *tree*. For our decoding purposes, it is noteworthy for occasionally blurring toward $|h|$.

In Extract 17.3 we can hear two instances of *I think* from Joey and Jack.

EXTRACT 17.3

```
01 || i THINK it was YEAR eLEven ||
02 || i THINK it's a bit more MEdical ||
```

Voices: Joey, Jack, UK.

To my ears, both versions of the word *think* undergo theta-blur which results in something close to |hɪŋ|.

Other processes at work in these speech units result in the following alternative hearings:

- in 01 Joey also does a syllablend (cf. Chapter 18.4.1) with *was year* sounding close to |wɜɪə|.

- in 02 Jack's *I think it's a bit* sounds close to the mondegreen *ah hingis bip.*

Finally in this section it is worth noting two other points. First that the theta-drop and theta-blur processes frequently occur in non-initial syllables such as the |θ| in *something* (cf. Cauldwell, 2013: 125). Second, you will often hear the theta-blur process at work in Cockney-related accents where, for example, the initial |θ| of *think* blurs to |f|, giving us *fink.*

17.5 T-drop and t-blur

In American English, the folk spelling *lil* for *little* gives us an example of a process called 't-drop', which we first saw in 17.2. This *lil* spelling and soundshape are well established, but they represent a general process of the blurring and dropping of |t| in the middle of words. In Extract 17.4 we can hear an example where |t| is preserved

EXTRACT 17.4

```
|| it was just a LITtle BIT ||
```

Voice: Sylvia from Romania.

Sylvia's *little* has something close to a tap, or a d-like sound – but nevertheless we still have something |t|-like, a t-blur. Notice also that the |t| at the end of *bit* takes on an |s|-like quality – the symbol used for this is |s̩|. We will use this symbol and the sound it represents in a classroom exercise explained in Chapter 22.4.2.

Now listen to Extract 17.5 which gives a British English example where the |t| is dropped in the middle of *little*. But it is not the only |t| that is streamlined.

EXTRACT 17.5

```
01 || and i JUST thought i'd || 6.3 sps [pause 0.53]
02 || WANT to do something a little bit DIFFerent || 8.5 sps
```

Voice: Jack, UK.

The |t| is dropped in *little*, blurred in *want to*, and it is blurred to a glottal stop in *different*.

As usual, there are other processes going on which are worth noting. In 02 Jack crushes the five syllables of *want to do something* into a mush that offers alternative hearings of *want.sue.some.n* |wɒnt sːu sm ŋ|, or *want.shoe.some.n* |wɒnt ʃu sm ŋ|. Notice that the |t| at the end of *want* blurs into an |s| which then leads us into a vowel |u| and then an |s| plus a nasal cluster |mŋ| for the word *something*. (For more on *something* cf. Cauldwell 2013: 125.)

Extract 17.6 features Jack again, here describing animals. His *pretty* undergoes t-drop, resulting in a monosyllabic *pre* |priː|.

EXTRACT 17.6
```
01 || they're STILL pretty WILD ||
```

Voice: Jack, UK.

This single-syllable version of *pretty* is very common, and may well present decoding problems to learners as it is a very frequent intensifier for adjectives in everyday speech.

We end this section with a list of other examples of possible t-blur and t-drop events.

- *settle* can be heard as *seddle* or *sell* as in
  - ```
    || we'll NEver seddle/sell down HERE ||
    ```
- *metal* can be heard as *medal* or *mell* as in
  - ```
    || it's the STRONGest medal/mell EVer ||
    ```
- *kettle* can be heard as *keddle* or *kell* as in
  - ```
    || SWITCH the keddle/kell off NOW ||
    ```
- *later* can be heard as *layder*, *layer* or *lair* as in
  - ```
    || i'll SEE him layder/layer/lair ON today||
    ```

The speech units for each example indicate a range of streamlinings that may happen for each word (e.g. *layder/layer/lair*). It is important to realise that the list of possible soundshapes is much greater than the examples shown here. Note also that the last soundshape in each example results in a dropped syllable – a 'syll-drop' – to which we turn our attention in Chapter 18.4

17.6 D-drop – d-blur

In Extract 17.7 you will hear three examples of d-drop or d-blur.

EXTRACT 17.7
```
01 || produced by GUY miEGE ||
02 || and GRADuate students ||
03 || it's a LOT HARDer || than PEOple THINK ||
```

Voices: Geoff, UK; Ellen, USA; Travis, USA.

In 01 Geoff gives us a soundshape of *produced* that is close to *pree-oose* |priːuːs| which is, to my ears, almost but not quite a single syllable. In 02 Ellen gives a soundshape of *students* that sounds to me definitely like a single syllable *stints* |stɪnts|. In 03 Travis gives us a version of *harder* which sounds to me something like AmE *horror* |hɑːrɚ|.

The d-drop process can create the following soundshapes, where the result of the process also results in syll-drops (cf. Chapter 18.4). Notice that I write below '*can* be heard' not '*is* heard'. The Jungle soundshapes shown below are possibilities – they are not certain to happen, and there are many possible intermediate stages of soundshape between the Greenhouse and Jungle forms which I have not attempted to represent here.

- *saddle* can be heard as *sall* as in
  o || DON'T sah-ull/sall the HORSE yet ||
- *medal* can be heard as *mell* as in
  o || the GOLD meh-ull/mell was aWARDed ||
- *model* can be heard as *moll* as in
  o || a GOOD mo-ull/moll of the BUILDing ||

17.7 K-drop – k-blur

The consonant |k| can also be dropped or blurred.

In Extract 17.8 you will first hear *because* from Jacklyn with a blurred version of the consonant at the beginning of the second syllable - |x| rather than |k| (where |x| is the sound at the end of the Scottish word *loch*), and then you will hear a re-created recording in which the |k| in *like* disappears entirely.

EXTRACT 17.8
```
01 || beCAUSE ||
02 || would you like a reCEIPT with that ||
```

Voices: Jacklyn, USA; Richard, UK.

In 02, the four syllables *would you like a* feature a dropping of the |k| in *like*, producing a soundshape for *like* that is close to *liar* |laɪə|. This sentence was repeated to me by an English teacher from the Basque country in 2016, who had first been confused, and then amused, by her ability not to understand it the first time.

The k-drop and k-blur processes can also create the following soundshapes:

- *like* can be heard as *liech* |laɪx| or *lie*
    - `|| i DON'T lie to SAY this ||`

- *because* can be heard as *be-chuz* |bixɔz| or *behuz*
    - `|| he SAID it behuz he LOVES you ||`

- *physical* can be heard as *fizzle*
    - `|| it was a VEry fizzle enCOUNter ||`

- *speak to you can* be heard as *spee chew*
    - `|| he SAYS he'll spee chew LAter ||`

The final example also features a 'Tuesday-blend' where *to you* becomes *chew* (cf. Chapter 18.4.1).

17.8 V-drop – v-blur

Brown (1990: 68) lists six examples of |v| being dropped from the words *five*, *have*, *of* and *leave*. In Extract 17.9 there is an example of v-drop in *have* from Jacklyn, and a v-blur from Jess.

EXTRACT 17.9
```
01 || my PARents wouldn't let me HAVE one || 8.5
02 || and they disCOVered that's what CAUSED it || 5.8
```
Voices: Jacklyn, USA; Jess, USA.

Jacklyn's *have one* sounds like *ha won* with the |v| dropped. Notice also that her second word *parents* sounds very close to a single-syllable *pairnts*, but it is also hearable as *pairs*. Alternative hearings are available in 01: for the syllables *-nt let me* it is *normally*, and for the syllables *-n't let me have one* it is *no may lee ha won*.

Jess's *discovered* features a v-blur where |v| becomes |w|-like, giving us something close to *discowered* |dɪskʌwɔd|. The speech unit also features two glottal stops: at the end of *what* and the final word *it*.

The v-drop/v-blur process can create the following soundshapes:

- *move* can be heard as *moo* as in
    - the COWS are mooing in the FIELD

- *level* can be heard as *lewel* as in
    - it's NOT a lewel PLAYing field

- *over* can be heard as *ower*, or *o'er* as in
    - || they're SOMEwhere ower/o'er THERE ||

17.9 P-drop – p-blur

The consonant |p|, when it does not begin a word, can blur towards something resembling |f|. In Extract 17.10 you can hear an example from Jack.

EXTRACT 17.10

01 || what QUITE a lot of people DO || 5.9 (8.8)

Voices: Jack (UK).

In this unit, Jack blurs the |p| at the beginning of the second syllable of *people* making it sound close to |f|. So if students report hearing *peefu*, then this is a successful hearing of the raw sound substance, a step on the way to decoding.

The p-blur can also create the following soundshapes:

- *couple* can be heard as *cuffle* as in
    - || he GAVE us a cuffle of DRINKS ||

- *opposite* can be heard as *offsit* as in
    - || she SAT in the offsit CORNer ||

For a technical description of the blurring of |p| cf. Cruttenden (2014: 172).

17.10 T-drop and cluster simplification

A consonant cluster, for example |st| in the word *constantly*, may be streamlined by the process of t-dropping resulting in a cluster simplification, where |st| becomes |s|, giving us *consantly* |kɒn.sənt.li|. In this section we will look at a number of examples of cluster simplification featuring t-drop, and in Section 17.11 we will examine the role which |s| plays in drowning the sound around it – the 'hiss effect'.

17.10.1 *constantly*

In Extract 17.11 you can hear Karam from California talking about water polo. She uses the word *constantly* three times. You will hear the three versions of *constantly* first, then the speech units in which they occurred.

EXTRACT 17.11
```
00 || CONstantly | CONstantly | CONstantly ||
01 || you're CONstantly TREADing WAter ||
02-03 || you're CONstantly || atTACKing or deFENding ||
04-05 || you're CONstantly || BATtling SOMEbody ||
```

Voice: Karam, USA. Row 00 gives the versions of *constantly* contained in the speech units 01–05.

The citation form of *constantly* contains three syllables, but experts disagree where to place the boundaries, so we will use |kɑːn.stənt.li| as our reference point. Karam is from the USA and she uses t-drop on the first |t|, resulting in a cluster simplification |kɑːn.sənt.li|. But if we turn our attention to the second |t| in *constantly*, we can hear that it, too, undergoes a streamlining process – a blurring of |t| occurs with glottal stops taking its place, giving us |kɑːnst.ən?.li|.

Other |st| clusters that can undergo t-drop simplification include:

- *most* becomes *mowss* as in
  - || it WAS the mowss DIFFicult one ||
- *first* becomes *firss* as in
  - || we GOT through the firss ROUND ||
- *just* becomes *juss* as in
  - || i juss NEver had a PET as a child ||

17.11 The hiss effect, the buzz effect and the creak effect

In the previous section, we treated the cluster simplification of |st| as an instance of t-drop. Where an |s| is a component of the cluster, there is another way of considering this type of simplification: we can treat this a case of the 'hiss effect', where the hissing of |s| can drown the surrounding sounds.

This happens frequently in consonant clusters – in Brown (1990: 66), eight of eleven consonant clusters in which |t| is dropped (elided) involve a preceding |s|. We will look at examples of the hiss effect operating on the word *asked* and in the word clusters *I just never*, *I used to play*, *it's the piece of*.

17.11.1 *asked*

The Greenhouse versions of the British and American English forms of *ask* are |ɑːsk| and |æsk| respectively. They have different vowels, but both share the final consonant cluster |sk|. Omira gives us an example in Extract 17.12.

EXTRACT 17.12

|| SO they'd ASK ||

Voice: Omira, Canada.

Sometimes, as in this case, when *ask* is prominent before a pause, the consonant cluster |sk| can be beautifully clear. But our focus is going to be on the simple past tense form *asked*. It ends with a triple-consonant cluster which is rarely pronounced with all its elements |ɑːskt|. The resulting cluster is often either |ɑːst| or |æst| with |k| omitted, or |ɑːs| or |æs| with both consonants dropped. In Extract 17.13 there are three speech units in which *asked* occurs as the first prominent syllable.

EXTRACT 17.13

```
01 || he ASKED me ||
02 || and she ASKED me to COME along to the INterview TOO ||
03 || he was ASKED ||
```

Voices: Terry, Ireland; Omira, Canada; Catherine, USA.

In units 01 and 02, the word *asked* has its three-element cluster reduced by two elements to |ɑːs|, and in 03 there is a final |t| giving us |ɑːst| before the pause.

Before we leave *asked*, we should note that there is a very common soundshape of which I do not have a recording: this is *akst* |ɑːkst|, where the |s| follows |k|. This soundshape dates back to the time of Geoffrey Chaucer (1343–1400). Here are two lines from 'The Canterbury Tales, The Knight's Tale'.

> Yow loveres axe I now this questioun,
> Who hath the worse, Arcite or Palamoun?

17.11.2 *I used to play*

Moving on to consider the hiss effect across a word cluster, in Extract 17.14 below we can hear the hiss effect drowning both the final element of the |st| cluster of *used* and the following word *to*.

EXTRACT 17.14

```
01 || i USED to play RUGby ||
02-03 || i USED to PLAY || the Oboe ||
```

Voice: Jack, UK.

In 01 I am confident, when I listen to the whole unit, that there is no |t| in the sequence *used to*. In fact, I hear something close to the mondegreen *you sue*. However, when I introduce a pause just before the end of |s|, then evidence for |t| emerges. In 02, similarly, if we introduce a pause just before the end of the |s| of *used*, then a |t| becomes audible. But to my ears, this is an artefact which comes from chopping up something that is inherently continuous. And for teaching purposes, it is vital to prefer the interpretation of the continuous sound substance.

17.11.3 *I just never*

Our next word cluster to suffer the hiss effect is *I just never*. Extract 17.15 contains an example from Jacklyn, from New Jersey USA complaining about not having a pet when she was young.

EXTRACT 17.15
```
|| I just never had DOG growing up ||
```

Voice: Jacklyn, USA.

We might expect the words *just* and *never* to become *juss never* with the |t| of *just* being dropped, but to my ears the hiss effect of |s| leads to the dropping of |n| at the beginning of *never* and we get *juss ever*.

17.11.4 *It's the piece of*

We move on to our next word cluster – *it's a piece of*. In Extract 17.16 there are two instances of the hiss effect: the |s| of *it's* and the |s| at the end of *piece*.

EXTRACT 17.16
```
|| it's the PIECE of techNOlogy i USE the MOST ||
```

Voice: Joey, UK.

The hiss of the |s| of *it's* drowns out the article (*the* or *a* – it's impossible to tell which) in front of *piece* and the |s| at the end of *piece* drowns out the following *of*. Finally, *most* at the end of this extract has no final |t|, but in this latter case, the recording has an extraneous noise which may have obscured this |t|.

17.11.5 The buzz effect

The voiced counterpart of |s| – |z| – can also act as a killer sound, as we will hear in Extract 17.17.

EXTRACT 17.17
```
|| it was just MOSTly ADmin work ||
```

Voices: Arun, (UK).

Arun's *it was just* features a buzz effect with |z|. There is an extra pulse to the buzz at the end of *was* |ɪwɔzz| which, for me, counts as an extreme streamlining of *just*. I am confident, when I listen to the whole unit, that Arun intended to say *just* and that he left sufficient sound substance to give me a rough hint that leads me to perceive it. But when I cut up the sound file and place a pause of 0.2 seconds between *just* and *mostly*, I am less confident. Thus the evidence for this is not absolutely clear. Consequently, *it was mostly* would be a reasonable hearing of this stretch of sound substance.

17.11.6 'Swonderful, 'Smarvellous

The hiss effect is used by writers of songs: a famous example is the song composed by George and Ira Gershwin 'Swonderful, 'Smarvellous'. The title consists of a shortened spelling of the words *it's wonderful, it's marvellous* in which *it's* is reduced to |s| and the surviving |s| attaches to the consonant of the following words *wonderful, marvellous* thereby reducing the number of syllables by one.

17.11.7 Other cases of the hiss effect

The hiss effect can result in the following changes of soundshape:

- *it's gonna be fun* can be heard as *scum be fun*
      || he SAID it scum be FUN tomorrow ||

- *it's like a bombsite* can be heard as *slike a bombsite*
      || they SAID slike a BOMBsite ||

- *it's a bit of a problem* can be heard as *spittuva problem*
      || they were TOLD spittuva PROBlem ||

- *it's not going to be long* can be heard as *snot gunna be long*
      || they ALways say snot gunna be LONG ||

17.12 Summary and what's next

In this chapter we have seen and heard how consonants can be dropped and blurred so that words can be streamlined to fit in with the speeds and rhythmic units which the speaker chooses to use.

We have only covered a sample of consonants, but the dropping and blurring processes can, in principle, apply to all consonants.

In Chapter 18 we will look at, and hear, another range of processes: the dropping of syllables (*Australia* becomes 'Stralia); the vocalization of |l| (*well* becomes *weh-oo*); smoothing of diphthongs and long vowels (*south* becomes *saath*); the lengthening of consonants to replace syllables; the 'Don't Repeat Yourself' principle; polarity problems (*can't* sounding like *can*); and finally the 'teeny' problem of distinguishing between the *thirteen/fourteen* and *thirty/forty* series of numbers.

17.13 Further reading

The following sources have more information on the streamlining processes mentioned in this chapter: Brown (1990 p. 79) on weakened consonants; Shockey (2003: 28) on stop consonants and (2003: 43) for d'eth-drop; Cruttenden, (2014: 172) on plosives and (2014:199) for d'eth-drop and the buzz effect. Note that these books do not use the same terminology that I have used in this chapter.

18 Streamlining II – smoothies to teenies

In this chapter we begin by looking at one of the streamlining processes that affect vowels – smoothing. We will then look at the following: a consonant that often turns into a vowel; occasions when it is difficult to judge whether a speaker is or isn't using a negative; and disappearing syllables. We will end with a 'teeny' problem.

The aim, as with every chapter in Part 3, is to help you develop your sensitivity to the nature of the sound substance of speech, so that you can fully engage with learners' problems of decoding.

18.1 Smoothing

Speakers often change the quality of the diphthongs or long vowels: thus |uː| becomes |ʊ|, |iː| becomes |ɪ| and |aɪ|, and |aʊ| become |a|. This very often happens with the first person pronoun *I* which is often spoken as |a| rather than |aɪ|. Wells (2008: 173) and Lindsey (2012) call this process 'smoothing', which we can hear in Extract 18.1, where Jack (UK) uses smoothing on both *I*, and *like*.

EXTRACT 18.1
```
01 || i like GOing to the GYM || 7.0 (11.0) sps
```

Voice: Jack, UK.

Jack breathes out before he begins *I like*, making it seem as if he is beginning the speech unit with |h|. Both syllables of *I like* are smoothed from |aɪ| to |a|, giving us something close to *hala*. And the word *going* is crushed into a very fast, almost monosyllabic blur giving us an alternative hearing of *I like going* as *halagin* |halagɪn|. Notice that the six-syllable cluster *I like going to the* goes at 11.0 syllables per second which is very fast indeed.

In extract 18.2 there are two further examples of smoothing, one each from the UK and the USA.

EXTRACT 18.2
```
01 || to SOUTH east Asia || 4.5
02 || a HUGE amount of LAND || 6.2
```

Voices: Corony, UK; Jess, USA.

Corony is from the UK, and in 01 *south* becomes a smoothie, something between |sɑːθ| or |saaθ| instead of the Greenhouse form with the diphthong |saʊθ|. In unit 02 Jess from the USA makes a smoothie of the second syllable of *amount* |əmaun| to |əman|. There is also an alternative hearing available here: the syllables *–mount of* are hearable as *man of* |manəv|.

Further examples of smoothing come from Karam from California in Extract 18.3. She is describing what happens between attackers and defenders in water polo, which I used to think of as a genteel, non-contact sport. But (a) it is definitely not a non-contact sport and (b) Karam goes beyond smoothing.

EXTRACT 18.3

```
00 || TRYing to | trying to ||
01 || you're TRYing to ||
02 || get aWAY from your deFENder ||
03 || who is GRABbing your SWIMsuit ||
04 || or trying to DROWN you or ||
```

Voice: Karam, USA. Her two instances of *trying to* are given at the beginning of the sound file.

Both occurrences of Karam's *trying to* are smoothies – their |aɪ| diphthongs become smoothed, but not to |a|. To my ears, the vowel in her first *trying to* is close to |ʌ| and the vowel in the second is between |e| and |ɔ|.

Although in the pronunciation class we may need to insist on the clear differentiation of diphthongs and simple vowels, in the listening classroom we need to teach students that different soundshapes, some with diphthongs, and others with smoothies, can represent the same word.

Other examples of smoothing are listed below.

- *really* can be heard as *rilly* where |rɪəlɪ| becomes |rɪlɪ| (cf. Chapter 15.5.1)
    - o || they WERE rilly HAPpy ||

- *royal* can be heard as *rawl* where |rɔɪl| becomes |rɔl|
    - o || he STUdied at the rawl aCAdemy ||

- *time* can be heard as *taam* where |taɪm| becomes |tam|
    - o || she LOVED her tam in LISbon ||

- *enjoy* can be heard as *enjaw* where |endʒɔɪ| becomes |endʒɔ|
    - o || she COULDn't enjaw his COOKing ||

- *sound* can be heard as *sand* where |saund| becomes |sand|
    - o || she couldn't STAND the sand of his VOICE ||

- *how are you* can be heard as *haa you* where |hauˈɑːjuː| becomes |hɑːˈjuː| (cf. Field 2008:156)
    - o || they just SHOUted haa you and ran aWAY ||

18.2 Vow-ell – vocalisation of 'l'

In the speech of many people, the dark or velar |l| towards the end and at the ends of syllables in words such as *old* and *well* is becoming vowel-like (vocalised). We will refer to this process as a 'vow-ell' (pronounced |ˌvaʊˈel|) – using the first three letters of 'vowel' and the three letters 'ell' to represent the consonant |l|. Extract 18.4 gives three examples of vow-ell from Dan.

EXTRACT 18.4

```
01 || that WASn't FILMED ||
03 || i CAN'T TELL you ||
03 || it was POP idol ||
```

Voice: Dan, London UK. These units are from different parts of his recording.

The words *filmed*, *tell* and *idol* all feature vow-ell |fɪʊmd| |teʊ| |aɪdʊ|, with *idol* – because it comes before a pause – being particularly easy to hear. The vow-ell process affects very common words such as *all*, *well*, *will*, *still*, *whole*, etc. And if your surname ends with *well* as mine does (Cauldwell) you are likely to hear this vow-ell very often. In Extract 18.5 you can hear Dan referring to someone who, at the time of writing, was a very famous TV personality.

EXTRACT 18.5

```
01 || SImon COWELL || was NICE ||
```

Voice: Dan, UK.

Dan gives us something close to |kaʊʊ| for this surname. Further examples include:

- *little* can be heard as *littoo* where |lɪtl| becomes |lɪtʊ|
    ```
    || there was VEry littoo LEFT ||
    ```

- *people* can be heard as *peopoo* where |pipl| becomes |pipʊ|
    ```
    || LOADS of peopoo turned UP ||
    ```

- *trouble* can be heard as *trubboo* where |trʌbl| becomes |trʌbʊ|
    ```
    || NO truboo at ALL ||
    ```

- *school* can be heard as *skoo* where |skuːl| becomes |skuːʊ|
    ```
    || LEAVing school was HARD ||
    ```

Vow-ell is a common process which adds to the range of soundshapes for words ending with |l|.

18.3 Polarisks – polarity problems

Occasionally, the speeds of spontaneous speech make it difficult to hear whether a negative or a positive meaning is being expressed. Expert listeners will (probably) get from the context an accurate understanding of what was meant, and what words were intended. But the evidence of the sound substance may be indeterminate, or indeed contain soundshapes which are symptomatic of the opposite polarity. We will use the term 'polarisk' |pəʊˈlæ.rɪsk| – derived from 'polarity' and 'risk' – meaning there is a risk of decoding problems around whether a positive or negative meaning is intended. The polarisks that I focus on below concern the negative forms of verbs and negative morphemes.

In Extract 18.6 we hear Dan again, talking about his experience of the TV programme 'Pop Idol'. He went to an audition for the first series, but the audition was not filmed.

EXTRACT 18.6
```
01 || that WASn't FILMED ||
02 || that WAS FILMED ||
```

Voice: Dan UK. 01 gives the original version; 02 has -n't edited out.

Dan's negative *n't* is non-prominent and it occurs after the |z| at the end of *was*. This creates a buzz effect that may – for students/learners – drown out the |n| that occurs immediately after it, so students may hear *was filmed* instead of *wasn't filmed*. The |n| is there in the sound substance (it lasts 0.12 seconds out of a total duration 0.93), but because it is non-prominent it may not be hearable by our students.

In Extract 18.7, unit 03 has the word *don't* but – to my ears – the sound substance only contains evidence for a |d| plus a weak vowel. Joey (recorded in 2003) is explaining why he values his mobile phone – by 'go anywhere' he means 'to find a landline'.

EXTRACT 18.7
```
01 || SO ||
02 || if you need to TALK to someone ||
03 || you don't HAVE to || [pause]
04 || GO anyWHERE ||
```

Voice: Joey, UK.

In 03 it is difficult to hear any evidence for the negative *don't*. Indeed, a reasonable (mondegreen) hearing of 03 is *you'd have to* with the sound substance *you daff to* |juːdæftə|.

Often the negative ending *n't* is dropped, or survives only in the quality and nasalisation of the vowel. In such circumstances we have polarisks – where learners may have difficulties perceiving the traces of the negative.

The following examples demonstrate different types of polarisk. The first two are similar to those that we have heard above.

- *aren't possible* can be heard as *are possible* or *arm possible*
    ```
    || they JUST are/arm possible toDAY ||
    ```

- *aren't treating it as* can be heard as *are treating it as*
    ```
    || the poLICE are/aren't treating it as MURder ||
    ```

In the following example *didn't* loses |t| and the |n| blends with the initial consonant of *know* to create a common polarisk:

- *didn't know* can be heard as *did know* or *din know*
    ```
    || he SAID he didn‿know/did know him at ALL ||
    ```

Similarly with *couldn't manage*:

- *couldn't manage* can be heard as *could manage*
    ```
    || they SAID they couldn't manage/could manage it toDAY ||
    ```

The weak forms *and* and *an* can sound identical to the negative morphemes *un-* and *–n't*:

- *and like* can be heard as *unlike*
    ```
    || he was TERRible and like/unlike just AWful to be with ||
    ```

- *it isn't ideal* can be heard as *it is an ideal*
    ```
    || this IS an/n't iDEAL ||
    ```

The *–ly* adverbs can merge with the negative morpheme *il-* to create a polarisk:

- *entirely illegal* can be heard as *entirely legal*
    ```
    || this ACtion is entirely LEgal/entirely‿ilLEgal ||
    ```

And lastly, although not a polarisk, an example in which an instruction can be heard as its opposite – both *off* and *on* drop their final segments, leaving the vowel |ɒ| or |ɑ| and making them sound identical:

- *turn off the heating* can be heard as *turn on the heating* |tɜːnɒðəhiːtɪŋ|
    ```
    || will you PLEASE turn on/off the HEATing ||
    ```

(The *Syllabus for Listening: Decoding* pages at www.speechinaction.com contain recordings of these examples.)

Although the speaker's positive or negative meaning may be entirely clear from the context, it may still be the case that the sound substance is indeterminate because it contains polarisks. Sound substance which, to expert listeners, contains negative soundshapes may in fact be unclear for learners.

For an example of a teaching activity on polarisks, cf. Chapter 22.4.4.

18.4 Dropping syllables – sylla-blends and syll-drops

There is a set of streamlining processes which involve syllables being blended together or dropped. The term 'compression' is used by Wells (2008: 173) to describe the loss of a syllable within words. Compression has happened over the history of the language, for example, *ang.e.ry* has become *ang.ry* (Wells, 2008: 174). As a result, pronunciation dictionaries recognise more than one form for a significant number of words. For example, *national* can be three syllables |næʃ.ə.nəl| or a compressed form with two syllables |næʃ.nəl|). Compression is a sufficiently user-friendly term to use, but as we have used the term 'syll-drop' (syllable + drop) frequently in the preceding chapters, we will continue to use this instead.

In everyday speech, we need to be alert to the fact that the syll-drop process can happen to any word. We saw and heard that *actually* and *absolutely* (Chapter 15.5) can have two-syllable versions, and that single-syllable versions are also possible – |ækʃ| and |æbs|.

In this section, we will look first at the blending of syllables, then at occasions when words lose their heads, middles or tails.

18.4.1 Syllablends

In Chapter 17 we mentioned the syllablend process, whereby syllables blend together, reducing the overall count of syllables by at least one. In this section we will look at two examples. First we focus on *and I've* in Extract 18.8.

EXTRACT 18.8

```
|| and i've done BITS and BOBS with my ART-teacher ||
```

Voice: Olivia, UK. 'Bits and bobs' means 'miscellaneous small items'.

Olivia streamlines this speech unit using the following processes to produce the syllablend:

- d-drop for the |d| of *and*

- n-blur (nasalisation) the |n| survives by blurring with of |æ| to give |æ̃|

- smoothing the diphthong of *I've* from |aɪv| to |av|

and this results in a syllablend giving us something close to the single-syllable |æ̃v| for the two syllables of *and I've*.

Perhaps the most well-known assimilations in ELT are those affecting the question-opening words *do you* and *did you*. With *do you* the |j| at the beginning of *you* blends with the |d| of *do* (the vowel of *do* having been dropped) to give an affricate |dʒ|. So we get |dʒuː| for *do* you and |dɪdʒuː| for *did you*. This type of assimilation has a technical name, 'yod coalescence' – where 'yod' refers to the symbol |j| and 'coalescence' means 'mixing', 'blending', 'mushing' or 'smudging'. A common way of demonstrating this process is to focus on the words *Tuesday* or *duty* where the old-fashioned

Greenhouse pronunciation would be |tjuːzdeɪ| and |djuːti|, whereas these days the Greenhouse forms are more likely to be |tʃuːzdeɪ| and |dʒuːti| *chewsday* and *jewty*. The teacher-friendly terms we can use to refer to the |tʃ| and |dʒ| versions of this process are 'Tuesday-blend' or 'duty-blend'.

Extract 18.9 gives three examples of *do you know* which feature the Tuesday-blend process.

EXTRACT 18.9

```
01 || do you KNOW(MMM) what i MEAN like||
02 || do you KNOW what I MEAN ||
03 || do you KNOW what I MEAN ||
```

Voices: Laura, UK. In 01 you can hear Richard agreeing with Laura, saying mmm.

As is almost always the case, there are other streamlining processes in play here. In 02 Laura makes the three syllables of *do you know* into one syllable, and in blending the vowels of *you* and *know* gives us something close to |dʒɜː| – which to my ears sounds like a Geordie version of *Joe*. In 03 the streamlining processes have even more extreme results, with just a faint hint of |dʒɜː|, giving us something between *joe te mee* |dʒəʊtəmĩ| and *yo tuh mee* |jəʊtəmĩ|, where the final |n| of *mean* is blurred and only survives in the nasalisation the vowel in *mean* |mĩ|.

In addition to being blended together, syllables can also be dropped. In the next three sub-sections we will look at three types of syll-drop.

18.4.2 Head-clipping

Head-clipping happens when a word loses its initial syllable. Classic examples of head clipping are *'cos* for *because* and *'phone* for *telephone*. Clipped forms such as these are now formally recognised in dictionaries. But head-clipping happens more often than pronunciation dictionaries allow (although, of course, it's not their job to allow for every soundshape). I am an avid listener to cricket commentaries and I frequently hear *'Stralia* for *Australia*, where the schwa of the first syllable is clipped. One scholarly name for this is 'apharesis' – which means 'a taking away'. I prefer to adopt the term 'clipping' from Brinton and Brinton (2010).

In Extract 18.10, you can hear Laura giving us a head-clipped version of *if you*. She is talking about how her mother, a dentist, was very good at reassuring patients that there would be very little pain.

EXTRACT 18.10

```
01 || if YOU ||
02 || WERE kind of ||
03 || WORried about the DENTist ||
04 || she was REAlly good at ||
05 || like HELPing you THROUGH it ||
```

Voice: Laura, Birmingham, UK.

In 01 we get *few* rather than *if you* – the vowel of *if* |ɪ| is head-clipped and the resultant |f| then attaches itself to |juː|, resulting in *few* |fjuː|. It is also worth noting that Laura's *dentist* runs into *she* and we get *dentishee* |dentɪʃiː|.

Head-clips can create the following soundshapes:

- *Australia* can be heard as *'Stralia*

    ```
    || i THINK stralia's going to WIN this ||
    ```

- *If I were you* can be heard as *fie were you*

    ```
    || i wouldn't GO if i/fie were YOU ||
    ```

- *I'm almost* can be heard as *amallmost*

    ```
    || i SAID i'm almost/mallmost FINished ||
    ```

- *and also in* can be heard as *nor so win*

    ```
    || he'll appear THEN and also in/nor so win sepTEMber ||
    ```

(The *Syllabus for Listening: Decoding* pages at www.speechinaction.com contain recordings of these examples.)

18.4.3 Mid-clipping

Middle clipping, or mid-clipping, occurs when weak syllables are omitted from the middle of words. Often it is just one, usually with schwa, as in *national* which can be *nash-uh-null* |næʃ.ə.nəl| or *nash-null* |næʃ.nəl|. But more extreme types of mid-clipping can also occur. In Extract 18.11 we will observe what happens to the word *everyone*.

Wells (2008: 286) comments that 'In very formal style occasionally' we get a four-syllable version |ev.ə.ri.wʌn|, but that the three-syllable soundshape |ev.ri.wʌn| is much more frequent. But in Extract 18.11, to my ears, *everyone* has two syllables.

EXTRACT 18.11

```
01 || EVeryone always SOUNDS so FRIENDly ||
```

Voice: Laura, Birmingham, UK.

It sounds close to *evan* |ev.ən| because the second syllable |ri| is dropped. Interestingly, *always* also drops from two syllables to one, but it is not a clean clipping – not like *because* becoming *cos*. It is rather that the |l| of *always* is vow-elled (vocalized) and colours the diphthong |eɪz| so that it becomes close to |ɔɪz| – and a reasonable (BrE), mondegreen hearing of *everyone always* becomes possible: *ever noise* |evənɔɪz|. Also:

- there is smoothing in sounds where the diphthong |aʊ| becomes close to |a|

- there is a mondegreen hearing of *everyone always sounds* as *ever noise sands*

- *friendly* suffers d-drop – sounding close to *frenly*.

In Extract 18.12 there are three further examples of mid-clipping.

EXTRACT 18.12

```
01 || trying to KEEP up the exerCISE that way ||
02 || and GET some exPERience) ||
03 || DIfferences beTWEEN ||
```

Voices: Olivia, Laura, Joey, (UK).

In 01 Olivia mid-clips *exercise* so that its three syllables |eks.ə.saɪz| become two |eks.saɪz|. A contributory factor is that the clipped syllable is a schwa, which is preceded and followed by |s| – an example of the hiss effect (cf. Chapter 17.11), where the strident noise of the |s| tends to drown out neighbouring sounds. Note also that Olivia makes the final syllable of *exercise* prominent and the first syllable (the normal place for the word stress) is non-prominent giving us a soundshape of *exCISE*.

In 02 the four-syllable *experience* |ɪk.spɪə.rɪ.əns| becomes |ɪk.spɪ.rəns|, losing its third |ɪ| and with the |r| being attached to the final syllable.

In 03, Joey is talking about the different cultural experiences he has in his mixed-race family. The word *differences* is shown as having either four |dɪ.fə.rən.sɪz| or three syllables |dɪf.rən.sɪz| but here it undergoes mid-clipping and we get a two-syllable version |dɪf.sɪz|.

Below is a list of mid-clips.

- *accidents* being heard as *accents* (mid-clipped |ɪd|)
    ```
    || there were TWO accidents/accents on the MOTorway ||
    ```

- *incidents* being heard as *instants* (mid-clipped |ɪ|)
    ```
    || THREE incidents/instants involving GUNS ||
    ```

- *afternoon* being heard as *aff noon* (mid-clipped |tə|)
    ```
    || they HAVE the afternoon/affnoon OFF today
    ```

- *ultimately* being heard as *ultimmly* (mid-clipped |ət|)
    ```
    || they WERE ultimately/ultimmly let DOWN ||
    ```

- *however* being heard as *howver* (mid-clipped |e|)
    ```
    || he WAS however/howver in LOVE at that time ||
    ```

- *minute* being heard as *mint* (mid-clipped |ɪ|)
    ```
    || JUST a minute/mint i'll GET it for you ||
    ```

- *excellent* being heard as *exsunt* (mid-clipped |ɔ|)
    ```
    || she PLAYED an excellent/exsunt game of FOOTball ||
    ```

- *physical* being heard as *fizzle* (mid-clipped |ɪk|)
    ```
    || it was a VEry physical/fizzle enCOUNter ||
    ```

- *cardinals* being heard as *carnals* (mid-clipped |dɪ|)

> || the SAINT louis cardinals/carnals are the BEST team ||

- *kilometres* being heard as *klommers* (mid-clipped |ɔt|)

> || we're THREE kilometres/klommers from HOME ||

A good place to gather your own collection of mid-clippings is in frequently repeated sections of news programmes on the radio: traffic reports and weather forecasts.

18.4.4 Tail-clipping

Words can also lose their final syllables, undergoing 'tail-clipping'. This is particularly common with verbal and adjectival words ending in *—ed*.

EXTRACT 18.13

```
01 || REAlly interest[ed] in MUSic as WELL ||
02 || i START[ed] working THERE ||
03 || such a MAjor || 04 || SURgic[al] operATion ||
```

Voices: Laura, Jess, and Joey (UK).

In 01, Laura is talking about her hobbies, and her *interested* |ɪntr.est.ɪd| undergoes tail-clipping, so we lose the final syllable |ɪd|.

In 02 Jess is talking about working with horses as a teenager. Her *started* features tail-clipping resulting in a single-syllable *star*. Meanwhile *there* undergoes d'eth-drop, and we get a mondegreen (reasonable hearing) *working air* |wɜːkɪŋ eə|.

In 04, we hear Joey talking about his experience shadowing a hospital surgeon as part of his school education. The adjective *surgical* undergoes tail-clipping and we get *surgic* – the *-al* blends into the initial vowel of *operation* giving us *surgicoperation*.

There are other processes which are noteworthy in unit 01:

- there is syllablending of the final vowel of *really* and the first vowel of *interest(ed)* giving us *realinterest*

- *in* becomes |ɪm| in anticipation of the first consonant of *music* giving us *imusic*

- *well* features both an vow-ell and a vowel close to |aʊ|, giving us *wow*.

18.4.5 Weak-form dropping

Single-syllable function words with weak soundshapes can disappear entirely. This very frequently happens with *to* and *of*.

In Extract 18.14 we can hear Jess and Arun dropping *to*. Jess is talking about her decision not to major in music at university, and Arun is talking about the final stage of climbing Mount Kilimanjaro. Both speech units are very fast – at 8.8 and 6.9 sps respectively.

EXTRACT 18.14

```
00 || want .. [to] .. do it || you have .. [to] .. start ||
01 || because then i deCIded i didn't want to do it at ALL ||
02 || and then you have to start CLIMBing in the DARK ||
```

Voices: Jess (USA) and Arun (UK). The first part of the extract (shown in Row 00) gives gapped versions of the word clusters with dropped weak forms.

In 01, Jess's *want* becomes something close to *one*, and *to* is dropped – it undergoes weak-form dropping.

In 02 the sequence of three syllables –*ing in the* seems to me to be a continuous stretch of sound substance which cannot be satisfactorily divided into three parts. To my ears, there are (at the most) two syllables and – if forced to do so – I would transcribe it as |ɪn.nə| with |ð| of *the* undergoing d'eth-drop and *in* being dropped completely. In 02 the word *to* is also dropped. It occurs between *have* and *start* and is swamped by the fricative sounds that surround it: the |v| of *have* is blurred to |f| and we get a soundshape close to *haff* |haf| – and this blends into the first consonant |s| of *start* creating a hiss effect (Chapter 17.9) which drowns out the word *to* which is between *have* and *start*. As a consequence, the three syllables of *have to start* become *haffstart*.

Weak forms which occur in clusters may be dropped in the sound substance, even though L1 and expert listeners may hear them as present.

18.5 Don't Repeat Yourself – D.R.Y.

In the normal speeds of spontaneous speech, economy of effort can extend to letting one syllable do the work of two. In this section we will look at instances where a sound or syllable is not repeated, and the single sound or syllable does the work of two. I term this 'D.R.Y.' for 'don't repeat yourself'. Extract 18.15 gives us two examples of this.

EXTRACT 18.15

```
01 || for my application ||
02 || not for an emergency situation ||
```

Voice: Joey, UK.

In 01 the vowel of *my* (a smoothie) is very similar to the first vowel in *application* so there is no need to repeat it, resulting in *mapplication*. In 02 the final syllable of *emergency*, and the first syllable of *situation* are very similar, and so Joey – following the D.R.Y. principle – does not repeat it, and we get *not for an emergen situation*. Reasonable (mondegreen) hearings are also available: *map location* for *my application* and *emergent situation* for *emergency situation*.

Other pairs of words in which the D.R.Y. process can occur are:

- *wish she'd* can be heard as *wisheed*
  ```
  || i DO wish she'd/wisheed GO now ||
  ```

- *there are* can be heard *as there*
  ```
  || i SEE there are/there THREE of them ||
  ```

- *that I use* can be heard as *thy use*
  ```
  || he SAW that i/thy use THIS medicine ||
  ```

In the sound substance, single sounds or syllables can do the work of two.

18.6 Teeny

A 'teeny' is a streamlining process which has a specific focus: the *–teen* series of numbers (13–19) and the possibility of confusion with the *-ty* series (30–90). The label 'teeny' is derived from the last syllable of *thirteen-nineteen*, and the last letter of the series *thirty-ninety*. These two series often share the same soundshapes, so *fifteen* can sound identical to *fifty*, and vice versa.

It may be obvious to expert listeners which one of the pairs *thirteen/thirty*, *fourteen/forty*, is meant because of the context in which the number is heard. For example, in a commentary on a tennis match, you will very often hear a score of 15–40, but you would never hear a tennis score of 50–40. But we need to differentiate what was meant, or intended, by the speaker from what the sound substance actually contains. It may well be meant to convey the meaning 15, yet have the soundshape of 50.

In Extract 18.16 Olivia is talking about the time she visited a turtle hatchery in Costa Rica. She did volunteer work there, and one of the tasks she had to do was to patrol the beach to see if any baby turtles were hatching. The frequency of the patrols was every 15 minutes. Below are two speech units in which she refers to the frequency of patrols.

EXTRACT 18.16
```
01 || FIFteen MINutes ||
02 || EVery fifteen MINutes ||
```

Voice: Olivia, UK.

In 01, I am fairly confident that I hear *fifteen* and that (although I don't know for sure) it is more logical that beach patrols are every 15 minutes, rather than every 50 minutes. But in 02 I am equally confident that the sound substance is *fifty* and not *fifteen*. I can assure you that Olivia is talking about the same patrols, and that the same number is mentioned each time. So we have two different soundshapes for the one word *fifteen* and, in the case of 02, it sounds like another number: *fifty*.

Yet again, the argument might be that the context will resolve the issue of what we are to understand from what Olivia is saying. But, once again, our focus is on the sound substance, and although the word *fifteen* is meant, it definitely has the soundshape *fifty*. This is something that can easily happen to *teen* numbers, particularly in front of words beginning with |n| or |m|.

- *thirteen names* can be heard as *thirty names*
     || there WERE thirteen names/thirty names sugGESTed ||

- *fourteen members* can be heard as *forty members*
     || we can't have MORE than fourteen/forty MEMbers ||

- *fifteen nil* can be heard as *fifty nil*
     || the SCORE was fifteen/fifty NIL ||

So in teaching decoding it is important to bear in mind that although we may be absolutely certain that the context requires one meaning, the sound substance may contain soundshapes of words which conflict with this meaning. For example, although the meaning of *thirteen* is clearly intended in the following sentence, the soundshape may actually be *thirty*: '*He's still only twelve, he's not a teenager yet. He'll be thirteen in May.*'

18.7 Return to *able*

We will conclude Part 3 by considering how some of the processes described in Chapters 15–18 might apply to the word *able* and the word cluster *be able to* which we first met in Chapter 15.2.2.

18.7.1 The single word *able*

The word *able* is a two-syllable word made up of three phonemes, and is given in pronunciation dictionaries (Wells, 2008) and Roach et al. (2011) as |eɪb.ᵊl| using five symbols: two symbols to represent the diphthong |eɪ|, a single symbol for the consonant |b| and a superscript schwa |ᵊ| to indicate that there may or may not be a schwa before the final consonant with the symbol |l|. Viewed as a single word, it can illustrate a number of streamlining processes:

1. the diphthong may be smoothed (cf. Chapter 18.1) to |e| giving us something close to *ebble* |eb.ᵊl|

2. the |b| may be blurred by the speaker's lips not making contact with each other, giving us something close to |w| thus *awol* |eɪ.wᵊl|

3. or the processes mentioned in 1 and 2 could work together to give us something close to *ewol* |ew.ᵊl|

4. the |b| may be dropped, either resulting in a single-syllable version close to *ale* |eɪl|, or perhaps retaining two syllables, giving us a version close to |eɪ.ᵊl|

5. the |l| may be vow-elled (cf. Chapter 18.2) thus giving us something close to *aboo* |eɪ.bʊ|

6. or the processes mentioned in 1, 4 and 5 could work together, giving us a version close to *eh-oo* |eʊ|, where smoothing, b-dropping, and vow-elling are all at work to create this soundshape.

In items 1,2, 4 and 5 of this list, streamlining processes may occur singly, whereas in items 3 and 6 they occur in combination. This may seem a lot of soundshapes for *able*, but there are more, as you can hear in Extract 18.17. To my ears, they sound close to (in folk spelling) *ebbu, awol, ale, ell, em/am* and *raybluh.*

EXTRACT 18.17

|| able | able | able | able | able | able ||

Voices: Karam, Jess (USA); Richard junior, Joey twice (UK); Jess.

As you listen, you will hear traces of the words which have occurred before and after the single word: the stream-like nature of speech means that very often the first and last sounds of a word are coloured by the neighbouring segments. This is particularly noticeable in the last *able* from Jess, which is preceded by the word *were* and the |r| runs into the beginning of *able* in a way which makes it difficult to edit it out. This is the reason it is best to work with units larger than a word to teach listening/decoding, and it is also why word clusters-in-speech-units are excellent units of speech to work with.

In the next three sub-sections we will look at the speech units from which each of these versions of *able* were taken.

18.7.2 The word cluster *to be able to*

Extract 18.18 features the speech units in which the first three versions of *able* in Extract 18.17 appeared.

EXTRACT 18.18

```
01 || to be able to TEACH || 8.6 (10.8)
02 || to be able to LIVE in || 8.5 (12.5)
03 || you HAVE to be able to SALsa dance || 6.7 (14.3)
```

Voices: Karam, Jess (USA); Richard junior (UK). The clusters are extracted, and are given at the end of the extract.

Note that, as is commonly the case, the clusters are at much faster speeds than the overall speeds of the speech units in which they occur. To my ears, in 01 the cluster sounds close to *be ebbluh*, in 02 it sounds close to a mondegreen *to be a little*, and in 03 it sounds close to *bee.yell.tuh*. The key point is that the soundshapes of the word *able* in each speech unit are hugely influenced by the properties of both the word clusters and the speech units in which they occur.

18.7.3 The word cluster *being able to*

Extract 18.19 gives us two examples of the cluster *being able to*. In both speech units *being* is one syllable, sounding close to *been*, and the vowel in *able* has become close to |æ|.

EXTRACT 18.19
```
01 || BEing able TO ||
02 || being ABle to underSTAND ||
```
Voice: Joey, (UK).

To my ears, in 01 the cluster sounds close to *been al too*, and in 02 it sounds close to *been am tuh*.

18.7.4 The word cluster *were able to*

The last *able* cluster— *we were able to* – comes from Jess in Extract 18.20.

EXTRACT 18.20
```
01 || so we were able to do LOTS of FUN things || 6.8 (8.8)
```
Voice: Jess (USA)

To my ears, the only sound to survive of *were* is |r| so that the four syllables of *were able to* become something close to *ray.bluh*, which we can describe as a double syll-drop.

This section started with applying some of the streamlining processes introduced in Part 3 to the word *able*. Doing this enabled us to generate a variety of soundshapes, some of which we then heard in Extracts 18.17–20. But the extracts contained additional soundshapes beyond the coverage of our description of streamlining processes. It is not the purpose (there simply is not room) of *A Syllabus for Listening: Decoding* to cover all eventualities. The aim has been to describe a sufficient range of streamlining processes to get you started on hearing the rough hints of words which occur in the raw sound substance of everyday spontaneous speech. Expert listeners find it easy to decode these rough hints and to understand the meanings conveyed. So easy, in fact, that most of them are completely unaware that the sound substance often consists only of rough hints. My hope is that after reading these chapters, and listening to the recordings, you will be able to hear these rough hints and help learners decode them efficiently so that their listening skills improve more rapidly than has traditionally been the case using conventional Greenhouse and Garden methodology.

18.8 Summary and what's next

In this chapter we have completed our look at the streamlining processes that create the soundshapes which may be unfamiliar to learners, and may cause them decoding difficulties.

The four chapters of Part 3 provide a partial description of a new model of speech –an ELT-friendly Spontaneous Speech Model (SSM) – which will be better able to describe what Nolan and Kerswill (1990: 295) characterised as 'the fluent continuous speech performance of everyday life'.

The chapters of Part 3 comprise the start of a description of what Cruttenden (2014: 320) called the 'less rule-bound' and the 'unpredictable' features of spontaneous speech:

> in casual speech they are **less rule-bound** and may contain **unpredictable** elisions such as those of |l| and |ð| in *Well, that's all right* |we ats ɔː raɪt| (emphasis added).

The description is designed to be used by teachers to help them demonstrate, and students practise, handling the relationship between Greenhouse, Garden and Jungle forms of speech. It provides a repertoire of tools which can be applied to individual words, to word clusters and to sentences. They can also act as an aid to finding decoding problems in any recording that learners find challenging, as we will see in Chapter 21.

In Part 4 we will look at the design and implementation of a variety of activities which can be used in the classroom to bring this syllabus to life.

Part 4 Education, tools and activities

Part 4 contains six chapters full of ideas, tools and activities to bring the *Syllabus for Listening: Decoding* to life.

Chapter 19 *Learner education and teacher-mindset* suggests ways in which you can help your students have a positive attitude to listening/decoding. Students need reassuring that (a) if they are struggling with a recording, then the struggle is an opportunity for learning and (b) they are not to blame if they cannot decode and understand – the sound substance is inherently difficult. As a teacher you need to have a mindset of openness to new ideas, and a willingness to question the received wisdom of the Careful Speech Model.

Chapter 20 *Teacher tools* introduces three tools. Two of them, 'the botanic walk' and 'the word-crusher' are tools to use at any time in class. The botanic walk uses the metaphor of the Greenhouse, the Garden and the Jungle to familiarise learners with the range of soundshapes that words can have. The word-crusher provides a framework for applying streamlining processes to words in speech units. The third tool – 'the accelerator' – is one for you to use to develop your own sense of the various speeds of everyday English.

Chapter 21 *Recordings, extracts and activities* explains how to choose extracts from recordings to focus on in class when teaching decoding, and describes practical activities that you can use with these extracts.

Chapter 22 *Pen-and-paper activities* looks at how to use our students voices, together with conventional pen-and-paper activities, to teach listening/decoding. We will look at how to convert familiar activities (e.g. minimal-pair pronunciation activities and games) into effective listening/decoding activities.

Chapter 23 *Visiting the sound substance dimension* identifies opportunities for slipping into and out of the sound substance dimension, moving constantly back and forth from the sight substance work which dominates time in the classroom. We also continue the work of Chapter 22 in using vocal gymnastics to see how playing with the sound substance can improve learners' listening/decoding abilities.

Chapter 24 *Internet and Digital* introduces one piece of software – Sonocent's *AudioNotetaker*, and three internet sites – TED Corpus Search Engine, YouGlish and TubeQuizard – which are useful for teaching listening/decoding.

19 Learner education and teacher-mindset

In the first half of this chapter (Sections 19.1 to 19.4) we look at steps you can take to educate your students so that they become efficient learners of listening/decoding. In the second half (Sections 19.5 to 19.7) we will look at the mindset that is most helpful to have as a teacher of listening/decoding.

The sections on learner education involve:

- managing expectations
- valuing discomfort as a sign that learning is taking place
- managing feelings
- removing the tendency of students to blame themselves

The sections on teacher-mindset involve:

- thinking for yourself
- trusting your own experience
- cherishing your doubts
- managing your status as an expert listener

19.1 Managing expectations

A major factor in teaching decoding is to manage learners' expectations about rules and explanations. They will probably expect that there is an explanation for everything, and that these explanations can always be expressed in terms of rules and exceptions. Unfortunately, this is not possible when dealing with recordings of spontaneous speech – things often happen for no obvious reason. The best way to approach this issue is to familiarise your students with the botanic metaphor of the Greenhouse, the Garden and the Jungle which was introduced in Chapter 2. Instructions on how to introduce this metaphor are given in Chapter 20. It is useful to do this as early as possible with a new class, so that when you and they encounter what appears (from the point of view of the CSM) to be some rule-breaking, you are in a position to smile confidently at the class and say such things as 'Well that's what happens when the speaker is going very fast' or 'That's what happens when the speaker focuses on communicating effectively' or even 'Well that's the Jungle for you!'

19.2 Valuing discomfort

Thorn (2009: 8) and Field (1998b: 14) report experiences where learners have been dismayed when they first listen to a challenging recording. Nobody likes the sight of people in discomfort. We want to help them, and – if it is in our power to do so – remove the causes of discomfort. But in the listening classroom, visible signs of discomfort (frowns, grimaces) may be positive signs either that learning is taking place, or that learners are ready to learn.

Personally speaking, I was not trained to cope with a classroom full of unhappy faces. But as students move from the happy social buzz of pre-listening activities (I was trained to do that!) to the private wrestling with decoding the stream of speech, it is very likely that any visible happiness will vanish.

That is why it is so important to support and encourage students through their encounters with the speeds and messiness of spontaneous speech.

One skill (or tolerance) that it is essential for us to have is to be able to work with students who are showing visible discomfort in the early and middle stages of a listening lesson. It is necessary to allow learners to feel challenged and stretched, and it will also be necessary for them to feel temporarily frustrated as they confront the challenges (which are, essentially, positive learning opportunities) of the listening task.

It is worth discussing explicitly with your students how they feel in the different stages of a listening lesson. One example of how this might be done is described in the next section.

19.3 Managing feelings

Some years ago, I taught a listening class to seven Japanese advanced learners of English (teachers of English from Japan). At the moment when they were deeply immersed in a difficult recording, and attempting to answer questions relating to it, I asked them to score their feelings on a five-point scale, with 'happy' at one extreme and 'unhappy' at the other. Later in the class, after doing the post-listening exercises of the type described later in Part 4, I asked them to make judgements on the same scale.

The 'Before' judgements were generally 'Unhappy', with five of the seven students giving a maximum score for unhappiness and none making 'Happy' judgements. In contrast, the 'After' judgements showed a marked swing towards 'Happy' with three students giving a maximum score for 'Happy' and none of them recording an 'Unhappy' judgement. Clearly, there was a major shift in feeling between the two points in the lesson where the judgements were given: the learners moved from being broadly 'unhappy' to broadly 'happy' after having successfully decoded a short extract of a recording that they had initially found difficult.

This survey was not very scientific – the 'happy' judgement could have been created by the imminence of the coffee break. But – although unscientific – it was useful for bringing into the open the feelings that these students experienced, making them discussable, and showing that (hopefully) every dip in happiness can be followed by a moment of learning, and a return to happiness.

So the steps to take include (a) discussing how they felt before, during and after the decoding activity; and (b) rating the activity for its usefulness in helping them increase their skills.

In essence, we need to have the personal and professional confidence to take our students from unhappiness to a state in which they believe they have learned something. They might even leave the classroom feeling less happy than when they entered it, but this does not necessarily mean that they have not learned anything.

A colleague reported that even students who felt they did not do well in a particular class 'have often said that later they have recognised some elision or a combined sound that we focused on in class' (Kezzie, personal communication, 2016). This shows that students can and do learn without necessarily feeling that they are doing well: discomfort and frustration are often important feelings in the overall learning process (cf. Cauldwell: 2002).

19.4 Removing self-blame

Learners tend to blame themselves for their deficiencies in listening, but it is absolutely not their fault that they find listening is difficult. Listening is problematic for them because decoding the sound substance, which flies by in real time at normal speeds is inherently difficult because of the features that we covered in Part 3. This is why it is important to show students directly, right from the start, what the inherent problems are – that the sound substance contains rough hints and mush, not clearly articulated words.

There are two steps that you can take to help melt away this self-blame: (a) demonstrate the inherent difficulty of the sound substance, and (b) deal with the 'only me' problem. These steps are described below.

19.4.1 Demonstrate the inherent difficulty

Some teachers find it helpful to use technology to delve into the sound substance in order to demonstrate to students that the sound substance often consists of rough hints of words rather than full Greenhouse soundshapes. A colleague in Hong Kong (James Pengelley, reported in Cauldwell, 2015) cut up sound files into small sections, asked his students to count the syllables, and then did mini-dictations. He subsequently reported that one of his students told him that doing this type of intensive listening and inspection of short extracts 'helped ... [the student] ... to understand why listening is so difficult, and where the mis-listenings come from and how some of the words change'.

19.4.2 Deal with the 'only me' problem

Some learners might find it helpful if you tell them what difficulties you have as a listener, both in English and in other languages. This is to stop them getting the 'only me' feeling. This is the horrible feeling you get when you are experiencing a particular inadequacy in your ability to do something: you feel that 'only you' have this problem, and everyone else is doing just fine.

Nobody I know finds listening to their native language unproblematic. In my case I find international airports a particularly interesting place to discover the limits of what I can hear, whether it is the announcements on the public address system, the conversations of people sitting behind me in back-to-back seating, or the unfamiliarity of the accents.

To avoid the 'only me' feeling of inadequacy around being a learner listener, tell learners about your own problems with listening to your own language, and your difficulties when listening to other languages, then invite them to discuss their problems with listening. (If you are a teacher whose first language is not English, you are probably better equipped to do this than a native-listener teacher.) Explain the 'only me' phenomenon to your students and then, during listening tasks, ask them at regular intervals 'Who is finding this difficult?' As they put their hands up, say to them, smilingly and confidently (and jokingly): 'Only me!' or (more seriously) 'See, you are not alone!'

We now turn to the teacher's mindset.

19.5 Teacher-mindset

A teacher's mindset is the sum total of attitudes they have towards their profession, the language, their students and the circumstances in which they teach. It is important to keep evaluating aspects of this mindset, and one of the best way is to be gently sceptical about what the 'experts' tell you. By 'gently sceptical' I mean a quiet postponement of belief until you have satisfied yourself – from the evidence of everyday speech – that what the experts say is true.

19.5.1 Think for yourself

Many of the statements made about everyday speech in textbooks, course books and in teacher-training materials are amenable to testing against the evidence of real life, or authentic recordings. So when you read a statement which proposes a simple causal relationship between the sound substance and a grammatical category such as 'questions', or the sound substance and meaning such as 'anger', you should immediately be on your guard. This is because in the Jungle there are no neat correspondences, and certainly no neat causal relationships of the type, 'when x happens, it means y'.

So when you read 'Falling tone means certainty and finality' and 'Rising tones mean uncertainty and continuity', you should be gently sceptical and query these statements, and then test them on examples you find in real life, or in authentic recordings.

You need to beware of invented examples (whether you or other people are the inventors) because these are (a) misleading and (b) very persuasive. Of course, you can 'prove' that rising tones mean 'listing' or 'questioning' if you invent a conversation, and act it out. The problem is that if you go to real-life recordings, the evidence is not nearly so clear-cut.

In sum, think for yourself – don't accept the pronouncements of the great and famous, and certainly don't shut down your capacity for independent thinking as you progress through to the senior ranks of the ELT profession.

19.5.2 Trust your own experience

If you are in the fortunate situation of being a language learner at the same time as being a teacher of English, you may be in an ideal position to help your students with their decoding problems – particularly in situations where you are having to cope with listening in the real world. If something works for you in coping with everyday listening in your new language, then you should consider using it in your teaching.

19.5.3 Cherish your doubts

Kezzie (the colleague mentioned above) told me that after her initial teacher-training course (CELTA) she 'never quite understood how listening practice ... [was] ... actually improving students listening skills.' She continued 'As my ... [training] ... hadn't mentioned any other way of 'teaching' listening, I thought maybe it was just one of those things' (personal communication, 2016).

Kezzie is articulating what happens as teachers become acculturated to the knowledge and practices of ELT: she felt doubtful about an issue, but rather than pursue a remedy, she accepted that it was just part of what people do in ELT ' ... it was just one of those things'.

It was only later, when Kezzie was doing a post-experience training (DELTA) course that she realised that her earlier dissatisfaction was justified. She was asked to compare the decoding work she had to do to understand a Scottish person's accent (which she couldn't understand) with 'normal top-down processing' activities, and she concluded that 'normal top-down processing isn't always going to help students improve their listening skills, as it hadn't helped us when we'd listened to a series of unintelligible accents, and we were native speakers!'

Kezzie goes on to say that she subsequently used decoding activities in her own classes and has had 'overwhelmingly more positive feedback' from students.

So, to continue developing as a teacher, cherish the doubts you may have about what you have been taught in your teacher training.

19.6 Language awareness is not enough

In a workshop I gave a few years ago, a participant asked me 'Is this information just for language awareness?' The question had an underlying assumption – that there is a type of knowledge about language that teachers acquire, but then not use with their students. This type of knowledge is often about how the language **really** works, as distinct from the rule-governed language that actually occurs in textbooks, and which we teach students. This separation should not be the case. If we want to improve the teaching of listening, it is not enough simply to increase our store of language awareness. It is important to turn this language awareness into teaching materials, and into classroom activities.

Therefore, as part of your development as a teacher, try and turn every 'language-awareness' activity into a learning activity that your students can do.

19.7 Managing your status as an expert listener

Managing your status as an expert listener can be challenging. An expert listener is someone who knows what the words are, and what meanings the speaker intended. By this definition you become an expert listener when you have the transcript of the recordings to refer to.

There are dangers inherent in making appeals to the context, and on what must have been intended (both the meanings and the words) by the speaker in the context. Making appeals to the context and the available meanings intended by the speaker is fine if you are working solely at the level of understanding meaning but, as our concern is with decoding, we and our students have to get to grips with the sound substance.

So you need to beware of the dangers of this 'logical' three-stage argument:

- because of the context, the speakers must have meant 'x'
- because they meant 'x', they must have said word 'y'
- because they said word 'y' it must have sounded like a clearly articulated 'y'

This can lead to an insistence, for example, that because someone is talking about the past and the places where they used to live, that they therefore:

- used past tenses such as *lived* and *settled*; and noun phrases such as *the move*
- they expressed these meanings with these words:
  - o 'I lived there for a while' not 'I live there for a while'
  - o 'I never settled down' not 'I never sell down'
  - o 'The move was difficult' not 'Move was difficult'

- therefore these words have the following soundshapes
- the past tense form |lɪvd| occurred with its ending |d| audible
- the full form of |setld| occurred with both |t| and |d| audible
- the definite article *the* occurred

Whereas in fact the speakers may well have actually said:

- *I live there for a while* (the |d| of |lɪvd| being inaudible)
- *I never sell down* (the |t| of |setld| being inaudible, final |d| merges with *down*)
- *Mmove was difficult* (the article *the* is replaced by a longer |m| – *mmove*)

These examples illustrate the possibility of the 'blur gap' (cf. Chapter 4) – the gap between what expert listeners 'know must be there' in the sound substance, and what is actually audible.

The first two steps of the 'logical' process (context, available meanings) are useful for arriving at an interpretation of meaning, but the third step ('the word must have sounded like this') is not at all helpful for listening/decoding.

19.8 Summary and what's next

Learners need reassurance about the difficulties of decoding the sound substance of speech. Compared to decoding the sight substance, it is immensely difficult. And because listening/ decoding is a less shareable activity (decoding has to happen in each individual's brain) than other activities, it is possible for each individual learner to feel privately bad about themselves as listeners. They need to be told, repeatedly, that many of the difficulties of decoding lie outside themselves.

We must be prepared for periods of learner frustration, and to have the methodological training and knowledge base to help learners through periods of discomfort and frustration so that they can progress to increasingly sophisticated levels of perception and understanding.

As teachers of listening it is helpful to be sceptical of any rule or explanation that claims a tidy relationship between form and meaning. Test any such statements against what you hear in spontaneous speech. If you have doubts about what you have been told, or about what textbooks and course books say about everyday speech, then hold on to those doubts. Do not forget them – investigate them. Learn from your own language-learning experience.

In Chapter 20 we will look at the tools that are useful for teachers to have to hand for use in both planned activities, and for those moments in a classroom when you need to deal with something that has just cropped up.

20 Teacher tools

This chapter will look at three tools that we can use to help with listening/decoding:

- the botanic walk
- the word-crusher
- the accelerator

Two of them, 'the botanic walk' and 'the word-crusher' are tools that you can use at any time in class. The third tool, 'the accelerator', is for you to use to develop your sense of speed, so that you can judge the speed at which you and your students are working during classroom activities. This is important because many of the activities described in Part 4 require both you and your students to work with streams of speech at fast speeds, in order to justify the streamlining processes that they are learning to handle.

An important aid to have to hand when using these tools is a metronome – either a mechanical one, or a digital one. Digital versions are available on the internet and as apps for smartphones. We will be using the beats of the metronome to help learners build their capacity to handle speech at a variety of speeds.

To begin with, however, we need to introduce the concept of 'vocal gymnastics'.

20.1 Vocal gymnastics

A key aid in learning to decode – of becoming familiar and comfortable with the sound substance – is to embody it: to have the experience of moving to its rhythms (tapping, swaying, chanting, dancing) and of experiencing it – making friends with it with different parts of your body, including your voice. It is often said 'If you can **say it**, you can **hear it**' and this is something that I believe in strongly, as long as (for the purposes of listening) the '**it**' that we say includes the Jungle domain.

For this reason, a good way to learn to handle the sound substance is through repetition in activities which resemble pronunciation activities, but which serve the goal of listening. Because the term 'pronunciation' has such strong connotations with correctness and with citation-form accuracy, it is not a good label to use for the kind of listening-goal activities which are presented here. The term we will use instead is 'vocal gymnastics', which refers to activities in which learners become comfortable at handling the variety and speeds of the sound substance by using their voices and bodies.

20.2 The botanic walk

The first tool is the botanic walk, an animation of the relationship between the three domains of the Greenhouse, the Garden and the Jungle (cf. Chapter 2). These domains respectively represent (a) isolated citation forms, (b) the genteel rules of connected speech and (c) the messy realities of everyday spontaneous speech.

The metaphor is a botanic one, and not everyone likes it or thinks it is appropriate. You can, of course, choose another set of terms. One other metaphor that comes to mind is from clothing: the three domains of the clothing metaphor might be Best, Smart Casual and Scruffy/Normal.

WHY USE IT?

The botanic walk is particularly useful because it shows the relationship between the soundshapes that we are familiar with in terms of pronunciation, and their relationship with the messy unfamiliarities of everyday speech.

20.2.1 Setting up the three domains

STEP 1

Write the words 'Greenhouse' 'Garden' and 'Jungle' along the top of the whiteboard, well spaced apart, so that you have to walk between them.

STEP 2

Place a picture representing each domain under each of the words. You can find appropriate pictures by doing a search on the internet. The important features of each picture are:

- Greenhouse – plants are clearly separate, in pots, and are healthy-looking

- Garden – plants and flowers of different types are seen together in close contact

- Jungle – the vegetation is chaotic, and it is difficult to see where one plant ends and another begins

STEP 3

Draw a line underneath the pictures from side-to-side across the middle of the board, allowing space above the line for you to write (you will need this space later). Under the line, write the sentence *I never did it in college.* Explain that *it* refers to swimming.

STEP 4

Stand by, and point to, the Greenhouse picture under the word *Greenhouse* on the left of the whiteboard. Explain that in this area, words exist as if they are beautiful, separate, perfect plants. Here the words are preceded and followed by a pause, and all of their syllables, consonants and vowels are clearly spoken.

STEP 5

Read aloud the sentence in the middle of the board slowly, with gaps between each word, making each word prominent, and with a clear falling tone starting on each prominence. Extract 20.1 gives you a recorded demonstration, the prominent syllables (six of them) are in uppercase letters.

EXTRACT 20.1

I, NEver, DID, IT, IN, COLLege

Voice: Richard, UK.

STEP 6

Move to, and point at, the Garden picture underneath the word *Garden*. Explain that in this area, words come into gentle contact with each other, and move together nicely as if in a gentle summer breeze.

STEP 7

Read aloud the sentence in the middle of the board at a moderate pace making clear the linking between *did* and *it*, (giving *did‿it*) and *it* and *in* (giving *it‿in*). Extract 20.2 gives a recorded demonstration.

EXTRACT 20.2

I NEver did‿it‿in COLLege

Voice: Richard, UK.

STEP 8

Move to, and point at, the Jungle picture underneath the word *Jungle*. Explain that words in this area rush past very quickly, running together in such a way that it is difficult to tell where one word ends and where another begins. It is even difficult to tell whether individual words have appeared at all.

As you do this, intersperse your explanation with increasingly fast versions of the sentence, making sure that they are messy by leaving out the |d| of *did* and the |t| of *it*, leaving a continuous mush of the vowel |ɪ|. Extract 20.3 gives you a recorded demonstration.

EXTRACT 20.3

i **NE**ver di‿i‿in **COLL**ege

Voice: Richard, UK.

If your students do not believe that this degree of streamlining can ever happen, then play them the original sound file in Extract 20.4, from Karam from California, who is talking about water polo.

i **NE**ver di̠i̠in **COLL**ege

Voice: Karam, US.

Having established the idea of these three domains, and their locations at the front of the classroom, we can put them to use by getting students to handle the different versions of this sentence.

20.2.2 Using the three domains

STEP 1
Go back to the left of the whiteboard, stand by the Greenhouse picture and ask the class what you said when you were in this position – it is the slow, paused, prominent version with falling tones. Have them say this version in chorus.

STEP 2
Stand by the picture of the Garden and ask the class what you said when you were in this position – this is the genteel, nicely-joined-together version. Have them say this version in chorus.

STEP 3
Lastly, stand under the picture of the Jungle and ask the class what you said when you were in this position. This was the fast version, with dropped consonants at the end of the words *did* and *it*. Have them say this in chorus. If they find it difficult to match the speed, then start slowly, beating out the timing for the prominences on the first syllables of *never* and *college*.

STEP 4
Now start walking backwards and forwards underneath the three pictures stopping at random under one of them, and ask your students, either individually or in chorus, to say the version which is associated with where you stop.

STEP 5
Then nominate small groups of students to say their versions in chorus.

STEP 6
Have students work in pairs. Tell them to write in their notebooks the words *Greenhouse*, *Garden* and *Jungle* across the top of a page. Then tell each pair to decide which of them is student A and which is student B. Student A points to each of the domains in turn, and then randomly, and student B has to say the speech units aloud. They then change roles, with B pointing and A speaking.

STEP 7

To finish, give each pair another speech unit to work with. For example:

```
|| i ALways did it in SCHOOL ||
|| we NEver did it in PAIRS ||
|| he SAID he did it in AUGust ||
|| they SAID they did it in two WEEKS ||
```

Have them prepare Greenhouse, Garden and Jungle versions of each speech unit and repeat Step 6.

HOMEWORK

For homework, you can set them tasks on TED Corpus Search Engine and/or YouGlish (cf. Chapter 24) and ask them to find Greenhouse, Garden and Jungle versions of speech units containing *did it in*. They should make a note of the URL where they found these versions, and be prepared to report back.

REMINDER

You will need to remind your class repeatedly that when they are producing language in the Jungle domain, they are doing this to improve their listening, not their pronunciation.

20.2.3 Extending the use of the three domains

IDEA 1

Every time you focus on a stretch of speech in your work with students, you can take that stretch for a botanic walk. Above, we have illustrated the technique using mostly the teacher's voice, but any time your students identify a stretch of speech from a recording that is giving them difficulty, you can help them take that stretch of speech for a botanic walk.

IDEA 2

When introducing new vocabulary, you can use the botanic walk to demonstrate a range of soundshapes for the new item. But for that, it might be more useful to use the word-crusher, to which we now turn.

20.3 The word-crusher tool — teaching new soundshapes

The word-crusher is a speech unit with two crush zones, in which we can create Jungle soundshapes. We have seen this type of speech unit in Chapter 15. It is shown in Table 20.1 below.

For the purposes of teaching listening, this table, and derivations of it, can be used both to demonstrate Jungle soundshapes of words which are already known, and to present selected items of new vocabulary. We begin with a description of the word-crusher itself, and then we'll look at some specific activities.

20.3.1 The word-crusher

The word-crusher consists of five columns, each representing a different component of the rhythmic pattern of a double-prominence speech unit. It is a great way of generating Jungle forms of words.

TABLE 20.1 THE WORD-CRUSHER – EXTRACT 20.5

	5	4	3	2	1
01	ba	BAM	ba ba ba ba	BAM	ba ba baa
02	(crush)	BANG!	(crush)	BANG!	(relax)
03	so	ALL	the way to the	STA	tion in fact

Row 01 shows a rhythmic pattern with the nonsense syllables *BAM* and *ba* representing the prominent and non-prominent syllables of the words in Row 03. Row 02 contains instructions on how to say the nonsense syllables which are given in Row 01. Notice that Columns 4 and 2 are the locations of the prominent syllables. Before and between them we have (in Columns 5 and 3) non-prominent syllables – *so* and *the way to the*. Columns 5 and 3 are the crush zones (also called 'squeeze zones') where words acquire their Jungle shapes and where the processes of streamlining (cf. Part 3) do their work in changing the soundshapes of words.

Importantly, the word-crusher is a self-contained pattern which is preceded and followed by a pause. And because Column 1 is followed by a pause, the speed slows, and the soundshapes in this column are usually somewhat clearer than they are in Columns 5 and 3. This is represented by a slightly longer spelling for the last syllable *baa* in Column 1.

The columns are numbered in reverse order, for reasons which will soon become clear.

As well as this double-prominence rhythmic pattern, there are larger and smaller patterns: quadruple-, triple- and single- prominence patterns. Quadruple units are difficult to fit on the page, so we will just look at a triple- and a single-prominence unit. Table 20.2 shows a triple-prominence speech unit, with prominences in Columns 6, 4 and 2.

TABLE 20.2 A TRIPLE-PROMINENCE SPEECH UNIT – EXTRACT 20.6

	7	6	5	4	3	2	1
01	ba	BAM	ba	BAM	ba ba	BAM	ba ba baa
02	(crush)	BANG!	(crush)	BANG!	(crush)	BANG!	(relax)
03	so	ALL	the	WAY	to the	STA	tion in fact

Table 20.2 contains the same words as the previous table, but there is a different rhythmic pattern – there is an extra prominence on *way*, giving us three prominences. Table 20.3 shows a single-prominence speech unit, using the same words.

TABLE 20.3 A SINGLE-PROMINENCE SPEECH UNIT – EXTRACT 20.7

	3	2	1
01	ba ba ba ba ba ba	BAM	ba ba baa
02	(crush)	BANG!	(relax)
03	so all the way to the	STA	tion in fact

There is now just one prominence in this speech unit, on the first syllable of *station*.

With the numbering in reverse order, we can make generalisations which apply to all three tables. Thus, whatever the size of speech unit:

- prominences occur in even-numbered columns

- non-prominences occur in odd-numbered columns

- the tone (falling, rising, level, etc.) starts in Column 2 and continues over the syllables in Column 1 (if there are any).

These different-sized tables form part of 'the Window on Speech' which is a method of both analysing recordings and of presenting speech units to learners. Cauldwell (2013: chapters 1–5) explains how to use it as an analytical tool, and there is more in Appendix 2.

Another important feature of these three tables is that they illustrate three different ways of saying the words *so all the way to the station in fact*. All three versions are legitimate ways of saying the words, and none of which is more correct than the other. All we can say with any confidence is that the triple- (and the quadruple-) prominence units would probably be clearer and more carefully articulated than the other two, and that the double- and single-prominence versions would probably be less clear, and less carefully articulated, and therefore more Jungle-like. We are going to focus on the use of the double-prominence unit because its simple shape makes it the easiest to handle for our listening/decoding purposes.

20.3.2 Filling the crush zones

An important means of learning to decode speech is to become familiar with the wide range of ways in which the same words may be said in different ways (cf. Field, 2008: 88). The word-crusher provides a way of doing this. Let us take the sentence *I never did it in high school*. We can put it into the word-crusher in a number of different ways.

The word-crusher is at its most crushing when we pack as many syllables as possible into the crush (or squeeze) zones: Columns 5 and 3 in Table 20.4. Note that this results in some of the cells being empty. (See Appendix 2 for an explanation.)

TABLE 20.4 A DOUBLE-PROMINENCE SPEECH UNIT – EXTRACT 20.8

	5	4	3	2	1
	(crush)	BANG!	(crush)	BANG!	(relax)
01		I	never did it in high	SCHOOL	
02	i never did it in	HIGH		SCHOOL	

In row 01, Columns 5 and 1 are empty because the first and last syllables are prominent and therefore have to go into the even-numbered Columns 4 and 2 respectively. But all the other six syllables are packed in-between them. Note that this produces a pattern which violates a CSM word stress rule (*high school*, as a compound noun, should have stress on *high*, but not on *school*) – but remember, we are preparing for the unruly Jungle here.

In Row 02, the cells in Columns 3 and 1 are empty because the last two syllables *high* and *school* are prominent, and have to occupy Columns 4 and 2. This means that the six syllables *I never did it in* have to occur in the crush zone of Column 5. Listen to Extract 20.8 and practise saying rows 01 and 02 out loud.

In conclusion, the word-crusher is a tool which you can use to help students practise different ways of saying the same words – but remember, the goal is not pronunciation, the goal is to improve their listening/decoding abilities by helping them become familiar and comfortable with the wide variety of soundshapes that words may have as they are streamlined in fast speech.

20.3.3 Whiteboard activity – *I'm going to London*

It is not always easy to present the word-crusher in tables, so here is a procedure to use from the front of the class, using the whiteboard.

STEP 1

Write the sentence below on the whiteboard, and place crosses above the first syllables of the words *going*, *London* and *weekend*. (It is a sentence that you might find in a pre-intermediate course book such as Redston and Cunningham, 2012). The crosses represent the prominent syllables, so we are looking at a triple-prominence speech unit, but without the table.

EXTRACT 20.9

```
     X          X               X
I'm  going to  London  at  the  weekend.
```

Voice: Richard, UK. There are three versions, with prominences at three speeds: 40, 50 and 60 beats per minute.

Say the sentence aloud, or use the recording, and ask students to repeat it in chorus.

STEP 2

Erase the sentence and write it up as the speech unit below, taking care that the prominent syllables are in capital letters and the non-prominent syllables – including the first person pronoun – are in lowercase. Tell the class that this is now a new speech unit.

EXTRACT 20.10

```
|| i'm GOing to LONdon at the WEEKend ||
```

Voice: Richard, UK. This version goes at a metronome speed of 60 beats per minute.

STEP 3

Using a metronome to help, model a careful, steady pronunciation of this, with the prominences occurring at 60 beats per minute. If your students find this difficult, then back-chain this unit using the recorded extracts to help you:

```
... the WEEKend
... at the WEEKend
... LONdon at the WEEKend
... to LONdon at the WEEKend
... GOing to LONdon at the WEEKend
i'm GOing to LONdon at the WEEKend
```

Then take it up to 50, then 60 beats per minute. This may look like pronunciation work, but because the word 'pronunciation' has such strong connotations of correctness and clarity, it is best to refer to all activities such as this one, which have a listening/decoding goal, as 'vocal gymnastics' (cf. Section 20.1 above). This is not pronunciation work because the purpose is to make learners familiar and comfortable with Jungle forms, which are often unclear and 'incorrect' in a conventional pronunciation sense.

STEP 4

Change this speech unit from a triple-, to a double-prominence speech unit by making *London* all lowercase – non-prominent – as in Extract 20.11.

EXTRACT 20.11

```
|| i'm GOing to london at the WEEKend ||
```

This results in *London* becoming non-prominent in a crush zone, in which there are four other syllables, making a total of six non-prominent syllables between the prominences in *GO* and *WEEK* – the six syllables being –*ing.to.lon.don.at.the*.

STEP 5

Let's be ambitious and set a target for our students to be able to handle this unit at a metronome speed of 60 beats per minute, thus preparing them to handle fast, messy speech in the Jungle. The aim is to match the prominent syllables (shown in uppercase) to each beat of the metronome speed of 60 beats per minute, crushing the other, non-prominent syllables between the beats.

Set the metronome going and conduct the class in choral repetitions. If the students complain that they cannot do it, stop and explain that all you want them to do is to get the prominent syllables on the beat, and to make any noise they like between the prominences. They should try to forget the words that they can see in Column 3, and simply make a vowel-like noise between the two prominences.

STEP 6

Then ask them to focus on the words *london at the*. Say them in a Greenhouse version, then a Garden version, and then make the following streamlining effects:

- drop the |d| from *London*, giving us something close to *lunnun* |lʌn.ən|
- streamline the word *at* by dropping the |t| and using schwa |ə| for the vowel
- blur *the* |ð| so that it becomes close to *duh* |də|
- run these streamlined soundshapes together

EXTRACT 20.12

|| ... london at the ... lun.nun.uh.duh || |lʌn.ən.ɔ.də|

Conduct them chorally on these non-prominent syllables. Precision is not required! Then come back to the full speech unit and get them to use this newly-learned mush in the crush zone of the full speech unit.

EXTRACT 20.13

|| i'm GOing to london at the WEEKend ||

STEP 7

As a final act of streamlining, get them to focus on the soundshapes of *London*, and streamline it even further so that it is a single syllable with a long |n| at the end *lunn* making *london at the* something closer to *lunn uh duh* |lʌnn.ɔ.də|.

EXTRACT 20.14

|| ... london at the ... lun.nun.uh.duh ... lunn.uh.duh || |

STEP 8

Explain that you are going to add a choice of destinations to this speech unit, and that you are going to need their help.

- Remind them of what they did to the word *London*

- Explain that you want to streamline other names of famous cities

- Write the names of three or four famous cities (more if you like) on the Greenhouse side of the whiteboard

- Then walk to the Jungle side and invite volunteers from the class to give streamlined shapes for these cities, by asking them to say these names as fast as they possibly can, and see what happens. Table 20.5 gives you some ideas. Precision is not required.

TABLE 20.5 GREENHOUSE AND JUNGLE FORMS OF CITIES

Paris	pa-iss	pæ.ɪs	Berlin	blin	blɪn
Dublin	dull-in	dʌ.lɪn	London	lun.n	lʌnn
Cardiff	car-iff	kɑː.ɪf	Edinburgh	em.bruh	embrə
Belfast	beffast	beʊ.fɑːst	Madrid	ma.rid	mæ.rɪd
Oxford	ossfud	ɒs.fəd	Cambridge	kay.midge	keɪmɪʤ

STEP 9

Put the class into pairs, and get them to practise the 'weekend' speech unit, replacing *London* with the names of other cities.

STEP 10

Write on the whiteboard another speech unit as shown in Extract 20.15, so we now have a miniature dialogue with one speech unit per person. Allan has the speech unit we have been working on, and Brian has a different speech unit, with prominences on *I'M* and *NOT* and all other syllables non-prominent.

EXTRACT 20.15

```
Allan || i'm GOing to london at the WEEKend ||
Brian || but I'M NOT going to london at the weekend ||
```

Voice: Richard, UK.

In Brian's speech unit, a falling tone starts on *not* and continues over the following nine syllables which are non-prominent. These non-prominent syllables are not crushed – they just slow down and get quieter as they approach the pause.

STEP 11

Model both speech units in Extract 20.15, and get the class to say them in chorus. Focus particularly on making Brian's prominent syllables extra loud, and the non-prominent syllables much softer and gradually slowing down and fading away to almost (but not quite) nothing as they approach the final syllable of *weekend*.

20.3.4 The word-crusher and new vocabulary – *reliable, volunteer*

A good time to use the word-crusher is when you introduce new vocabulary. There won't be time to treat all new vocabulary in this way, so it is best to choose just one or two words. Three-syllable and four-syllable words are particularly good to focus on, because their length offers more opportunities for streamlining. It is helpful to have the Greenhouse citation form to hand, either in a dictionary sound file or in symbols. But for our listening/decoding goal it is important to demonstrate what other soundshapes each word might have. Let us look at two items of vocabulary: *reliable* and *volunteer*.

You need to add other words on either side of the words themselves. This is because the natural state for any spoken word is to be streamed together with other words which will influence its soundshape. Most dictionaries have example phrases or sentences in which the headword appears, but not all of them are ideal for listening/decoding purposes. We need a sentence (or phrase) which will fit the five columns of our word-crusher, and will allow us to have our target word in the middle column (the crush zone) of the table, the one which occurs between two prominences. This makes the word non-prominent, and therefore gives us a reason to apply the streamlining processes which will change its soundshape.

For *reliable* I have found in the Macmillan Dictionary online *I heard this from a very reliable source*; and for *volunteer* I have found (from the Longman Dictionary of Contemporary English) *I need some volunteers to help with the washing-up.*

RELIABLE

Let's remove the first three words of our sample sentence, which will give us a slightly more manageable *from a very reliable source* which can fit into the word-crusher as shown in Table 20.6. Notice that our target word *reliable* is in Column 3, and it shares this crush zone with the second syllable of *very*.

TABLE 20.6 A DOUBLE-PROMINENCE SPEECH UNIT – EXTRACT 20.16

	5	4	3	2	1
01	from a	VE	ry reliable	SOURCE	

The Greenhouse form of *reliable* has four syllables, with the word stress on the second syllable |riˈlaɪ.ə. bᵊl|. In order to do the streamlining in column 3, we need some streamlining information from Part 3.

- the diphthong |aɪ| may be smoothed to |a|, resulting in |riˈla.ə. bᵊl| (cf. Chapter 18.1)

- the second and third syllables may blend together (a syllablend cf. Chapter 18.4.1) thus resulting in a syll-drop (cf. Chapter 18.4) thus |ri.la.bᵊl|

- the |b| of the final syllable may be blurred towards |w|, resulting in |ri.la.wᵊl| (cf. Chapter 18.7)

- the final segment |l| may undergo vow-ell streamlining (becoming a vowel), resulting in |ri.laɪ.ə.bʊ| (cf. Chapter 18.2)

- the first syllable |ri| is the same as the syllable that precedes it |ri| from *very* and may therefore be subject to the D.R.Y. process (cf. Chapter 18.5) whereby the speaker uses one syllable to stand in the place of two, resulting in something close to *veri-liable* |veri.laɪ.ə. bᵊl|

- and if all of the above apply simultaneously we get something close to |veri.laə.wʊ|

The list above may look like steps towards a correct answer, or like instructions to arrive at one, and only one, streamlined form. The truth is that there are many streamlined forms for any word, or word cluster – far too many to list. The best way to consider such descriptions of streamlining processes at work is that it presents **only one possibility among many**. These are guides, not rules, to the kind of streamlining processes that can apply in the Jungle. As you work with these examples, do not insist on precision.

Having prepared the Jungle version, you can then use the steps of the activity described above in Section 20.3.3, starting with a three-prominence version shown as unit 01 in Extract 20.17, and ending with the Jungle version shown in unit 02.

EXTRACT 20.17

```
01 || from a VEry reLIable SOURCE ||
02 || from a VE.ri.lae.wu SOURCE ||
```

Speech unit 02 must be spoken fast, in order to justify the amount of streamlining that has been applied to it.

Remember (your students will need constant reminding of this) that the goal of any activity involving streamlining processes is listening. Although students will be using their voices, they will be doing vocal gymnastics in the service of listening, not pronunciation.

VOLUNTEER

The word *volunteer* has three syllables |ˌvɒ.lənˈtɪə| with word stress (cf. Appendix 1) on the first and third syllables in both the noun and the verb form. It can have prominences on both of these syllables (cf. Row 01 in Table 20.7), or on either one of them (Rows 02 & 03) or on none at all (Row 04).

TABLE 20.7 STRESS-SHIFT – EXTRACT 20.18

	5	4	3	2	1
01	can i have a	VO	lun	TEER	please
02	does	AN	yone want to volun	TEER	
03	can i have a	VO	lunteer to clean the	BOARD	please
04	i	NEED	a volunteer to clean the	BOARD	please

Voice: Richard, UK. Note that in Unit 01, can i have a sounds like kaffa.

The four rows give us four different soundshapes of *volunteer*. For the purposes of streamlining, we will focus on Row 04 where the three syllables of *volunteer* share the non-prominent crush zone with four other syllables: *volunteer* is preceded by *a* and it is followed by *to clean the*.

- the long vowel in *clean* is likely to be smoothed to |ɪ|, giving us |klɪn| (cf. Chapter 18.1)
- *the* in *to clean the* is likely to undergo 'd'eth-drop' (cf. Chapter 17.3), resulting in something close to *tuh cleanuh* |təklɪnə|
- the initial consonant |v| is likely to blur towards |f|, thus resulting in something close to |fɒ.lən.tiə|
- there may be a mid-clip (cf. Chapter 18.4.3) with the weak syllable |lən| disappearing, leaving us with something close to *fonteer* |fɒn.tiə|
- applying all these processes simultaneously will give us |fɒn.tiə.tə.klɪn.ə|.

Remember, this procedure presents only one possibility among many.

Having prepared the Jungle version given in Row 4, you can then use the steps of the activity described above in Section 20.3.3, starting with a four-prominence version shown as unit 01 in Extract 20.19 and ending with the Jungle version shown in 02.

EXTRACT 20.19
```
01 || i NEED a volunTEER to CLEAN the BOARD please ||
02 || i NEED a fontier to klinuh BOARD please ||
```

It is really important that the Jungle version is practised at a high speed, because one of the main justifications for doing this kind of activity is that these streamlining processes are caused by the high speeds at which speakers produce language in everyday speech.

Again, you will need to remind your students that such activities are to help them with listening, not pronunciation.

20.4 The accelerator

The activities described in the preceding sections require that you and your students speak at fast speeds, otherwise there is little justification for the streamlining processes to operate. It is also useful for you and your students to develop a feel for the changes of speed that occur in recordings. This is because when you see a transcript of a recording, it is a sight substance that you can read at your own pace. But the sound substance of the recording will have many changes of pace, none of which are under your control, and some of which will contribute significantly to your students' ability, or lack of it, to decode.

It is best to compute speed of speech in syllables per second, rather than words per minute (cf. Cauldwell, 2013: 97). This is because we are working (typically) with very short stretches of speech, and this gives a measure of speed which more accurately reflects the rhythm of each speech unit.

It is useful to create for yourself a benchmark that you can call to mind to help you judge speeds. Table 20.8 gives you some benchmarks for 'slow', 'average', 'fast' and 'very fast' speaking speeds.

TABLE 20.8 AVERAGE SPEAKING SPEEDS IN SYLLABLES PER SECOND

	SLOW	AVERAGE	FAST	VERY FAST
Syllables per second (sps)	2.0	4.0	5.3	6.5–10.0+

The figures for speeds are best thought of as being the central point of a range – so that 4.0 as the speed for 'average' is the centre point of a range which goes from 3.0 to 4.7 syllables per second.

Extract 20.20 has been specially constructed to demonstrate these different speeds. The speeds of the units vary from 2.0 (slow) to 10.0 sps (very fast).

EXTRACT 20.20

```
01 || and then they FInally bought a BIG house || 2.0
02 || and then they FInally bought a BIG house || 4.0
03 || and then they FInally bought a BIG house || 5.3
04 || and then they FInally bought a BIG house || 6.5
05 || and then they FInally bought a BIG house || 8.0
06 || and then they FInally bought a BIG house || 10.0
```

Voice: Richard, UK.

This recording can be used as a reference to help you build up your sense of speed. Coming back to this regularly, and repeating what you hear, will help develop this sense. It is important to do this, because working at speed on vocal gymnastic exercises justifies the use of streamlining activities in pursuit of the goal of listening.

The inspiration for the demonstration of different speeds in Extract 20.20 comes from Jess, from the USA, in speech unit 06 from Extract 20.21.

EXTRACT 20.21

```
01 (slow)       || UM || 1.9
02 (slow)       || FOR || 1.7
03 (slow)       || aBOUT || 2.6
04 (slow)       || two YEARS || 2.9
05 (very fast)  || mmHMM || 7.2
06 (very fast)  || and then they FInally bought a BIG house || 7.5
07 (very fast)  || a BIgger house for US || 6.5
08 (very fast)  || to be Able to LIVE in || 8.8
09 (average)    || so we MOVED || 4.6
10 (very fast)  || for THAT REAson || 7.6
```

Note how the speeds vary from speech unit to speech unit. This is very characteristic of everyday spontaneous speech, and yet it is rarely a feature of textbook or course book recordings.

20.5 Summary and what's next

In this Chapter we have looked extensively at activities involving two key tools: the botanic metaphor of the Greenhouse, Garden and the Jungle; and the word-crusher. Using these tools effectively does not require a recording (although they can help): the teacher's voice, and the students' voices in vocal gymnastic exercises are sufficient.

It is also important to note that they can be done with students at any level.

In Chapter 21, we move on to consider the practical aspects of finding and using useful extracts from recordings.

21 Recordings, extracts and activities

For many teachers, recordings are an essential component of the listening lesson. The first half of this chapter addresses the issue of how to find extracts in any recording which provide opportunities for learning about the wide variety of soundshapes that words have, and learning to handle the speeds and messiness of spontaneous speech. The second half of the chapter describes activities to use with extracts from recordings.

In the first half of this chapter – up to and including Section 21.5 – we will consider:

- the different levels of a recording
- what type of recording is suitable
- how long it should be
- the role of the transcript
- how to identify opportunities for learning the sound substance

In the second half of this chapter – from Sections 21.6 to 21.12 – we will describe a number of activities:

- repeated listenings
- gap-fills
- dictation
- gleeps (to be defined later)
- raw sound
- getting up to speed
- drafting phenomena

Some of these terms may be unfamiliar to you but do not worry, they will be defined in the relevant section below. We begin with a reminder.

21.1 Levels – a reminder

There are three levels at which you can work when using recordings: first, at the level of the meaning(s) intended by the speaker; second, focusing on the words that the speaker intended us to hear; and lastly, focusing on the sound substance which is continuous, fast and mushy. These three levels are represented in Table 21.1.

TABLE 21.1

	LEVEL
1	meaning
2	words
3	sound substance

Each of these levels can be probed using three different questions:

1. What did the speaker mean? 'We've turned down the invitation'

2. What words did the speaker say? 'Sorry we can't come tomorrow'

3. What were the soundshapes? *kangkum* or *khankum* – 'Can come' or 'Can't come'?

Our decoding activities are focused on the relationship between the bottom two levels: the relationship between the sound substance and words. The bottom level may contain only rough hints and mush, but learners, when they need to decode, have to match these rough hints to words at level 2, and thereby (after taking in contextual factors) arrive at the meaning(s) at level 1.

21.2 The recording is a treasure trove of soundshapes

CONVENTIONAL APPROACHES

In conventional approaches to listening comprehension, the course book recording is regarded as **a repository of meanings** which have to be captured as they fly by embedded in the rapidly vanishing sound substance. The capturing consists of gathering clues, building meanings and thereby constructing responses to the tasks set. Prior to the process of capturing meanings, students are primed in some way (contextualisation, prediction) to expect a certain range of meanings of which they have to select one. Therefore the emphasis is very much at the level of understanding meaning.

Often there is little recognition that there is a sound substance to be learned. The acoustic substance of the recording is regarded as a vehicle for carrying meanings, but the physical features of the vehicle itself are given little attention.

DECODING

For the purposes of decoding, we need to view the recording somewhat differently: every recording is a repository – sometimes a treasure trove – of soundshapes of the language. Even the slow, scripted recordings found at beginner and pre-intermediate levels will contain Greenhouse and Garden forms which can be used as the starting point for activities. The recording is likely to contain repeated words which will have different soundshapes on each occurrence, and word clusters are likely to be spoken moderately fast (in recordings for beginner and elementary levels) or very fast, and in very streamlined ways (in authentic recordings or those for more advanced learners). There will be changes in speed, accelerations and slowing down.

21.3 What type of recording? – Authentic?

AUTHENTIC RECORDINGS

Increasingly, textbooks are featuring authentic 'real world' unscripted recordings which contain Jungle phenomena. However, the accompanying tasks and instructions to teachers continue to be based on the Careful Speech Model (CSM, cf. Chapter 13). This results in a conflict – an incompatibility between the contents of the recording and the descriptions of it that are given in, or implied by, the accompanying materials. So although the increasing number of authentic recordings in course books is to be welcomed, we need to improve our ability to describe what happens in these recordings, and not rely on the terms and concepts taken from the CSM which we use to teach pronunciation.

SCRIPTED RECORDINGS

Scripted recordings are also likely to contain at least some features of the Jungle. Although they may not contain drafting phenomena (*uh, like, and that sort of thing*) which often make a significant contribution to the sound substance of the recording, they will almost certainly contain word clusters which occur in short bursts that are spoken faster than the words around them. Extract 21.1 contains two examples from scripted materials at advanced and upper-intermediate.

EXTRACT 21.1
```
01 || where there were STREET LIGHTS || 5.0 (12.5)
02 || you KNOW what i MEAN || 7.5
```

Unit 01 from *Pronunciation for Advances Learners of English*, (Brazil, 1994); 02 from *Outcomes Upper Intermediate* (Dellar & Walkley, 2010).

Unit 01 is from advanced materials by Brazil (1994, unit 1) which contains the word cluster *where there were* which sounds like *weatherwuh* |weðewɔ| and which goes at 12.5 syllables per second – more than double the speed of the speech unit in which it occurs. Unit 02 is from an upper-intermediate course book by Dellar and Walkley (2010). The Jungle feature of this clip is in the drafting nature of the wording, and the smoothing of the first person pronoun. Its speed, 7.5 sps is also very fast. So scripted materials can contain Jungle-like phenomena

But even the slowest, most carefully scripted recording can be taken as the starting point for work on decoding, simply by the teacher taking words for a spin – the botanic walk from Greenhouse through the Garden to the Jungle (cf. Chapter 20). It's up to the teacher, in such cases, to create fast-speech decoding activities based on the original recording.

21.4 Time – how long should a recording be?

FOR WORK ON MEANING

The recordings which are the main focus of ELT course books are often minutes long. Field (2008: 58) writes of a medium-length recording being about three minutes long (enough for eight evenly spaced comprehension items).

FOR WORK ON DECODING

The length of the extract of the recording that forms the basis of decoding work needs to be very much shorter – seconds rather than minutes long. This is because decoding an extract of even a few seconds duration requires intense concentration. Therefore any decoding task needs to be short, sharp and achievable, so that learners can get a sense of satisfaction on successfully completing the task.

In the activities suggested in the sections which follow, the typical length of the extract which is the focus of decoding is very short – between one second (sometimes less) and up to ten seconds. The good news is that appropriate short extracts can easily be found in the longer recordings that accompany course books.

21.5 Mining recordings for extracts

There are two basic ways of choosing what parts of a recording to focus on for decoding work. The first is for you, the teacher, to select appropriate passages to work with; the second and often the best way is to allow students to select the passages themselves.

21.5.1 The teacher decides

USING THE TRANSCRIPT TO FIND WORD CLUSTERS IN FAST SPEECH

Most course book recordings come with a transcript, and you can use the transcript to find ideal material. As you listen, follow the recording by moving your pencil along the words and lines of the transcript, and underline those passages where there are noticeable changes in speed. When you have finished listening, review the transcript, and look at those parts that you have underlined for word clusters – familiar words grouped together.

Then select a ten-second (or shorter) section to work with – the section should be challenging in terms of speeds and soundshapes, but not contain items of unknown vocabulary. The purpose is not to teach vocabulary, but rather to teach explicit knowledge of the sound substance and of the soundshapes that words can have, together with the skill of being able to handle them and hold them in the mind (even if only in mush form) for the purpose of practising decoding.

USING THE TRANSCRIPT TO FIND REPEATED WORDS

Again, using the transcript, look for words that are said more than once. Then identify them in the recording and using a wave editor such as Audacity, cut out the speech units (the rhythmic units in which they occur) and then cut the words themselves out of those rhythmic units. Then get students to do some vocal gymnastics imitating them, mouthing them in different ways, savouring and relishing the different soundshapes, and making an earworm (cf. Chapter 23.4).

21.5.2 Soft-focus listening

There is another way of identifying extracts which involves listening without the transcript and without paying attention to the meanings being conveyed. This is 'soft-focus listening' where you attend, deliberately, to the sound substance itself, while resisting the temptation to recognise words and understand meanings. You listen for the ups and downs, changes in volume, changes in clarity, changes in speed and differences in flavours.

21.5.3 Students decide

WITHOUT TRANSCRIPT

Rather than have the teacher identify extracts to work with in advance of the class, Field (Field 2008: 162) suggests getting students to identify extracts to work with. There are a number of ways you can do this. You can roll through a recording (video or audio) and, as you do so, ask students to shout out or raise their hands when they have the greatest difficulty working out what words were said. (cf. 21.9 below).

Identifying passages to work with can also happen after comprehension work has been done. It is always worthwhile asking students – after they have answered the 'meaning' questions – what it was in the recording that they heard which led them to choose their answers.

WITH TRANSCRIPT

Also, as students follow the transcript doing a 'last listen' for checking understanding, they can underline problematic passages in the transcript that they struggled to understand when they were just listening. Then you can take a vote on which passages to work with, and work with those passages which get the most votes.

21.6 Repeated listenings

For Field, 'The learning process partly entails playing and replaying problematic passages…' (2008b: 162). This is indeed a very useful thing to do. When learners can see the words as they listen repeatedly to the problematic passages, they get to match the particular soundshapes that are on the recording to their mental picture of the sight substance of these words. This work enlarges the store – the cloud – of possible soundshapes that needs to surround all the words in each learner's mental dictionary.

However, for this experience to really help learners with future encounters with the same words in different contexts with different speakers and soundshapes, we need to do more than a rapid repeated re-hearing of a single instance. Learners need to engage with, and handle vocally, the sound substance and not only imitate it, but also play with different versions of how it could have been said. We will cover how this might be done later (cf. Chapter 23.4).

The key thing to remember is that you are teaching the sound substance, that words have multiple soundshapes, and that working hard to hear them in one situation, on one recording – even if successful – is not necessarily enough to help them successfully decode the same words on future occasions.

21.7 Gap-fills

Gap-fill exercises involve taking a short section of the transcript of a recording and creating gaps by removing single words or preferably groups of words. The students' task is to listen to the recording and write the words they hear in the gaps.

21.7.1 Gap-fills as a testing tool

Gap-fill exercises involve an incomplete sight substance that provides, in written form, the co-text of the gapped words. There are three potential problems with gap-fills: first, that learners could succeed by guessing from what they know of the context and co-text, together with their knowledge of the language; second, that the gap-fill becomes an exercise in sight-substance reconstruction (and not about the sound substance); third, that the teacher fails to take active steps to ensure that the exercise is not a test (as Anna's teacher from Chapter 11.4 failed to do: 'Well done – you got the right answer, so let's move on').

You might think it odd that the first potential problem concerns 'guessing correctly', but remember we are engaged in teaching the sound substance – we are working at the level of decoding, not the level of meaning.

21.7.2 Gap-fills as the start of teaching

Gap-fill is a testing technique, but it can become an extremely effective teaching technique as soon as you explore the differing perceptions that learners have about the words that they think have occurred in the sound substance.

In doing so, you will learn a great deal about their strengths and weaknesses in terms of perception and understanding. My experience is that their difficulties lay in what were for me surprising places: they did not recognise words which were (supposedly) in their active vocabulary, and they reported hearing words which could not have fitted the context, or words which contradicted the meanings that they had successfully arrived at.

21.7.3 Gap-filling familiar words – an activity

Following Thorn (2009, 2013) and Sweeney (2017), I suggest that gap-fill work should focus on familiar words which are perceptually difficult – word clusters, and any known words which occur in the crush zones of speech units.

An activity that you can do at any time, either using a prepared handout, or on the board at the front of the class, is to focus on a stretch of speech that contains a perceptually difficult run of words which lead into a word which is clearly audible. For example, let us take the following speech unit.

EXTRACT 21.2
```
01 || even though it is for READing || 8.0
```

Voice: Geoff, UK.

In this unit, the first five words are spoken very fast and are therefore likely to provide decoding difficulties.

STEP 1
On the whiteboard, draw a long continuous line where you will eventually write the words *even though it is for*, followed by the word *reading* with the first syllable in uppercase, to represent a prominent syllable.

```
_____|READing|
```

STEP 2
Play the extract a couple of times, and ask the class to make a noise of their choosing (e.g. humming) to substitute for the mush of non-prominent syllables, while telling them that they should aim to say the word *reading* on time. Make sure that they get their noise of preference as long as (no shorter, no longer) the timing of five missing words. It may take several attempts to get to this point.

STEP 3
By this time they may be hearing *tis* for *it is* quite clearly – if they say that they do, then react positively ('Yes good, but wait a minute') and ask them how many syllables there are altogether.

STEP 4
Play the extract another couple of times, encouraging them to tap their fingers to the rhythm of the unit. Elicit guesses as to the number of words, and then divide up the horizontal line with six vertical slashes – which gives us five spaces.

Then ask them where *tis* goes (it is shared between gaps 3 and 4, which hold *it* and *is* respectively), and then ask them to mimic the sounds they hear as you play the extract again.

STEP 5

Play the extract several times and accept all suggestions for what the words are that go in the gaps. You can write the 'wrong' ones above and below the gaps and the 'right' ones in the gaps themselves. It is important, following the principle of valuing alternative hearings, to respect all suggestions from the class. This is because they may well have alternative hearings of the sound substance that are well founded. For example, they may report hearing the word *know* instead of *though*. And although *know* does not fit as far as meaning is concerned, this may be an accurate perception of the sound substance in which *though* undergoes d'eth-drop (cf. Chapter 17.3) and is linked to the preceding |n| of *even*, giving us *even-ough* |iːvɔnɔʊ|.

STEP 6

Add in the first letters of the remaining words, resulting in something like this:

```
|e   |th   |'t|is|f  |READing
```

Replay the extract several more times, and elicit from the class (a) what sounds they hear, and (b) which words go in the gaps.

HOMEWORK

After such intensive decoding work in the classroom, you can set your students homework, for example, finding other examples of *even though it is* from websites such as TED Corpus Search Engine (2017) or YouGlish (2017) (cf. Chapter 24). The task could involve:

- finding five examples from videos which interest you

- making a note of the URLs of these videos, and the time in the video where you hear *even though it is*

- writing a short commentary on the sound substance (one line of notes such as 'Garden with Jungle-like bits', or 'Mountainous, not monotonous')

- writing a short paragraph on why the video interests them e.g. 'I like cooking, and this chef is a hero of mine.'

Searching the internet for multiple examples is one way of getting around the problem of the single instance. Another way of avoiding this problem is to take the words concerned for a botanic walk (cf. Chapter 20.1).

21.8 Dictation for decoding purposes

Dictation is the art of resolving the invisible sound substance into a visible sight substance. The danger with dictations is that the construction of accurate written words and sentences becomes the sole focus of attention. For decoding purposes, we need to ensure that the sound substance comes into play as much as possible.

Field (1998a: 24) and Thorn (2009: 9) suggest mini-dictations, in which the teacher plays a recording then stops it, either at a random place, or at a pre-planned place, and asks students to write down the last few words – five or six, but the number need not be precise. The idea is that the length of the gap is appropriate for the amount of sound substance your students can retain in their minds as they attempt to decode, so that this does not become a test of memory capacity.

21.8.1 Maximising the value of mini-dictations

There are two important things you can do to maximise the value of dictations. First, you need to have a sense of where the extract lies on the botanic spectrum – is it a Garden-like stretch of speech, or is it a Jungle-like stretch? Then, at the end of the activity, you can maximize the usefulness of the task by getting students to take the extract for a botanic walk – giving Greenhouse, Garden and Jungle versions of the words they have written down. Second, it is a good idea to maximize your students' handling of the sound substance by encouraging them to vocalise what they hear before writing anything down. If they do not recognise individual words easily, they should just mimic the sound substance without worrying about what words it contains. The description of the next activity gives you an idea how you might do this on a systematic basis.

21.9 Speechstream activities – Gleeps

Sullivan (2017) describes 'speechstream' techniques which she uses in classes for adult immigrants in New Zealand. She takes videos of TV programmes and finds bits of fast speech that her students can neither understand nor decode. (She says: 'When they can't hear it, rejoice!'). For Sullivan this is a wonderful circumstance – the perfect opportunity for learning. She gets the class to mimic stretches of the non-understood speech stream (Sullivan calls these moments 'gleeps' – it's her term). The students do this vocally, and with hand and arm gestures. This voice gym work is bottom-up processing without understanding. Sullivan wants the non-understanding and pre-verbal handling to go on for some time, and she deliberately delays the resolution into words.

Her reason for doing this is to prevent the pronunciation component of the students' L1 language system being an obstacle to hearing 'what is really there' in the sound substance. She argues that this helps the brain networks of adult learners to revive the early-life plasticity used to acquire the sound system of their L1 as children.

Sullivan's justification for this approach takes us into the brain – but away from the parts that are to do with conscious learning to the procedural system, including the basal ganglia – a key group of neurons which are used to process muscle movements. Sullivan argues that the substance of language is physical – hence the vocal mouthing, and hand/arm gestures.

Sullivan advises 'maybe five minutes of voice gym work and then resolve into words and meaning'. She also asserts 'When they want to understand too early, this is an obstacle to learning.'

Sullivan notes that the most important feature of a gleep activity is to begin with a 'total lack of understanding', although she acknowledges that this is 'difficult and counter-intuitive'. It requires learner-training and commitment to get them to not try to understand (2017: 14), but they certainly get value from such work. They tell her that in later hearings the recording has been slowed down – when in fact it has not, the cerebral network has simply relaxed, as it is easily decoding identified sounds and is riding along comfortably. Although it is a demanding exercise, requiring intense focus and effort, Sullivan's students soon request this 'speechstream' work as part of their daily schedule, once they experience the improvement in their listening ability.

For more, read Sullivan (2017).

21.10 Raw sound

Grinberg devised activities which address 'the raw sound' (sound substance) of the language to develop his students' 'auditory acuity' (2017).

His method is to take a recording of about 45 seconds ('the full recording'). He then prepares a transcript which students use either on their own or in pairs. Using sound-editing software, he prepares between six and ten short extracts (up to one second in length) of words, word pairs, and word fragments ('short fragments'). He then prepares slightly longer versions of the short fragments which include the immediate co-text ('long fragments') within which the short fragments are contained.

Grinberg plays the full recording and students follow the transcript as they listen. He then plays the first short fragment once or twice, and the students' task is to find and circle the syllables or words in the transcript that they hear in the short fragments. He goes through the rest of the short fragments one-by-one. He then reviews the answers with the whole class and, as he does so, he plays the longer extracts alongside the relevant short extract.

The key feature of this procedure is the choice of both the full recording and the short fragments. The full recording needs to have Jungle features and the short fragments need to focus on parts of the recording that contain examples of these features. They may occur as different soundshapes of single words, word clusters, or stretches of sound substance that start in one word and end in the middle of a subsequent word.

To maximise the value of this procedure it is a good idea to get students to vocalise – to sound out quietly to themselves – what they hear as they go through this activity.

21.11 Coping with speed

One of the biggest problems that learners report is that of speed. Even if they know a great deal about the variety of soundshapes that words can have, and can successfully produce them, acquiring the skill of catching them at speed requires separate work. But speed is also the reason why most of the streamlining processes apply.

In the sub-sections which follow, we will look at two activities which prepare learners to handle fast speech.

21.11.1 Wordless rhythms

The rhythms of language are often compared to other types of rhythm: heartbeat, drumming, walking and other repetitive physical movements. And we can use learners' experience of these other types of rhythm to help them handle the speeds of normal speech. Using non-verbal rhythms, we can help learners to master the speed component of short extracts of the sound substance before they actually start to handle the words that are contained within it.

As with Sullivan's speech stream activities, this can be done on the raw sound substance, without any reference to the words it contains, and it can be done with the learners' eyes open or closed. Students can use their voices to hum along with the sound substance, following its speeds (e.g. the faster the louder, the slower the quieter) and following the pitch contours by going higher and lower along with the voices on the recording.

The physical movements can involve clapping, tapping their fingers, gesturing by waving their arms in the air and shadow boxing so that the punches occur in time with the prominences. Sullivan encourages her students to do Irish dancing in the mouth!

One way of thinking of this is that we are preparing the learners' short-term memory to retain, and process quickly, any stretch of speech which comes their way (cf. Kjellin, 2017).

21.11.2 Using a transcript

Speed work can also be done using a transcript such as the one shown in Extract 21.3. This extract lasts about ten seconds and consists of ten speech units. Presenting an extract in this way has two advantages: first, it is unfamiliar to students, so they are less likely to treat it as a normal reading task; second, it indicates the way in which the speed of speech changes moment-by-moment.

The speed is shown in syllables per second (sps) at the end of each speech unit, so the slowest speech unit is 01 at 1.6 sps and the fastest is 07 at 9.4 sps. The speech units start slowly, with stepping stones (cf. Cauldwell 2013: 85) in units 01 and 04, during which the speaker dwells on words while deciding what to say next. And then, once he has decided what to say, he speeds up dramatically in units 07–10. This pattern of starting slow and ending fast is common in spontaneous speech. If you are a course book author, writing a script for actors to record, it would be well worth including instructions to the actors to vary their speaking speed in this way, in order to make the recording sound more natural.

EXTRACT 21.3

```
01 || THIS IS || 1.6
      [pause 1.0]
02 || a MANual || 5.3
      [pause 0.5]
03 || FOR BOTH|| 1.8
04 || READing || 3.8
05 || and WRITing || 4.0
06 || efFECtively || 7.1
07 || it's a MANual || 9.4
08 || well well it's MORE of a manual for WRIting in fact || 8.3
09 || even though it is for READing || 8.0
```

Voice: Geoff, UK.

Show the students the script (either on a handout, or projected on the whiteboard) and do a vocabulary check. Then play the extract twice and ask students for their comments. Have them tap the table in time with the prominent syllables as they listen again – play it as often as it takes for them to get the tapping in time. Next get them to vocalise in a way of their (or your) choosing as they listen – this could be humming, buzzing, going 'BAM ba ba BAM' or 'la-la-LA'. The point of the vocalisation is to get them to ride the stream of the sound substance at the original speeds. This will acclimatise them to the natural rhythms which are commonly found in spontaneous speech. Next, get them to simultaneously vocalise the sound substance and tap in time to the prominences. Play the extract as often as necessary to get them comfortable and familiar with its changing speeds.

Lastly, ask students to move on to saying the words in time without tapping, first focusing on the prominent syllables, and then the non-prominent ones. Afterwards, if they have any energy left, ask pairs of students to personalise the dialogue by replacing *manual*, *reading* and *writing* with words of their own choosing. They then practise performing them at the speeds of the original.

Unlike a standard listening comprehension lesson, this method of using vocal gymnastics and body movements with a known text will help students acquire the skill of handling spontaneous speech. For a step-by-step description about how to choose and teach an appropriate extract, see Pinard (2014).

21.12 Drafting phenomena

If your recording is of truly spontaneous speech it is likely to contain a lot of drafting phenomena, such as *like*, *kind of* and *you know*, which go very fast. This listening task requires a transcript with all the lines double-spaced (so that students can write notes between the lines), and with the fast drafting phenomena (*like, kind* of, and repetitions) edited out. The crucial feature of the transcript is that there should be no gaps indicating where the drafting phenomena had occurred. The students' task is to listen to the recording as many times as needed to identify the location of the drafting phenomena. The following are examples of the type of questions you might ask in such a task:

- Between which words does *you know* occur?

- How many times can you hear *like*?

- There are six versions of the word *like*: where are they, and which ones sound like *lack* and *lick*?

When you review the answers, always play the relevant part of the recording (a very short extract) and encourage your students to vocalise the words in the sound substance, saying them quietly to themselves, as they hear each repetition of the extract.

21.13 Summary and what's next

In this chapter we have covered a variety of activities that can be used with the sound substance of a recording and which will help your students decode speech more effectively, at speed. These activities can follow immediately after conventional work on meaning, in the same class, or they can occur as a follow-up in a later class.

The essential thing is that you make time for such decoding activities.

In Chapter 22 we will look at how conventional pen-and-paper activities can be used for the purpose of teaching decoding of the sound substance.

22 Pen-and-paper activities

In this chapter and the next we will look at how we can use our students' voices, together with conventional pen-and-paper activities to teach listening/decoding.

The activities are designed to help learners explore the cloud of soundshapes that belongs to, and surrounds, every word and word cluster that we find in the sound substance. We are exploring how approximate, indeterminate and variable the sound substance can be.

We describe how to:

- exploit minimal-pair activities
- use limericks to practise drafting phenomena
- exploit the transcript of a recording
- present and practise streamlining processes (e.g. d'eth-drop, the hiss effect)
- practise shifting prominences a game of dice

Each activity needs to be conducted at high speed, where the relevant words and speech units are spoken as fast as learners can manage. This is because fast speeds are the main reason for streamlining: if you are not going fast, then there is little reason to streamline.

Throughout all these activities, you will need to remind your students frequently that they are working towards the goal of listening/decoding. The activities may look, sound and feel like pronunciation activities, but they are best thought of as 'vocal gymnastics' – with students using their voices to become familiar and comfortable with the sound substance of Jungle speech.

22.1 During pronunciation activities

Whenever pronunciation minimal-pair work involves repetitions of the same phrases, you can encourage your students to vary the way in which they say them. For example, the 'Street maps' activity in Hancock's Pronpack 3 (Hancock, 2017: 32) requires students to identify locations of cafés by naming streets which have minimal-pair names. The task is to use this frame:

It's on the corner of _____ and _____ (opposite _____ Park).

Clearly, the activity will require multiple repetitions of *It's on the corner of* and *opposite*, both of which can be said in a variety of Jungle ways, while the street names are said with Greenhouse accuracy (e.g. *Bowl Street, Pole Street*).

Before the activity starts you can get students to play with a variety of ways of saying this frame in chorus. Extract 22.1 contains extremely clear Greenhouse versions (01–02), a Garden version (03), and extremely streamlined versions (cf. 04–05).

EXTRACT 22.1

```
01 || IT'S ON THE CORner OF … || OP PO SITE ||
02 || it's ON the CORner OF … || OPPosite ||
03 || it's ON the CORner of … || OPPosite ||
04 || 'sonna CORner of … || oppsit ||
05 || 'sonna CORnuff … || offsit ||
```

Voice: Richard, UK.

Notice that the Greenhouse versions do not need to be boring citation forms: units 01 and 02 feature mountainous versions (lots of ups-and-downs in pitch) of the citation forms.

The streamlining processes which apply in 04 and 05 are:

- *'sonna* results from the hiss effect (cf. Chapter 17.11)

- *oppsit* results from mid-clip (cf. Chapter 18.4.3)

- *cornuff* results from D.R.Y. (cf. Chapter 18.5)

- *offsit* results from p-blur (cf. general comment in Chapter 17.12)

Another activity from Hancock (2017: 45) similarly requires students to distinguish between the Greenhouse forms of pairs such as 'long jumper' (athlete) and 'long jumper' (clothing). Each of the six items in this exercise is preceded by a short stem such as *This is a …* or *My sister went out with a …* and *I didn't see …* which are easy to turn into Garden and Jungle forms. Extract 22.2 gives both Garden and Jungle forms of three of the six stems.

EXTRACT 22.2

```
01 || this is a picture of a BLACK bird ||
02 || sizza pitcher ovuh BLACK BIRD ||
02 || did you see the BUTCHer's shop ||
04 || dijewsee/diyousee a BUTCHer's SHOP ||
05 || my sister went out with a LONG jumper ||
06 || ma sissuh wenow wiffa LONG JUMPer ||
```

Voice: Richard, UK.

The odd-numbered units, 01, 03 and 05, give Greenhouse/Garden versions; the even-numbered units 02, 04 and 06 give Jungle versions. It is in the Jungle versions in 02, 04 and 06 that these streamlining processes apply:

- *sizza* results from the hiss effect on *this is a* (cf. Chapter 17.11)

- *dijewsee* results from a Tuesday-blend on *did you see* (cf. Chapter 18.4.1)

- *diyouseea* results from a d-drop on *did you* and d'eth-drop on *the* (cf. Chapter 17.6, 17.3)

- *ma* is a smoothie (cf. 18.1) *sissuh* results from the hiss effect on *sister* (17.11)

- *wenow* results from two t-drops on *went out* (cf. Chapter 17.10)
- *wiffa* results from an eth-blur on *with a* (cf. general comment in Chapter 17.12)

Students may say that they do not want these Jungle versions to influence their pronunciation. You will need to remind them constantly that the reason for the activity is to improve their listening/ decoding.

22.2 Limericks

Limericks are a popular device in teaching pronunciation (e.g. Mankowska et al., 2009; Vaughan-Rees, 2010). They are normally thought of as having a strong rhythm which – in our terms – is Garden-like. But they can be used to help make the transition between the Garden and the Jungle.

22.2.1 Drafting phenomena

Drafting phenomena occur at moments when speakers edit what they say as they are speaking: pauses, restarts, repetitions and references to speaker and listener roles (*you know, I mean*). It is useful to think of drafting phenomena as consisting of two different types: slow, level-tone stepping stones on syllables such as *um* and *uh* and on words such as *and* and *so*; and very fast non-prominent, difficult-to-perceive elements of the stream of speech such as *like* and *yeah* and clusters such as *you know* and *I mean*.

This limerick in Extract 22.3 consists largely of drafting phenomena, with the only clues to context being the words *feeling, tough* and *rough*. The purpose of the task is to help learners become familiar and comfortable with the rapid type of drafting phenomena *you know, I mean* and *like*.

STEP 1
Give students the script of the limerick and ask them to read it to themselves slowly, making the syllables in bold prominent. Explain that the limerick does not mean much – it simply demonstrates a selection of drafting phenomena.

STEP 2
Then play Extract 22.3, in which the drafting phenomena are spoken at fast but entirely normal speeds (averaging 5 syllables per second). In this limerick *wow* rhymes with *know*.

EXTRACT 22.3

I **mean** you **know** yeah like **wow**!
Um **wow** yeah I **mean** yeah you **know**
That was **sort** of like **tough**
And **kind** of like **rough**
I mean **um** you know **yeah** like **wow**!

STEP 3

Once students have mastered this, give them the limerick in Extract 22.4 and practise it Garden style.

EXTRACT 22.4

There **was** a young **den**tist called **Tim**
Who **cleaned** people's **teeth** in the **gym.**
On the **run**ning ma**chine**
He **brushed** their teeth **clean**
Now **Tim's** very **slim** in the **gym.**

STEP 4

Once this version is mastered, give them the version shown in Extract 22.5. This version has drafting phenomena inserted which are spoken much faster than the other words of the limerick. The students should practise saying the extract in such a way that the rhythm of the limerick is preserved, as demonstrated in Extract 22.5, and the drafting phenomena are slipped in very quickly.

EXTRACT 22.5

like There *um* **was** a young **den**tist called *like* **Tim**
I mean Who **cleaned** people's *you know* **teeth** in the **gym.**
you know On the **run**ning *kind of* ma**chine**
He *sort of* **brushed** their teeth **clean**
Now *yeah like* **Tim's** very **slim** in the **gym.**

It is important, once again, to remind your students that they are doing this to improve their listening/decoding. These are vocal gymnastic exercises which – although they are using their voices – are not aimed at improving their pronunciation. Students may ask why they should bother with drafting phenomena, since they are not meaning-bearing. The answer is that they often occur in the sound substance of spontaneous speech, and one of our goals is to teach everything that occurs in the sound substance to help them with listening/decoding.

22.2.2 Word clusters

The limerick in Extract 22.6 contains the word clusters *there was this*, *did not go to*, *just went* and *so he went to the*. It is derived from an extract of spontaneous speech (cf. Cauldwell, 2013: 108) where Dan describes losing his voice when he started to sing solo in public.

EXTRACT 22.6

There **was** this **man** called **Dan**
Whose **sing**ing did **not** go to **plan**
His **voice** just went **aaahh**
So he **went** to the **bar**
'Poor **you**!' said his **best** friend **Diane**

STEP 1

Give students the script of the limerick and ask them to read it slowly, making the bold syllables prominent.

STEP 2

Then play them Extract 22.6 and encourage them to repeat the limerick at the same speed as the extract.

STEP 3

Give them the script of Extract 22.7 – this is a version of the same limerick, but there are only two prominences in the first two lines, and in lines 3 and 4 there is just one. In the first four lines, the words before the first prominence are treated as word clusters, and they are going to be streamlined to make them into Jungle forms.

STEP 4

Ask them to read the limerick to each other, making the words before each prominent syllable as fast as possible.

EXTRACT 22.7

There was this **man** called **Dan**
Whose singing did **not** go to **plan**
His voice just went **aaahh**
So he went to the **bar**
'Poor **you**!' said his **best** friend Di**ane**

STEP 5

Then play the recording, and ask students what they notice about the opening words of the first four lines. The list below shows what they should notice.

- *there was this* sounds close to *airwaziss*

- *whose singing did* sounds close to *hoossingindit*

- *his voice juss went* sounds close to *hisvoyjusswen*

- *so he went to the* sounds close to *soywentuhthuh*

STEP 6

Ask them, in pairs, to prepare a performance of the Jungle version of the limerick, with one student performing the Jungle parts with the word clusters, and the other performing the parts with prominent syllables:

- Student 1: *airwaziss* – Student 2: ***man** called **Dan***

- Student 1: *hoossingindit* – Student 2: ***not** go to **plan**.*

Again, you need to remind your students that the goal of this activity is the listening/decoding of word clusters, not pronunciation.

22.3 Transcript

Although the transcript of a recording is – because it is written – essentially a misrepresentation of the sound substance (cf. Chapter 12.7), it can nevertheless be a useful tool for decoding work. Below are two ways in which this might be done.

22.3.1 Find the syllables

This is an adaptation of the activity by Grinberg introduced in Chapter 21.10. You can use this activity with any sentence or paragraph that students have in front of them. The example below is from a pre-intermediate course book, but you can use the technique with any text at any level.

STEP 1

Give students the text below but without the underlining. Note that the first two underlined stretches are single syllables (-*stan* and -*layed*) and that the remaining three underlined stretches use segments and syllables that belong to neighbouring words (-*cy foo-*, -*ical sup* and -*st wee-*)

Ask them to read the paragraph aloud to themselves, savouring the words (enjoying the feeling of each word in their mouths) as they do so. (Remember, they do not see the underlining.)

> In Pakistan, heavy rain has delayed relief efforts as the army tries to get emergency food and medical supplies to the victims of last week's floods, which destroyed towns and villages in the north of the country. (Redston & Cunningham 2012: 165)

NB The underlined stretches do not necessarily contain word-stressed syllables. In fact it is best if they are a mixture of stressed and unstressed syllables.

STEP 2

Then you say each underlined stretch of sound substance in turn and then ask learners to identify the word(s) in which the stretches of sound substance occur. The list below shows what their answers should be.

- *stan* |stæn| – *Pakistan*
- *layed* |leɪd| – *delayed*
- *cy foo* |sifuː| – *emergency food*
- *icalsupp* |ɪklsʌp| – *medical supplies*
- *stwee* |stwiː| – *last week's*

STEP 3

Then ask pairs of students to prepare – on their own – a similar task, either on the same paragraph (but they must choose different syllables), or another paragraph. When they have finished their preparation, re-set the classroom, so that the students who designed the task are now separated and are paired up with a different classmate. In the new pairs, the students run their activity in the same manner in which you ran the whole-class version.

22.3.2 Predict from transcript

This activity involves looking at the transcript, before listening to a recording, to predict which sections will be fast and mushy, and which will be clear and intelligible. The best way to do this is in two parts, with part 1 preparing students by helping them get accustomed to the voices on the recording, so that they can do the main section of the activity in part 2.

STEP 1

Choose two short extracts (between 5 and 10 seconds, the first much shorter than the second) from a recording, and prepare a transcript for each. The transcript should have numbered lines so that students can refer to them easily. Both extracts should contain stretches of speech from the same person. Students are going to focus on just this one voice.

STEP 2

Give the transcript of the first extract, Part 1, to the students and ask them to predict, in pairs, which sections of the transcript they expect to be Jungle-like and which sections they expect to be Garden-like. Ask them to read the transcript to each other according to their predictions. After a few minutes' work, elicit opinions from the whole class.

STEP 3

Play the recording twice, and ask if there were any surprises for them. Then have the students read the transcript to each other in the style and timing of the original. Extract 22.8 gives an example of one such text.

EXTRACT 22.8

Part 1: First day there, I went for a staff meeting. And they said uh, right we don't have a technology teacher, we don't have any technology teachers.

Voice: Emily, UK.

On hearing it they might comment that (as my students did):

- *uh* sounds like *the* or *that*

- *we don't have any* sounds like *we have many*

STEP 4

Give students the second extract, Part 2, and ask them to read it to each other slowly and clearly, and then at increasing speeds.

STEP 5

Now that they are familiar with the words of Part 2, remind them of the Jungle sections of Part 1, and ask them to predict which sections of Part 2 will be most Jungle-like, which most Garden-like, and which most Greenhouse-like.

STEP 6

Play them the recording as many times as they need to make their judgements. Extract 22.9 gives an example which follows on from the previous extract.

EXTRACT 22.9

> Part 2: So um now you're head of technology for the entire school of about fifteen hundred pupils. And we don't have any equipment to do technologies so you have a blackboard and this workbook and um yeah just get on with it.

Voice: Emily, UK.

This time they might comment that:

- *fifteen hundred* sounds like *fifty hundred*
- *pupils* sounds like *peoples*
- they cannot hear *any* in *any equipment*

STEP 7

Ask them, in pairs, to prepare a performance of one of the extracts, either Part 1 or Part 2, with one student making the extract as Jungle-like as possible and the other student making the extract as Greenhouse/Garden-like as possible.

Again, you will need to reassure them that they are doing this to help them with listening/decoding rather than pronunciation.

22.4 Jungle processes – streamlining

We now move to activities which focus on some of the streamlining processes that were covered in some detail in Part 3, Chapters 17 and 18.

22.4.1 D'eth-drop

D'eth-drop is a very common streamlining process which affects function words such as *the, there, then* and so on which begin with |ð|, the symbol known as *eth* (cf. Chapter 17.3). This activity practises (for the goal of listening/decoding) the occurrence of d'eth-drop in the word clusters which occur at the beginning of four clauses.

STEP 1
Begin by playing the example speech unit (or a similar example of your own) such as the one in Extract 22.10.

EXTRACT 22.10
|| and then THAT was THAT ||

Voice: Dan, UK.

After playing the example, tell students about the streamlining that happens here: d'eth-drop has occurred at the beginning of the three words *then*, *that* and *that*. Tell them that d'eth-drop can also occur after |l| — *all there* can become something close to *all air*; and after |s| — *stops there* can become something close to *stops air*.

STEP 2
Show students the transcript of Extract 22.11 and ask them to read the speech units slowly, savouring the words in their Greenhouse and Garden forms. This extract is a version of the end of the 'Pied Piper' fairy tale.

EXTRACT 22.11
01 || and then they FOUND themselves in a big CAVE together ||
02 || and then the PIper stopped PIping ||
03 || that was the LAST that we SAW of them ||
04 || all those POOR young CHILDren ||

STEP 3
Ask them to look carefully at each speech unit, and to identify opportunities for 'd'eth-drop'. As they do so, they should speak the speech units at increasing speeds in order to justify these streamlining effects.

- in 01 *and then they* should become *aneney* |əneneɪ|
- in 01 *found themselves* should become *fownemselves* |faʊnemselvz|
- in 02 *and then the* should become *anenuh* |ənenə|
- in 03 *that was the* should become *thatwasuh* |ðæʔwɔzə|
- in 03 *last that* should become *lass at* |lɑːsəʔ|
- in 04 *all those* should become *allose* |ɔːləʊz|

STEP 4

Ask students, in pairs, to prepare a performance of these four speech units, first as Greenhouse/Garden versions, and then as a Jungle version.

You will need to remind them that this activity is designed to help improve their listening/decoding – it is not aimed at improving their pronunciation.

22.4.2 T-drop, t-blur

Lots of things happen to |t|. Because I am Irish by birth, I like |t| to become like an Irish |t| which sounds as though it is blended with |s| – indeed the symbol that is used to represent this sound is |ʂ| ('s' *with right tail*). Below is a list of this and other things that can happen to |t|:

- blur into a tap resulting in *letter* becoming *ledder* |leɾə|
- blur into an Irish |t| resulting in *letter* becoming close to *lesser* |leʂə|
- blur into a glottal stop resulting in *letter* becoming *leh-uh* |leʔə|
- be dropped entirely (t-drop) resulting in *letter* becoming *lair* |leə|

Here is an activity which gives students the chance to become familiar and comfortable with these variations in the |t| sound.

STEP 1

Play the four speech units in Extract 22.12 one at a time, and ask students to focus on the soundshape of *letter*. The speech units of the extract contain the streamlining processes given in brackets at the end of each line. Students listen and imitate them.

EXTRACT 22.12
```
01 || the LETter came YESterday || [tap]
02 || the LETter came YESterday || [Irish t]
03 || the LETter came YESterday || [glottal stop]
04 || the LETter came YESterday || [t-drop]
```

Voice: Richard, UK.

STEP 2

Give students a copy of the transcript of Extract 22.13. Play this extract and ask students to decide which of the occurrences of |t| are a tap (they write **1**) an Irish t (**2**) glottal stop (**3**) and a t-drop (**4**). The answer to this activity is given in the Answer Key.

EXTRACT 22.13
```
01 || it's BETter if you WAIT over THERE ||
02 || just TAKE a SEAT ||
```

```
03 || she's GETting it for you NOW||
04 || and i'll SEE you in a little WHILE ||
```

Voice: Richard, UK.

STEP 3

Elicit the answers from the class, then play the extract one speech unit at a time, and have the class repeat each unit in chorus, ensuring that they use the 'Irish t', glottal stop, taps and t-drops as appropriate for each speech unit.

STEP 4

To end the activity, the students say all four of these speech units to each other four times: first all the speech units should have taps, then they should all have Irish |t|, then glottal stops, and finally t-drops.

Remind them that this activity is for listening/decoding, not pronunciation.

22.4.3 Hiss effect

The hiss effect occurs when the fricatives |s z ʃ| and the affricates |tʃ dʒ| dominate or even obliterate neighbouring sounds. For example, the cluster *is that it's very* may well become *isassferry* |ɪzasferɪ|. Particularly vulnerable is |t|, whether it occurs after |s| as in *most* (*most sensible way* becomes *mowsensible way*), or before |s| as in *it's* (*it's wonderful* becomes *'swonderful*). Table 22.1 shows a matching activity which practises the hiss effect.

STEP 1

Give pairs of students a copy of Table 22.1. Explain that the task is to match the mush of the folk spellings on the left of the table with the sentences on the right. (Each item of folk spelling only applies to the underlined part of its corresponding sentence, not to all of it.)

TABLE 22.1

	Folk spellings	Symbols		Sentences	
A	isassis	ɪzasɪs	1	He says it's going to be great	
B	scum be	skəmbi	2	It's in the kitchen	
C	sinner	sɪnə	3	I think it's just awful	
D	speesuh	spiːsə	4	Look and see that he's gone	

E	issshuss	ɪssʃʌs	5	They used to have a nice house	
F	you suffer	juːsʌfə	6	He was the first to go	
G	cease	siːs	7	She said it's a piece of cake	
H	uhfurssuh	əfɜːsə	8	The problem is that it's very fast	A

STEP 2

Drill the folk spellings, making sure that students are able to produce them at different speeds – but do not decode them.

STEP 3

Tell them that item A: *isassis* goes with item 8: *The problem is that it's very fast*, and that it corresponds to the words *is that it's*. Ask them to mouth and savour Garden and Jungle versions of the sentence so that they can produce both clear and mushy versions.

STEP 4

Ask students to work in pairs to find which sentences in the right-hand column the other seven folk-spelling items belong to. The answers are given in the Answer Key.

STEP 5

Elicit answers from the class. Then ask them to perform the sentences in Garden and Jungle styles.

Remind them that the activity is designed for listening/decoding practice, not for pronunciation.

22.4.4 Polarisk

A polarisk |pəʊˈlæ.rɪsk| occurs when words and syllables which indicate negative meaning (e.g. contracted *did not*, and prefixes such as *il-* in *illegal*) are often streamlined to such an extent that it is difficult to determine from the sound substance alone whether a positive or a negative meaning is intended (cf. Chapter 18.3).

The task here is to identify potential problems in the speech units of Extract 22.14, recreate them, and then suggest ways – both as a speaker, and as a listener – that any confusion can be avoided.

STEP 1

Display the speech units of Extract 22.14 on the whiteboard. Ask students to say the speech units aloud to themselves, making sure that they make the differences between prominent syllables loud and clear, and the non-prominent syllables fast and unclear.

STEP 2

Play the extract two or three times, and ask students if the lines of the transcript contain an accurate transcription of the sound substance.

EXTRACT 22.14

```
01 || unLIKE the REST of them ||
02 || he wasn't KNOWN to the seCURity services ||
03 || what he did was ACTually ilLEGal ||
```

Voice: Richard, UK.

The extract has been deliberately recorded so that an equally reasonable transcription would have no negative morphemes such as *un-* in *unlike*, *-n't* in *wasn't*, and so on.

- 01 *and like – unlike* – potential confusion arises because the negative prefix *-un-* $|n|$ sounds like the weak form of *and*

- 02 *was known – wasn't known* – potential confusion arises because the $|t|$ at the end of *wasn't* is dropped and the resulting $|n|$ combines with, and may overlap the $|n|$ at the beginning of *known*

- 03 *actually legal – actually illegal* – potential confusion arises because the $|ɪ|$ at the end of *actually* combines with, and may overlap the $|ɪ|$ at the beginning of *illegal*

STEP 3

Then display the speech units of Extract 22.15 and follow the same procedure: students read the extract aloud to themselves, then they listen two or three more times.

STEP 4

Tell them (if they do not already realise) that the recordings were the same both times, and that the sound substance is neither clearly version 1 (negative version) nor clearly version 2 (affirmative version).

EXTRACT 22.15

```
01 || and LIKE the REST of them ||
02 || he was KNOWN to the seCURity services ||
03 || what he did was ACTually LEGal ||
```

Voice: Richard, UK.

STEP 5

Ask students, in pairs, to practise saying both Extract 22.14 and Extract 22.15 in Greenhouse/Garden and then Jungle styles, starting with slow, clear versions, and then spending time working at speed to make the negative syllables unclear. Remind them that this is not to improve their pronunciation, but to improve their listening/decoding.

STEP 6

Elicit from the class how they would ensure that they, as speakers, would be able to deliver both a clear negative version, or a clear positive version. They should suggest

- 'say *unlike* and *and like* in the Greenhouse or Garden form'

- 'say *was known* and *wasn't known* in the Greenhouse or Garden form'

- 'say *actually legal* and *actually illegal* in the Greenhouse or Garden form'

STEP 7

Then elicit from the students how, as listeners, they would check what was actually said in order to avoid misunderstanding:

- Excuse me, did you say AND LIKE, or UN LIKE?

- Sorry, did you say WAS KNOWN or WAS NOT KNOWN?

- Excuse me, did you say LEGAL or IL LEGAL?

They should practise saying these sentences in their Greenhouse/Garden form because these questions need to be clear and intelligible.

22.4.5 Consonant death

The purpose of this activity is to help students with areas of the Jungle where whole sequences of consonants disappear. To do this we take a sentence and remove all the non-initial consonants – except for the last word, which we leave intact.

STEP 1

Write the sentence below on the Greenhouse (left-hand-side) of the whiteboard and, as you do so, say each word in its Greenhouse (carefully articulated) form. Encourage students to repeat these Greenhouse forms after you as you write them.

WOULD YOU LIKE ANy HELP?

STEP 2

Then go the middle of the whiteboard and write up a Garden version – but this time using uppercase letters for the first and last words, and then a second Garden version emphasising the linking.

WOULD you like any HELP?
WOU‿jew‿lie‿kenny HELP |wʊʤuːlaɪkenihelp|

Ask students to repeat after you as before.

STEP 3

Then move to the right-hand-side of the board and write a repeat of what you wrote in the

Garden section, but this time you cross out all syllable-final consonants, except on the last word

WOU~~LD~~ you li~~ke~~ a~~ny~~ HELP
WOU you lie a-e HELP |wʊjuːlaɪeːhelp|

Drill this so that learners can say it very fast.

STEP 4

Then ask the students to look at Table 22.2 (in a handout), which contains this sentence, along with two others. Remind them that columns 5 and 3 are crush zones (also known as squeeze zones). Ask them to cross out all syllable-final consonants in columns 5 and 3 (except |s|). They begin with the sentence that you have already worked on.

TABLE 22.2

	5	4	3	2	1
01		WOULD	you like any	HELP	
02	let me	KNOW	if you need a	DIFF	erent style
03	jackie's	AL	ready bought a white	DRESS	today

They should do the following:

- *you like any* becomes *you lie a-e* |juːlaɪjei|

- *let me* and *if you need a* become *lemme* and *iyouneeya* |lemi| and |ɪjuːniːə|

- *Jackie's* and *ready bought a white* become *jahees* and *rayee bore a why* |dʒæiːz| + |reibɔːrəwaɪ|

STEP 5

Elicit answers from the class, and make changes on the board.

STEP 6

Pairs then perform these speech units at speed, taking particular care to make the words in the crush zones of Columns 5 and 3 unclear and crushed.

Remember, always finish with some speed work. Speed is the main reason for streamlining, so if you are not going fast, then there is no reason to streamline.

22.5 Dice it up

The purpose of this activity is to practise different patterns of rhythm of speech units by placing prominences on different syllables. This is necessary because in the Jungle, prominence placement is very unruly (cf. Appendix 1 for the difference between prominence and word stress).

STEP 1
Write a phrase or sentence with six words on the whiteboard – for example

```
this is the way we go
```

STEP 2
Give a volunteer student two dice, then ask him or her to throw them and tell you what the numbers are. If the dice show 'two' and 'four', then you say the sentence with prominences on the second and fourth word and get the class to repeat in chorus:

```
this IS the WAY we go
```

STEP 3
Ask for another throw of the dice. If the dice show 'one' and 'six', then you say the sentence with the prominences on the first and sixth word:

```
THIS is the way we GO
```

And if the throw of the dice gives 'three' and 'four':

```
this is THE WAY we go
```

If the throw of the dice gives you the same number ('two' and 'two') then you can either ask the student to throw again, or say a single-prominence version of the sentence, with double the loudness and pitch movement on the prominent syllable.

So two 'four's would give

```
this is the WAY we go
```

(Do not worry if this seems an unlikely way to say these words. Remember, anything can happen in the Jungle.)

STEP 4
Then turn this activity over to pairs of students, using the following seven speech units all of which have six words. Most of the words have only one syllable, but *feeling* in 04 and *very* in 06 have two. The prominence should go on the first syllables (the word stress) of these words if the dice require it. Notice that the speech units have a horror story theme. Encourage rapid, panicky speech.

HORROR STORY

```
01 i don't know where we are
02 i think we might be lost
03 do you know where we are
04 i am feeling a bit scared
05 let's not go down there please
06 it looks very damp and dark
07 please let's get out of here
```

STEP 5

Have each pair join another pair to form groups of four. Tell one pair to be the dice-throwers, and the other pair to be the speakers. The dice-throwing pair throws the dice and instructs one member of the other pair to say the first sentence/speech unit. The dice-throwers then judge whether this sentence was correctly spoken, i.e. that the prominences fell on the syllables that correspond to the dice numbers. Then they do the same – as fast as possible – for the next sentence.

Students might object that the words *the* or *a* would never in real life receive prominences. Tell them that for the purposes of this listening/decoding activity, and indeed in spontaneous speech, anything can happen.

22.6 Summary and what's next

This chapter has demonstrated how listening/decoding can be improved by direct teaching and practising of streamlining processes. These activities share the overall goal of all listening/decoding activities, namely to make learners familiar and comfortable with the features of normal, fast everyday speech. Throughout I have emphasised the need to do vocal gymnastics, and to work at speed. The sound substance has to be animated by the voices of the students in your class, so that they become gradually more familiar with the unruly nature of the Jungle. In Chapter 23 we will continue looking at how we can find opportunities to do this.

23 Visiting the sound substance dimension

In the language classroom the sound substance comes second – by a long way – to the sight substance of writing: the sound substance is taught and learned through the obscuring veil of writing (cf. Chapter 1). This chapter gives you ideas for increasing the amount of work on the sound substance in the language classroom.

The two substances, sight and sound, are parallel dimensions between which you and your students can shift back and forth at a moment's notice, for activities which can vary in length from a few seconds to a minute or two. This shifting between dimensions does not require a recording. Ideally, every time a short stretch of language is **looked at**, it also should be **sounded out** – vocally played with – in ways which respect its multi-shaped and invisible fleetingness. We will look at opportunities to go dimension-hopping in these items:

- rubrics
- back-chaining
- rounds
- earworms
- classroom management
- introducing new language
    - vocabulary
    - grammar
- reading
- streamlining of the week
- mondegreens

We will also continue the work of Chapter 22 – using vocal gymnastics to see how playing with the sound substance can improve listening/decoding.

23.1 Rubrics – mountainous and monotonous

One example of an opportunity to slip momentarily into the sound substance dimension are the rubrics (instructions) given in the students' course books. We will use one rubric to illustrate two vocal gymnastic exercises – the 'monotonic drone', and 'making mountains'.

Rubrics which use the same words throughout a book (e.g. *explain briefly*, *discuss in pairs*, and so on) can be used to switch from the sight substance to the sound substance dimension. The art is to play with the soundscape of the rubric, exploring other possible ways in which its component words, and the rubric as a whole, might be said.

Take this rubric from New Cutting Edge Upper Intermediate (Cunningham & Moor 2005: 18)

Close your book and explain briefly to your partner what you learnt from the article.

STEP 1

First read the rubric aloud in Greenhouse form, but make your reading entertaining, by bouncing around your vocal range by going first high then low in pitch (this is 'being mountainous') and using a variety of tones. An example is given in Extract 23.1.

EXTRACT 23.1

```
01 || CLOSE YOUR BOOK ||
02 || AND exPLAIN BRIEFly TO YOUR PARTner ||
03 || WHAT YOU LEARNT FROM THE ARTicle ||
```

Voice: Richard, UK.

STEP 2

Next read the rubric in a smooth drone (this is 'being monotonous'), as if you are stirring double dairy cream into slowly melting thick chocolate (to make chocolate mousse). Extract 23.2 gives you an example. Blend words wherever possible, giving particular emphasis to the sounds which happen where words are smoothly blended into neighbouring words (connected speech rules are at work here).

EXTRACT 23.2

```
closeyourbookand_explaimbrieflytoyourpartner
wha_chewlearntfromthearticle
```

Voice: Richard, UK. Note that what you undergoes Tuesday-blending (cf. Chapter 18.4.1).

Students repeat after you, and then produce their own monotonous versions.

STEP 3

Move into the Garden, mixing the best of the linking of the monotonic drone in Extract 23.2 and the mountains of Extract 23.1. Extract 23.3 demonstrates one way in which this might be done. Students repeat after you, and then perform their own mountainous versions.

EXTRACT 23.3

```
01 || CLOSE your BOOK ||
02 || and exPLAIN BRIEFly to your PARTner ||
03 || what you LEARNT from the ARTicle ||
```

Extract 23.3 provides only one way of reading this rubric. Other versions are possible. For example, you can vary the pitch of every prominence, and vary the tone on the last prominence in each speech unit (on *book*, *part-* and *art-*).

Students repeat after you, and then perform their own Garden versions.

STEP 4

Now move on to a Jungle version – an example is given in Extract 23.4 which is very much faster, and far less mountainous, than the Garden version in Extract 23.3.

EXTRACT 23.4
```
01 || close your BOOK ||
02 || and exPLAIN briefly to your PARTner ||
03 || what you LEARNT from the article ||
```

Voice: Richard, UK.

In the soundscape of Extract 23.4, there is one fewer prominence per speech unit than in Extract 23.3. There are also some other significant differences due to the streamlining processes that have occurred:

- the contours of the tones are very shallow

- in 01 *book* ends with a glottal stop

- in 03 *what you* |wɒtʃuː| is a Tuesday-blend (cf. Chapter 18.4.1)

STEP 5

Students repeat after you, and then perform their own Jungle versions.

Extract 23.4 gives only one of many possible Jungle versions. When the same or a similar rubric occurs again, you can ask your students to perform the rubric in different ways. For example, you can give a monotonic drone and then ask them to give you a mountainous version, followed by a Jungle version.

23.2 Back-chaining

As with rubrics in course books, classroom instructions also provide many opportunities for vocal gymnastics. We will use an instruction from Willis (1981) to demonstrate a key technique for handling speed, namely 'back-chaining'.

As has been mentioned frequently, it is vital that speed work is a major component of all vocal gymnastics. The technique of back-chaining not only helps with speed, it is also a very useful tool for making long speech units manageable.

The technique involves drilling short sections of a stretch of speech starting from the end and proceeding backwards, adding further short sections until learners master the whole speech unit. Extract 23.5 gives a three-prominence speech unit example of an instruction that a teacher might give.

EXTRACT 23.5 BACK-CHAINING

```
                                            || ... we'll STOP ... || x 3
                              || ... and then we'll STOP ... || x 3
                    || ... the TASK and then we'll STOP ... || x 3
          || ... just FINish the TASK and then we'll STOP ... || x 3
```

Voice: Richard, UK.

This back-chaining technique can be used on any speech unit that students find challenging, and not just classroom instructions.

23.3 Round

A 'round' is a song or chant in which two or three people sing exactly the same words and tune, but start at different times, so that when all the participants are singing they are at different points in the song, and the resulting sound is (usually) harmonious. Well-known examples include 'Row, row, row your boat' and 'Three blind mice'.

The purpose of this activity is to familiarise learners with different soundshapes associated with the word cluster *have you got any*. The activity is best done in small groups of three or four students, but it will start with a whole-class phase. Although a round is usually associated with singing, we will ask students to chant.

Table 23.1 has three versions of *have you got any change*. Row 01 has a Greenhouse version, row 02 has a Garden version, and row 03 has a Jungle version. In Row 02 *have you* is shown as *haffew* |hæfjuː| and *got any* is shown as *gotenny* |gɒteni|; in Row 03 *have you got any* is shown as *haffew gonny* |hæfjuː gɒni|. (The words have undergone the following streamlining processes: *have* – v-blur (cf. Chapter 17.8), so that it sounds close to |f|, and the three syllables of *got any* have undergone t-drop (cf. Chapter 17.5) and syllablend (cf. Chapter 18.4.1) to give us *gonny*.

TABLE 23.1 EXTRACT 23.6

	1	2	3	4	5
01	HAVE	YOU	GOT	ANy	CHANGE
02	haffew	gotenny	haffew	gotenny	CHANGE
03	haffew gonny	haffew gonny	haffew gonny	haffew gonny	CHANGE

Voices: Richard and Jane, UK.

STEP 1

Show your students the table, and explain what is in each row. Explain that this is a shopping context, where one friend asks another for some coins in order to pay a small amount of money for a soft drink. Elicit from them what other words might occur in other contexts instead of *change* in column 5. Write them on the whiteboard, (possibilities include *children, food* and *friends*) and say that we will use this list at the end of the activity.

STEP 2

Start a regular beat using your hand to tap the table and say *one, two, three, four, five*; and then, going at the same rhythm, say the words in Row 01, then 02, and then 03.

STEP 3

Then conduct the whole class in doing exactly the same as you have just done in chorus.

STEP 4

Divide the class into three groups and name them A, B and C. Tell group A that, on your signal, they should start with Row 01, and B and C should keep quiet, waiting for your signal to start. When group A gets to the end of Row 01, you then signal to group B to start on Row 01 so that they are chanting at the same time as group A who are now on Row 02. And when group A is starting on Row 03, you signal to group C to start. Have them continue the round until all groups have said all the rows at least three times.

STEP 5

Divide the class into groups of three. Ask each group to decide who is student A, B or C.

STEP 6

Explain that they are going to perform the round as a group. On your signal, student A will start tapping the rhythm and will then read Row 01 at the rhythm he/she has established. As student A is about to start Row 02, student B starts Row 1. Last to join in is student C who starts speaking

Row 1 as student B is on Row 02. By now student A should have started the Jungle version in Row 03, and all three students are contributing to the round, simultaneously chanting their respective lines.

STEP 7
Each group continues the round, until – after four repetitions – first student A, then B and finally C stop chanting.

STEP 8
Then student B starts tapping again at a faster speed, and she/he speaks Row 1 to the new faster rhythm. Students C and A join in as described above, as B reaches the end of each row.

STEP 9
To end the activity, ask students to substitute the word *change* with their choice of the other words you wrote on the board at the start of the activity. They then chant this different word as they go through the rows.

Rounds such as this are an important feature of Cauldwell (2016). Some groups of students do not react well to this type of activity (particularly in early-morning classes), others enjoy it immensely.

23.4 Earworms

An 'earworm' is a short, catchy piece of music which sticks in your head and keeps repeating itself. I find that music by Hank Williams sticks around in my head (*Why don't you love me like you used to do? How come you treat me like a worn-out shoe?*). When I asked friends for advice on a cure, they said that the only cures were (a) another earworm (Abba's *Waterloo* or Boney M's *Brown Girl in the Ring*) or (b) time – you just have to wait until it goes away.

If we can capture this earworm mechanism and plant playful variations of word-cluster-loaded speech units into learners' brains, then we will be helping them to become familiar and comfortable with fast speech. Extract 23.7 is an example, using the words *Would you like a receipt with that?*

EXTRACT 23.7
```
|| would you like a receipt with that ||
```

The extract contains nine versions (including Greenhouse, Garden and Jungle versions) with interpolations of playful mondegreens *july* and *liar* for *would**you**like* and *like‿a*.

STEP 1
Play the recording (it's just over twenty seconds long) several times, encouraging the class to join in and get up to speed. Getting up to speed can mean them wiggling their fingers in time or conducting each recording.

STEP 2

Ask them to count how many times they hear the question. Also ask them which words occur that are not in the transcript. (Accept all answers.)

STEP 3 HOMEWORK

Ask them to memorise this earworm (explain the reason – it is to make them familiar and comfortable with fast spoken English), and to say it to themselves as they walk home from class. Tell them you will ask them to repeat it in the next lesson, but with different words replacing *a receipt*. (Possibilities include *a bag, some chips, some salad, some salt* and *some ketchup*.)

If your class includes students who are interested in rap or other kinds of rhythmic music, you can appoint one or more of them to listen for opportunities in class to make an earworm of rhythmic chunks of language which occur in the course of your teaching. You can use their skills to take the opportunity to slip into the sound substance dimension by creating an earworm.

You will need to remind them that the purpose is to improve listening/decoding, not their pronunciation.

23.5 Classroom language

Teaching typically involves many activities which are both routine, and repeated. These repetitions present opportunities for helping learners to become familiar and comfortable with the Jungle mode of speech. The tools you need for these activities are the botanic walk (cf. Chapter 20.2 – Greenhouse, Garden, Jungle), the word-crusher and the process of consonant death.

At the beginning of the first lesson of a week, a common way to open a class is to ask students questions such as *Did you have a nice weekend?* or *Did anyone do anything interesting?* You might then say *Could you open your books, please, at page ten?* Then you might say: *By the end of the lesson you'll be able to…* and later: *Now this is about what we did last lesson* and *Just finish the task and then we'll stop.* (All examples are from Willis, 1981.)

One way of exploiting these classroom instructions is to say them in the three modes (Greenhouse, Garden, Jungle) the first few times that you need to give them. And when students have become accustomed to hearing the three versions, you can ask them to contribute different versions – you say a mountainous Greenhouse version (see Section 23.1), and then they give Garden and Jungle versions.

EXTRACT 23.8

- JAffa nice weekEND

- DENnyone dooWENnything INtresting

- couyouwopenyuhBOOKS pleess appage TEN

23.6 Introducing new language

There are many types of activity that occur in a language teaching lesson: vocabulary, grammar, reading, and so on. Below I illustrate how conventional ways of doing these activities can be adapted so that they include the sound substance dimension.

23.7 Vocabulary

When introducing new vocabulary, choose one of the new words and take it for a botanic walk (cf. Chapter 20.2). Choose a word to which you can easily apply some streamlining effects.

Redston and Cunningham (2012: 10) have a list of seventeen words for free-time activities which include: *museums, running, basketball, festivals* and *chess*. Of these, I chose the three-syllable word *festivals* because it seems to me to be easily subjected to three streamlining processes:

- the hiss effect (cf. Chapter 17.11) of |s| can drown out the |t|, resulting in *fessivals*

- the hiss effect can also drown out the vowel |ɪ| of the second syllable, and therefore cause a syll-drop (cf. 18.4), leaving just two syllables – *fessvals*

- the |l| can undergo the vow-ell process (cf. 18.2) resulting in *fessvoos*.

But in order for these streamlining processes to be justified, we need more than just the word itself; we need some co-text – neighbouring words to go in front of and after it. Preferably, these should be words which frequently collocate with this word, and which will enable us to get it into a squeeze zone between two prominences. The Longman Dictionary of Contemporary English gives us the following example: *the Swansea festival of music and the arts* which, in Garden mode, would be a four-prominence speech unit as in Extract 23.9.

EXTRACT 23.9

|| the SWANsea FEStival of MUSic and the ARTS ||

Voice: Richard, UK.

This speech unit would be ideal for practising clear intelligible pronunciation, complying as it does with the Careful Speech Model (cf. Chapter 13.1). For the purpose of listening/decoding it needs to be placed in the word-crusher (cf. Chapter 20.3) with just two prominences and with *festival* in a crush zone in the non-prominent Column 3, as shown in Table 23.2.

TABLE 23.2 EXTRACT 23.10

	5	4	3	2	1
01	(crush)	BANG!	(crush)	BANG!	(relax)
02	the	SWAN	sea festival of	MUS	ic and the arts

STEP 1

Drill a slow version of the speech unit, but make sure that the prominent syllables (columns 4 and 2) are much louder and clearer than the non-prominent syllables, and ensure that the syllables in column 1 -*ic and the art* slow down and become quieter.

STEP 2

Slowly speed up, drilling the class as you go, and encouraging them to gesture (tap their desks, shadow box) the rhythm. You will end up with something like *fessvoof* for *festival of*, in which four syllables become two: *fes.ti.val.of* becomes *fess.voof*. The streamlining has involved the following processes:

- *fes.tiv.al* – *fess.i.val* – hiss effect/t-drop
- *fess.i.val* – *fess.val* – hiss effect/syll-drop
- *fess.val* – *fess.voo* – vow-ell
- and |v| – from *of* – is blurred to |f| and added to *fess.voo* to give *fess.voof*

This is only one of many possible Jungle versions. Do not insist too strongly on accuracy here.

When you are searching for examples to use in the word-crusher, it is a good idea to look for clauses with word clusters and a content word which you can use in a crush zone. The best such sentences are ones in which you can use to fill the five columns, and have word clusters in column 5 and a content word in column 3 (these columns are the crush zones).

Remember, the goal is listening/decoding, not pronunciation.

23.8 Grammar

The sentences which occur in grammar teaching also provide opportunities to use our word-crusher tool. For example, Cunningham and Moor (2005: 37) have an activity of seven items which practises the continuous aspect of different tenses. In the sixth item, students have to choose the better of two endings to a given sentence. Both of the *so*-clauses give us an opportunity for vocal gymnastics.

My car's broken down,
- so I'll go to work on the bus next week
- so I'll be going to work on the bus next week

The second clause is the right answer for this test of grammar. But both can fit neatly into the word-crusher, as you can see from Rows 02 and 03 in Table 23.3.

TABLE 23.3 EXTRACT 23.11

	5	4	3	2	1
00	(crush)	BANG!	(crush)	BANG!	(relax)
01	so i'll go to	WORK	on the	BUS	next week
02	so i'll be going to	WORK	on the	BUS	next week

Follow the steps given in the previous section for the work on Table 23.2. The processes to apply are:

- in Column 3, d'eth-drop (cf. Chapter 17.3) for *on the* giving us |ɒnə| for both speech units

- unit 01, Column 5, a syllablend (cf. 18.4.1) for *so I'll go to* which becomes *swalguhtuh* |swælgətə|

- unit 02, Column 5, the hiss effect (cf. 17.11) for *so I'll be going to* which becomes *swalbeegunna* |swælbɪgənə|

Crucially, you should point out to students that although the grammatical difference illustrated in the words in Column 5 (*so I'll go to* vs. *so I'll be going to*), will be clearly audible in the Greenhouse and Garden modes of speech, it may become very unclear in the Jungle.

You will need to remind them that this activity is not about improving their pronunciation, it is about improving their listening/decoding.

At the end of a reading/writing exercise, a couple of minutes spent on vocal gymnastic exercises such as this – a brief visit to the sound substance dimension –can make a nice transition between activities in the classroom.

23.9 Reading – crushing sentences

After a reading activity, take an appropriate clause (containing a word cluster and a content word) from towards the end of the reading text. It is best that it comes from towards the end of the text, as by then there is a lot of contextual information in play which can justify having content words non-prominent.

For example, Redston and Cunningham (2012: 6) contains a reading passage about the famous British chef, Jamie Oliver. The passage has five paragraphs which give key events from his biography in chronological order. In the last paragraph we have *At the moment Jamie is writing a new book of recipes.* In Garden mode, we might read it as in Extract 23.12.

EXTRACT 23.12
```
01 || AT the MOMent ||
02 || JAmie is WRITing ||
03 || a NEW book of REcipes ||
```

But because there is so much contextual information in play, we do not need to make all of these syllables prominent. We would be justified in having just one double-prominence speech unit:

EXTRACT 23.13
```
01 || at the moment jamie is WRIting a new book of REcipes ||
```

The justification for all these non-prominent words is as follows:

- *at the moment* – the previous paragraphs are clearly leading up to the present time
- *Jamie* – his name has been mentioned several times, and therefore does not need to be prominent
- *a new book of* – it is clear from earlier in the passage that he is also a writer

We can fit this speech unit into the five columns of the word-crusher as shown in Table 23.4, and we may get something close to *uhthumomenjemmyiz* in column 5, and *tinguhnubukuf* in column 3.

TABLE 23.4 EXTRACT 23.14

	5	4	3	2	1
00	(crush)	BANG!	(crush)	BANG!	(relax)
01	at the moment jamie is	WRI	ting a new book of	RE	cipes

23.10 Reading – mush replaces words

Give students a paragraph from a reading text which you have doctored, by putting in mondegreens (cf. Chapter 6.1) and folk spellings where the text allows. For example, here is a paragraph from Redston and Cunningham (2012: 27), with some mondegreens written in folk spelling – these are shown in italics in this extract.

This is a paragraph from an interview with a British traffic warden, whose job is to issue fines to motorists who park their cars illegally.

> … we have radios so we can get help when we are in trouble. And now some wardens *ashyaff* video cameras *ass par off air* uniforms. *Sofa knee one guess* aggressive, it's on camera. Strangely *summer fur* most aggressive people are parents *wennair* collecting *air chillin fum* school.

Ask students to read this paragraph aloud to each other. Explain that the 'words' in italics are Jungle forms – a mush of several words – which they have to read unclearly, very quickly and without any prominences or stresses – only then will they begin to make sense. If students struggle with this, then get them to think of each italicised part as a crush zone, which is part of a speech unit just before a prominent syllable.

TABLE 23.5

	3	2	1
01	(crush)	BANG!	(relax)
02	ashyaff	VI	deo cameras

The folk spellings introduced in this paragraph will not work for everyone, so feel free to devise spellings which work for you and your students.

Here are the patches of mush translated into the actual words used.

- *ashyaff* – actually have
- *ass par off air* – as part of their
- *Sofa knee one guess* – So if anyone gets
- *summer fur* – some of the
- *wennair* – when they are
- *air chillin fum* – their children from

23.11 Other activities

Now that we have a syllabus for listening/decoding you can set work for students to do on the sound substance of everyday speech in much the same way that you would for the written language.

23.11.1 Streamlining of the week

You nominate a streamlining process of the week, give examples, and ask students to contribute their examples throughout the week. For example, you explain d'eth-drop (cf. Chapter 17.3) and ask your students to find examples on the internet (see next chapter), or find examples in a written text (e.g. a newspaper article) which they then perform for the class at the end of the week. Or, after doing a reading, you direct their attention to a sentence which contains streamlining possibilities, and you ask them to perform a sentence in Garden and then Jungle modes, in ways which illustrate the streamlining effects which are in focus.

23.11.2 Mondegreens

A mondegreen (cf. Chapter 6) occurs when one set of words is heard as a different set of words: for example, my students heard *I beg your pardon* as *Big Bang.* Such mondegreen moments present an opportunity to work in the sound substance dimension. We'll take this example and see how it might be exploited.

STEP 1
Write the intended words *I beg your pardon* on the board, towards the top, making sure that the words are well spaced. Ask the class to say these words in Greenhouse and Garden modes.

STEP 2
Then tell the class that you are going to write *big bang* on the board. Begin by writing these two syllables immediately below *pardon.*

STEP 3
Turn to the class, looking puzzled, and ask them if that is the best place for the words to go. Did they hear the two syllables of *par.don* as the two syllables of *big bang*? The answer is 'No'.

STEP 4
Elicit from them that they probably heard *beg* as *big* and therefore *big* should go under *beg* and *bang* should go under the first syllable of *pardon.*

STEP 5
Focus on *pardon* and *bang.* Ask how many syllables each has (*pardon has* two and *bang* has one).

STEP 6
Then give students a handout of Table 23.6 or project it on the whiteboard. Talk your students through it row by row. Row 01 has the original and Row 08 has the mondegreen. (As you explain, ask students to vocalise quietly to themselves the soundshapes that occur.) Rows 02–08 display intermediate stages between the original version and the mondegreen:

- 02 drops the non-prominent words *I* and *your*

- 03 changes *pardon* (d-drop, plus syllablend cf. Chapter 18.4.1) to *parn* |pɑːn|

- 04–06 changes the vowel in *beg* to create other words

- 07 arrives at the mondegreen syllable *big*; *parn* becomes *pang*

- 08 changes *pang* to *bang*

TABLE 23.6 EXTRACT 23.15

01	i	BEG	your	PARdon
02		BEG		PARdon
03		BEG		PARN
04		BUG		PARN
05		BAG		PARN
06		BOG		PARN
07		BIG		PANG
08		BIG		BANG

STEP 7

Ask students, in pairs, to read the table row-by-row, starting slowly, and gradually speeding up.

As they vocalise the area of sound between the original version and the mondegreen, they are exploring the world of in-between-ness, using their own voices to prepare them to be familiar and comfortable with the variability of everyday speech.

You can collect mondegreens that the students and yourself encounter, and write them on a poster on one wall of the classroom. Having written evidence of the mondegreens will provide a good record of these moments of learning. And revisiting them, and asking students to vocalise their way from the original to the mondegreen and back again, will be a useful exercise in experiencing, and learning to be familiar and comfortable with, the Jungle.

YouTube videos can also be a good source of mondegreens, because many of them have transcripts which are automatically generated by software, and sometimes they give mondegreen versions of words that do not fit in the context. So when you have given your students tasks which involve YouTube (cf. Chapter 24), you can ask them to make a note of any mondegreens they encounter, and report back to class.

23.12 Summary and what's next

The classroom is a language-rich environment, but it is dominated by the sight substance. In this chapter I have shown how you can slip into the sound substance dimension briefly and regularly in order to give it a more constant presence in the classroom.

Every classroom activity presents an opportunity to do this. During or after work of any kind, whether it be grammar, reading, writing, listening or pronunciation, there are opportunities to slip into the sound substance, and into the Jungle. You can encourage students to go wild with their speech in the Jungle as both an energising activity, and as a transition activity. These activities should take up very little classroom time, once students become familiar with the routines.

In the next chapter, we will look at the digital resources now available on the internet which are beginning to transform the teaching of listening.

24 Internet and digital resources

Digital and internet resources now exist which make it easy to search recordings and find many examples of the same words spoken by people from very different backgrounds (and therefore very different voices) in a wide range of contexts. This chapter reviews some of these resources, and suggests ways in which they can be used.

- Sonocent's AudioNotetaker, which can serve both the teacher in the classroom and the textbook or course book author.

- YouGlish, a pronunciation site, which you can search for words and clusters and hear them in videos.

- the TED Corpus Search Engine (TCSE) which indexes thousands of TED talks and makes them searchable.

- TubeQuizard which provides pre-made decoding activities focussing on clusters and processes, and enables you to create your own.

This chapter is likely to go out of date as far as links are concerned, so the particular resources that I write about here may no longer exist when you read this. But there will be others in their place. The purpose of this chapter is to alert you to the types of resources that are out there, and to suggest types of activities to accompany them.

The key idea is that teachers and students should use these resources with an informed, active engagement with the sound substance. This will involve focused questioning ('What did that word sound like?'), gap-filling, and physical re-enactment of what has been heard using vocal gymnastics.

Over recent decades, developments in technology have created the potential for greatly improving the teaching of listening. But there are a number of obstacles which have delayed, and continue to delay, the implementation of these improvements. One is that many course book recordings are still scripted and performed by actors, and do not contain those features of spontaneous speech which cause learners problems. Also, they are often created towards or at the end of the course book-authoring process, when it has already been decided what the recording will contain, how it will be used and what the authors will say about it. So even if there are any interesting soundshapes, soundscapes, and changes of speed, these will not be a focus of the course book exercises. In addition, any comment on the audio is likely to be worded in terms of the Careful Speech Model (cf. Chapter 13), with the danger that it might be in conflict with the evidence of the recording.

There are now course books which are built around pre-existing recordings (e.g. the Keynote series from Heinle Cengage) which have recordings and transcripts which are available at the start of the authoring process. But the lack of a metalanguage for the sound substance phenomena of everyday speech means that the exercises in the course book remain locked into the CSM. Part

3 of *A Syllabus for Listening: Decoding* has provided this missing metalanguage and Part 4, of which this chapter is the last, contains ideas which will enable you to circumvent some of the problems caused by the current methods of producing and treating recordings.

In my experience of writing materials, it is vital to stay close to the recording and to listen to it repeatedly. The reason for this is that as you are drafting your commentary on the sound substance, or the activities which are based on the recording, you can continually check that the sound substance does indeed contain the features that you have written about.

It is very tempting, once the transcript is created, to rely on it, and on your memory of what it sounded like, without going back to the recording to check. And failing to go back and check on the recording and relying on the transcript will predispose you to hear things a certain way, which may well differ from what the recording actually contains.

24.1 AudioNotaker from Sonocent

AudioNotetaker from Sonocent (you have to buy the application) makes 'staying close to the recording' very easy. Although it was not designed for this type of listening/decoding work, it is an excellent aid for both course book authors and for teaching. Its virtues are that you can always see the transcript and the audio side by side. The audio has equal status with the transcript, so you can immediately check a detail of the recording without having to search through all of, or long stretches of, the full recording.

24.1.1 AudioNotaker and the textbook author

I wrote enthusiastically about AudioNotetaker in Cauldwell (2013: 300), and I remain hugely enthusiastic. It is easy to learn and use and it is particularly wonderful for finding and labelling key moments in long sound files, as I explain below.

FIGURE 24.1 EXTRACT 24.1

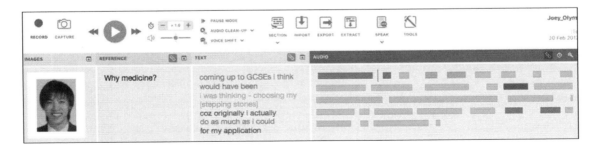

Figure 24.1 shows a screenshot of part of an AudioNotetaker file. The top row contains controls for recording, and for importing text, sound and images, as well as tools for playback (you can vary the speed). The thin row just below the controls shows the headings for the four panes which take up the bottom half of the image, and which form the main working areas.

The Image pane sits on the left-hand side, and can contain images or slides from a presentation. To the right of the Image pane there are two text panes: the Reference pane, which I have used to label the topic of the recording at this point as 'Why medicine?', and the Text pane. The Text pane contains the text of a number of word clusters which are contained in the recording. These are colour-coded to match the colours of the chunks of the audio recording in the fourth working area: the Audio pane. (Apologies, this book is in black and white – but you can download this file from the online Appendix to this book).

The sound file is presented in the Audio pane as rectangular chunks. These chunks are pause-defined units, which you can treat as if they are text: you can colour-code the chunks, cut, copy and paste them. You can navigate around the recording using your trackpad and keyboard just as quickly as you can a written document.

If, for example, you have imported a recording and you are listening to it for word clusters spoken quickly, you can colour code the chunks in which they occur in real time as you listen, just by tapping one of the numbers 1–6. If you hear something unexpected that you want to revisit, you can assign that chunk another colour, and revisit that chunk of audio, and other similarly coded chunks, after you have finished your first listening.

AudioNotetaker is an excellent tool for transcribing recordings – you can swiftly type, back up the audio and listen again, and resume typing. You can also use it to create activities to use in class, or for students to do as homework.

24.1.2 Activity: detecting different soundshapes

Figure 24.2 shows an activity designed to get students delving into a short extract of a recording and listening to the sound substance. The specific task here is to detect different soundshapes of the words *just started*, *voice just*, *everyone* and *didn't*. The Image pane shows the speaker, the Reference pane contains the questions students have to answer, the Text pane contains the transcript, and the Audio pane contains nine chunks of sound – nine seconds in total.

FIGURE 24.2 EXTRACT 24.2

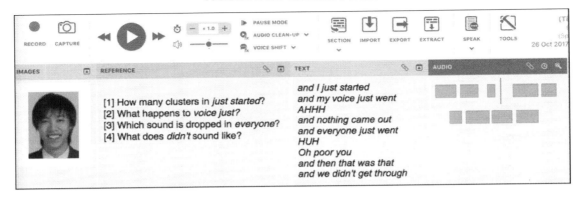

Voice: Dan, UK. This recording featured in Cauldwell, (2013: 108).

The purpose of the activity is to alert learners to the fact that:

- the two |st| clusters in *just started* become one, giving us *justarted* – an instance of D.R.Y. ('Don't Repeat Yourself' cf. Chapter 18.5)

- the end of *voice* and the beginning of *just* combine to give us something close to |vɔɪʒəs| an instance of the hiss effect leading to a blurring of |dʒ| (cf. 17.11)

- in *everyone* the |v| is dropped giving us something close to |erɪwʌn| (cf. 17.8)

- *didn't* is streamlined by d-drop (cf. 17.6) and t-drop (cf. 17.5) to *din*; and before the |g| of *get* the |n| becomes |ŋ| giving us something close to *ding*

The advantage of presenting the activity in AudioNotetaker is that learners can zoom around the audio chunks in the Audio pane, using the arrow keys on their keyboard. They can explore the sound substance by slowing it down, and they can compare different parts of the recording by colouring, copying, cutting and pasting the chunks of audio as if they were text. And, of course, they may hear things entirely differently to you, so they can annotate and colour-code their own interpretations of the sound file. They can also record their own versions alongside the original, should they wish. Although pronunciation is not our focus, this feature makes such exercises possible. This is an application that you have to pay for, but you can download a fully-functional 30–day trial version for free.

24.2 YouGlish – cluster – *to be able to*

YouGlish is a free platform which enables you to find multiple examples of words and word clusters (indeed any string of words) spoken in videos (mostly YouTube) which are available on the internet. You can select from three different accents of English: British, US and Australian.

At the time of writing, if I search for *to be able to* I get nearly 54,000 US versions just over 4,500 British versions and around 1,900 Australian versions of this cluster.

FIGURE 24.3

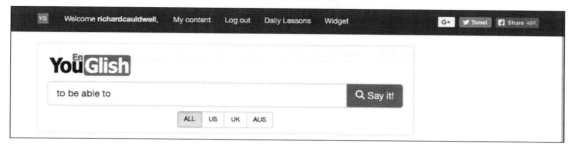

When you click 'Say it!', you get the first video, with the transcript below it and the cluster highlighted. You can play the segment as often as you like, or backtrack to the preceding five seconds, or simply let the video continue. You can opt to listen in either a slowed-down or speeded-up mode. You can also set up an account and save selected extracts. It is a bewitching, engrossing and wonderful platform. But you have to be disciplined to get the best out of it. Be clear in your objectives, and set clearly defined tasks. One such task type is given in the next section.

This site brings together both the sight- and soundshapes of words, so that learners can associate multiple soundshapes, soundscapes and rhythmic versions of the same string of words with the sight substance. It is an excellent resource for both learners and for teacher education.

The site presents itself as a pronunciation site, but (in my view) is much more valuable as a listening/decoding site.

24.2.1 Activity – *to be able to*

This activity is best done in a computer cluster, where students can go online. They may do this activity as individuals or in pairs, but in pairs is best. This activity would be a great follow-up to any work you may have done with them on the sections earlier on, which involve *able*-clusters (cf. Chapters 15.2.2 and 18.7).

STEP 1
Give students Table 24.1 in a handout.

TABLE 24.1 YOUGLISH

	Column 1 word clusters	Column 2	Column 3 Comments
1	If you wanna keep your sanity, you have to be able to back away		
2	... need to be able to decide for what's what and the best way to do that is understand		
3	They need to be able to adapt to situations		
4	They need to be able to put all those together		
	(A) to be ebble to (B) to be abboo ˈeɪbʊl to (C) to be al to (D) to be ell to		

Explain that they are going to do a matching task involving Columns 1 and 2 (described in Step 2), where they have to listen and identify the different soundshapes of *to be able to*. Then they are going to listen again and make comments (in answer to questions given in Step 9) on each version of *to be able to*.

STEP 2
Have students read aloud the words in Column 1 at a variety of speeds, placing prominences on different syllables.

STEP 3
Have them read the contents of the last row of the table at a variety of speeds, but mostly very fast.

STEP 4
Instruct them to go to the YouGlish website and search for the words shown in Column 1 of Table 24.1 – they all contain the cluster *to be able to*, but in searching they need to add the word(s) in front of and following this cluster in order to identify the relevant extract.

STEP 5
They listen carefully to each extract at both normal and slow speeds (vocalising what they hear), paying particular attention to the words *to be able to* in each of these extracts.

STEP 6
They decide which versions of *to be able to* they hear, and match the versions given in folk spelling in Column 2 with the words given in Column 1.

STEP 7

Elicit answers from the class, without saying which are right or wrong. If there is disagreement, ask them to listen again.

STEP 8

Give them the answers (which are in the Answer Key).

STEP 9

Direct their attention to Column 3, and tell them they have to listen again to the extracts, and to the soundscape which precedes and follows each extract and make comments in answer to the questions below. They need not answer all of the questions.

- Which words are made prominent by the speaker in the soundscape around these words?
- Which words sound Greenhouse-like, Garden-like, and Jungle-like?
- Which words are spoken fast and/or less clearly?
- Do you hear any mondegreens?
- Do you find the accents easy to understand?
- What soundshapes are typical of this accent?
- Which words (if any) are repeated?
- Is there a difference between what you see the speaker's mouth doing and what you hear?

Examples of comments your students might make are given in the Answer Key.

24.3 TED Corpus Search Engine – *absolutely*

TED talks, founded in 1984, are a very influential set of talks on many different topics. The name TED is an acronym for Technology, Entertainment and Design. It is a very powerful educational tool, and the Heinle Cengage *Keynote* series of course books (e.g. Dummet et al., 2017) feature these talks prominently.

Many TED talks have been indexed in the TED Corpus Search Engine (Hasebe, 2015). This search engine (henceforth TCSE) can search, at the time of writing, 2,400 TED talks. You can enter a term, for example a word or string of words such as *absolutely wonderful*, and the search will return a list of the TED talks in which the words *absolutely wonderful* have occurred. For *absolutely wonderful* there are four occurrences in all, whereas *absolutely* on its own gets 704.

Figure 24.4 shows a screenshot relating to one of the four talks which feature *absolutely wonderful*.

FIGURE 24.4 TED CORPUS SEARCH ENGINE

				Total : 4 hits in 4 / 2431 talks [0.707 seconds]		Help	Prev 100	Next 100

#	ID	Line	Time				
1	1291	290 [0.88]	14:19 [15:38]	▤	▶	⁄	And it was absolutely wonderful.

The line for this talk displays the following information (from left to right):

- #1 is the reference number for the line.

- ID 1291 is the reference number for the TED talk.

- Line 290 with [0.88] below gives the line number in the transcript where the words occur, and the duration of the 'segment' in which it occurs.

- The numbers 14:19 give the time in the talk where the words *absolutely wonderful* occur, and the numbers [15:38] give the duration of the whole talk.

- The symbol of the lined square, when clicked, gives a pop-up window with details of the talk.

- The arrow symbol, when clicked, will play a video of the relevant segment.

- The paper clip symbol gives you a hyperlink to the segment.

- The words *and it was absolutely wonderful* show the search term and the other words which occurred with it in this segment.

There is also a very handy pop-up box which gives information about the talk: this one is by Charles Limb, who is a doctor and a musician. The title of his talk is 'Building the Musical Muscle'. Even more useful is the fact that the information includes a figure for the speed of the talk in words per minute 235.45 – very fast, (for comparison, 163.00 is 'slow'). There is also a measure for readability: FK 63.86 'easy' (FK = Flesch-Kincaid readability test).

One way of thinking of the TCSE is as a scholarly version of YouGlish, because it contains many more research-type options. For example, you can search for different forms of the same word using square brackets, so [excite] will give you *excite, excites, excited* and *exciting.*

Many TED talks are scripted, so they will not be wholly representative of spontaneous speech. But some, like Sir Ken Robinson's 'Do schools kill creativity?' (TED 66) certainly contain very fast stretches. His talk is fast (208 wpm) and is rated very easy for Readability (FK index 68.67). This relative ease (by this measure) combined with the fast speed of delivery, makes talks such as this one ideal for decoding work, and for noticing Jungle phenomena.

TCSE is also suitable for doing activities of the type shown for YouGlish in Table 24.1.

24.4 Tubequizard – activities on streamlining processes

Tubequizard (Sergeeva & Sukhomlin, 2017) is a web service which enables you to find or create gap-fill quizzes from YouTube videos. It is particularly good for decoding work. Like TCSE and YouGlish, it searches the transcripts of videos, and the focus is primarily on listening. The basic technique is gap-fill, but as I explain below, the gap-fill activity can be enhanced so as to avoid the single-instance problem (cf. Chapter 21.6).

Figure 24.5 shows the choices you get on the home page.

FIGURE 24.5 TUBEQUIZARD

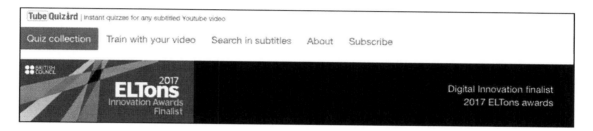

The important choices on the top menu of the home page are:

- Quiz collection – this is a selection of ready-made quizzes.

- Train with your video – this enables you to generate a ranges of quizzes from a subtitled video of your choice.

- Search in subtitles – this enables you to search YouTube videos for words or phrases which can then be turned into quizzes.

Lower down the home page there is a menu shown in Figure 24.6. This shows that in the Quiz collection, you can filter your search by language level (A2–C2), by category (business, education, entertainment, and so on); and variety of English (US, UK, etc).

But for us, the most wonderful filter is one labelled 'type' which enables you to search for activities in five categories: Grammar for listeners, Pronunciation for listeners, Vocabulary in context, Grammar in context and Spelling.

FIGURE 24.6 TUBEQUIZARD MENU

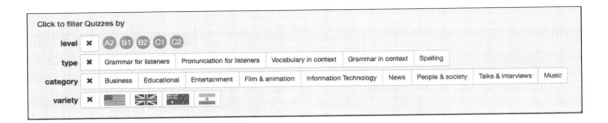

The key category for our purposes is the second category, 'Pronunciation for listeners', where we can focus on word clusters.

24.4.1 Pronunciation for listeners

Using the word 'pronunciation' when writing or talking about teaching listening/decoding is not something I favour. However, it is fairly commonplace, and if it leads people to resources like these, then we can be thankful. Clicking on 'Pronunciation for Listeners' gives you a selection of videos, each labelled with sub-categories such as:

- Disappearing sounds: |t| and |d| – in words such as *and, that, what, could.*

- Disappearing sounds: *and.*

- Top 20 two-word chunks – word clusters such as *you know, I mean, I think.*

- Difficult three-word chunks – *I don't know, a lot of.*

To explain further what this Tubequizard offers, I will describe my experience with one of the prepared quizzes. I have chosen 'Pronunciation for Listening', a nine-item quiz for B2 and above, (quiz id 118) the trailer for 'Pirates of the Caribbean: Dead Men Tell No Tales' (Trailer #1: Bruckheimer et al., 2017).

The learner's task is to listen and fill in the gaps. The instructions read:

> Research shows that people often say frequently used expressions very fast, and so they can be difficult to catch. Listen and fill the gaps with frequently used two-word expressions.

Having selected this quiz, you see lines of the transcript which, when clicked, will play the relevant video for that part of the transcript. You click on a line and the video plays (you can click to hear each line as often as you would like) and your task is to fill in each of the nine gaps with the two-word expressions that you hear. You type in the words, click 'check', and then you will see whether you have the correct answer or not – if not, the answer is shown to you.

It is worthwhile describing my experience with this particular activity for a moment. I did not get all the answers right first time – I had problems with gaps 2 and 5. In gap 2 (the underlined words were gapped): *They're searching for a Pearl* I heard *for Pearl* – with no indefinite article. I thought *Pearl* was a character's name, and did not need an article, and to my ears *for Pearl* (with no article) is a reasonable hearing of the sound substance.

If you know or assume that *pearl* is not a character's name, then you will be predisposed/primed to hear *for a pearl* (with an article); and if you know or assume that *pearl* is a proper name, you will be predisposed/primed to hear *for Pearl* (with no article). The point is that the sound substance is in-between (indeterminate) and on its own terms – purely as sound substance – can be reasonably heard to be either.

It is necessary to point out here that this recording is rich in both sound effects (explosions), music, voice types and voice qualities – fierce sinister whispering and growling, and Johnny Depp's choice of a comic version of a particular type of British accent.

The problem I had with Gap 5 was with the words *to be* in *From this moment on we are to be allies.* And despite playing it a couple of times, I could not hear anything that would fit. My first impression was that there was only one word, and it was the word *see*. But of course this doesn't fit the context – or what the instructions had told me, which was that I should use a two-word expression. So I replayed it, but still did not get it. I then checked the answer and had an 'Oh, of course!' moment. Subsequently, on every replaying of this section, I am locked in to hearing only *to be,* and it is difficult for me to believe that I could ever have heard anything else. But, of course, there are streamlining processes at work here in the sound substance (t-blur and b-blur) which makes *see* a reasonable hearing of the sound substance.

I have spent time explaining my encounters with gaps 2 and 5 because they illustrate a learning process that it is important for learners to go through, and which will help us get around the testing problem that gap-fills present. We need to delve intelligently into and around the gaps that are to be filled, by getting learners themselves to pay careful attention to their own mental processes as they experience these encounters with the sound substance. We need to persuade them to do these activities slowly, and if possible to capture their perceptions every step of the way. We also need to encourage them to observe their own reactions and perceptions, and make a note of what they hear, or think they hear. They should not discard anything – so they must resist the temptation to think things like 'I thought that was *see* and it is in fact *to be?!* Silly me!' We should stress that it is not 'silly them' at all: it is a perception worth noting down, and reporting in class.

Here are some questions that you can ask students to consider and report back on.

- What did you hear the first time you played it?

- Did you hear something different on later plays?

- How else could these words sound? What other words did they remind you of?

- Is the soundscape (cf. Chapter 13.1) in which they occur mountainous or monotonous?

- What other words could this stretch of speech sound like?

- What bodily movements (if any) could you use to move to this soundscape?

- What else of interest has happened in the soundscape around the gap?

- Did the gapped words sound like they were Greenhouse, Garden or Jungle forms?

24.4.2 Creating your own quizzes

Perhaps the best thing about Tubequizard is that you can edit any of the pre-existing quizzes, changing them from (as in the example above) 'Chunks: two-word expressions' to 'Grammar in context: articles', where the task is automatically changed to require learners to supply definite and indefinite articles. If I do this for the trailer of *Pirates of the Caribbean* example, we have this line from Johnny Depp's character (Captain Jack Sparrow), in which the indefinite article is gapped out.

> You'd have seen **a** lot more if you'd kept your cakehole shut.

(02:18 seconds into the trailer) The word *cakehole* is a slang word for *mouth*.

Now, this activity gives us eleven gaps to fill, of which the line above contains just one, but it is vital to get a feel of the soundscape in which the gapped words appear.

EXTRACT 24.3
```
01 || you'd have SEEN a LOT MORE ||
02 || if you'd KEPT your CAKEhole SHUT ||
```

Voice: Not the original recording – Richard UK.

When you ask students what they notice they might comment on:

- the initial |k| of *cake* sounds more like |h| or a k-blur |x| (cf. Chapter 17.7)

- in 01 *you'd have* sounds like *you da*

- in 02 *you'd kept* sounds like *you kept*

- in 02 *kept* |t| becomes a glottal stop

- the soundscape is mountainous with peaks on *more* in 01 and *cake* in 02

The gap should not be the sole focus of the task. There is usually so much more of interest in the surrounding soundscape.

24.5 Summary

This is the chapter that is most likely to be out of date by the time you read it. But there will be resources of the same type available. The key ideas you need to bear in mind are that the goal is to train both yourself and your students to listen for the sound substance, and its characteristics, and not just for meaning. The sound substance contains many soundscapes (monotones to mountains) and many soundshapes – words which are flexi-forms, multi-flavoured and multi-coloured. And this sound substance is a separate entity from the sight substance. It is teachable, it should be taught, it should find a place in textbooks and course books, which continue to lag behind on this issue, despite the fact that, these days, they contain many more 'authentic' recordings.

Encouragingly, however, many teachers around the world are increasingly teaching wonderful listening lessons, and giving conference presentations about helping their students with decoding. Among them are (at the time of writing) Chinn and Willoughby (2016), Grinberg (2017), Sergeeva (2015), Sweeney (2016, 2017). I am grateful to all of them for their influence on this book.

24.6 Finally

The Speech in Action website has resources to accompany this book – worksheets for classroom activities, and much more – **www.speechinaction.com**.

Answer key

Chapter 11

Transcript of Emily's recording

They said uh right we don't have a technology teacher
we don't have any technology teachers. So um
so now you're head of technology for the entire school of 'bout fifteen hundred pupils
and we don't have any equipment
to do technologies.

Chapter 22

SECTION 22.4.2

EXTRACT 22.13

```
01 || it's BETter if you WAIT over THERE || 2: the 't's are taps.
02 || just TAKE a SEAT || 3: this 't' is a glottal stop
03 || she's GETting it for you NOW|| 1: the 't's are Irish 't's.
04 || and i'll SEE you in a little WHILE || 4: the 't' is a t-drop.
```

SECTION 22.4.3

A	isassis	ɪzasɪs	1	He says it's going to be great	B
B	scum be	skəmbi	2	It's in the kitchen	C
C	sinner	sɪnə	3	I think it's just awful	E
D	speesuh	spiːsə	4	Look and see that he's gone	G
E	issshuss	ɪssʃʌs	5	They used to have a nice house	F
F	you suffer	juːsʌfə	6	He was the first to go	H
G	cease	siːs	7	She said it's a piece of cake	D
H	uhfurssuh	əfɜːsə	8	The problem is that it's very fast	A

Chapter 24.2.1

	Column 1 word clusters	Column 2 Folk spellings	Column 3 Comments
1	If you wanna keep your sanity, you have <u>to be able to</u> back away	(D) to be ell to	
2	... need <u>to be able to</u> decide for what's what and the best way to do that is understand	(A) to be ebble to	
3	They need <u>to be able to</u> adapt to situations	(B) to be abboo l eɪbʊ l to	
4	They need <u>to be able to</u> put all those together	(C) to be al to	

Below are some comments that students might make about the extracts, and the soundscapes around them.

- 1 US English.
  - o The speaker seems to do a lip-closure for the |b| of *able*, but the effect of the lips is inaudible.
  - o The following words have prominences in the extract and the soundscape around it: *then, sanity, away.*
- 2 US English.
  - o The speaker repeats the words *to be able to* and has a stepping stone 'ah' after the repetition of *to be able to.*
  - o The transcript contains a mondegreen: the transcript has decide for but the speaker says the word *decipher.*
- 3 British English.
  - o The following words are less clear in the extract and the soundscape around it: *need, work, adapt situations*
- 4 Australian English
  - o The speaker repeats the syllables *all those to-.*

Appendix 1 – Word stress and prominences

It is important to understand the relationship between word stress and prominence. Word accent is a property of the word in the Greenhouse – the isolated citation form. Thus the two-syllable words *going* |ˈɡəʊ.ɪŋ|, *looking* |ˈlʊk.ɪŋ|, *slightly* |ˈslaɪt.li| and *detail* |ˈdiː.teɪl| all have word stress on their first syllables.

Speakers highlight a word by making it more noticeable than the other words around it and, as a consequence other words may become less noticeable. If a speaker chooses to emphasise or highlight a word, they make the word-stressed syllable prominent; if they choose not to highlight a word, they make it non-prominent. So prominence is a property assigned to a word by speakers at the moment of speaking, in contrast with word stress which is a property of a word in the Greenhouse or citation form.

Table A1 illustrates the relationship between prominence and word stress. The odd-numbered columns contain one or more non-prominent syllables, and the even-numbered columns contain one, and only one, prominent syllable.

TABLE A1 – EXTRACT 25.1

5	4	3	2	1
this is	ONE	i'm going to be looking at in slightly more	DE	tail in fact

The two-syllable words *going*, *looking* and *slightly* are not highlighted by the speaker, therefore the syllables which would be stressed in the citation form are non-prominent. However, the words *one* and *detail* are highlighted:

- *one* is a single-syllable word, and therefore the prominence goes on that syllable in Column 4

- *detail* is a two-syllable word so the speaker makes the first syllable (the one with word stress) prominent, and this is shown in Column 2

- the second syllable of *detail* is non-prominent, so it goes in Column 1 together with the words *in fact*.

In sum:

- word stress is a property of the word in isolation (Greenhouse/citation form)
- prominences are assigned by speakers as they speak
- prominences are used to highlight words
- prominences go on the syllables which have word stress
- prominences apply to single syllables
- if speakers choose not to highlight a word, the syllable which is stressed in the citation form will be non-prominent
- word stresses are potential prominences.

Appendix 2 – Window on speech

A full presentation of the 'Window on speech' can be found in Part 1 of *Phonology for Listening, Teaching the Stream of Speech* (Cauldwell, 2013). In that book, The Window on speech was used to analyse recordings of spontaneous speech: it is a way of hearing, analysing and presenting the sound substance of speech in terms of speech units rather than clauses or sentences.

Briefly, a speech unit ends and another begins when (a) there is a pause or (b) a tone (fall, rise, etc) occurs or (c) where there is a change of rhythm. In deciding where tone unit boundaries occur, no attention is paid to the grammatical structure of the words involved. Boundaries are a feature of the soundscape, and can occur anywhere.

The main roles of the Window on speech in *A Syllabus for Listening: Decoding* are as both a presentational device, particularly in Part 3, and as a teaching aid in Part 4.

The three most common sizes of speech unit (single-, double-, and triple-prominence) were described in Chapter 20. A number of points which were not covered there are illustrated in Table A1 using the pattern of a double-prominence speech unit.

TABLE A.1 EXTRACT A.1

	5	4	3	2	1
01	so	ALL	the way to the	STA	tion in fact
02		ALL	the	WAY	
03		TO	the	STA	tion
04		THAT'S		TRUE	
05		OH		YES	

Table A.1 shows the different rhythmic patterns that double-prominence speech units can have.

Row 01 shows a complete pattern for the double-prominence speech unit, with syllables in all the cells. Note that columns 4 and 2 have only one syllable in them, because these are prominent syllables – the ones that the speaker has chosen to highlight.

Row 02 has empty cells in columns 5 and 1, but still counts as a double-prominence speech unit. This is because columns 4 and 2 contain prominent syllables.

Rows 03, 04 and 05 likewise are all double-prominence speech units because, although they have cells without non-prominent syllables, they all have prominent syllables in columns 4 and 2.

In sum:

- prominent syllables occur in even-numbered columns

- as a consequence, the even-numbered columns contain only syllable only

- non-prominent syllables occur in odd-numbered columns

- the cells in odd-numbered columns can contain more than one syllable

- the tone (fall, fall-rise, rise, and so on) starts in Column 2, and continues over the syllables in Column 1 (if there are any).

Appendix 3 – Voices

Below is a list of the people whose voices are used in *A Syllabus for Listening: Decoding.* The information includes their first name, nationality, the region where they were brought up, and their age when they were recorded.

Arun	UK	Birmingham	19
Catherine	USA	Texas	50s
Corony	UK	London	30
Emily	UK	Birmingham	20s
Geoff	UK	Birmingham	30s
Jack	UK	Birmingham	19
Jess	USA	New Mexico	30s
Joey	UK	Birmingham	19
Karam	USA	California	20s
Laura	UK	Birmingham	19
Olivia	UK	Birmingham	19
Omira	Canada	Vancouver	20
Philip	UK	Bristol	50s
Richard	UK	Birmingham	60s
Richard junior	UK	Birmingham	20s
Sylvia	Romania	Ploiesti	20s
Suzanne	UK	Birmingham	20s
Dan	UK	Epsom, near London	20s
Toby	UK	Hertfordshire	30s
Richard II	UK	Birmingham	20s
Ashley	USA	Richmond Virginia	20s
Ellen	USA	Georgia	20s
Jacklyn	USA	New Jersey	20s

NB The region given for each speaker indicates where they live, or where they were brought up. It is not a reliable indicator of the speaker's accent.

Appendix 4 - Adverbs

additionally	a dishy	ədɪsʃi
apparently	appantly	əpæntli
automatically	automagically	ɔːtəmædʒɪkli
certainly	surtuny, surtny, surny	sɜːtəni, sɜːʔni, sɜːni
definitely	defnally, deafnee, defly	defnəli, defni, defli
eventually	venchly	ventʃli
fortunately	fortunely	fɔtʃuːnli
generally	jenny	dʒeni
literally	litchruhlee, litry	lɪtʃrəli, lɪtʃri
obviously	ovsli	ɒvsli
originally	origli, origi, ridgely, ridgey	ɒrɪdʒli, ɒrɪdʒi, rɪdʒli, rɪdʒi
openly	openi	əʊpəni
probably	prabli, prali	prɒbli, prɒli
properly	proply	prɒpli
recently	reesunly, reesly	riːsənli, riːsli
regularly	reguly	reɡjuli
shortly	shorey	ʃɔːri
stupidly	stupilly	stjuːpɪli
suddenly	sunly	sʌnli
ultimately	ultimully, ultimmly,	ʌltɪməli, ʌltɪmli
unfortunately	unforchly, unforshutly	ənfɔːtʃli, ənfɔːʃətli

Appendix 5 – Word clusters

Two-word clusters

Below is a list of examples of two-word clusters of function words and other frequent forms which are commonly squeezed together into short bursts of spontaneous speech.

and i	8	in a		to come	
and the		in the	4	to the	17
and then	13	is a		was to	
as well		it was	5	we were	
at the	18	lots of		what it's	
because the		of a		what they	
but it		of the	7	when i	
did you		on it		when you	
do you	10	on the	12	where it	
don't know	16	or so		which i	
for a		out for		which is	
for about		since he		which was	
go and		so they		who had	
have to	19	sort of	9	with a	
i didn't		that i		with the	
i don't	6	that there		you are	20
i mean	2	that had		you can	
i really		there were		you could	
i think	3	there's a		you didn't	
i was	11	through the		you know	1
if you	15	to be	14	you were	

The first person pronoun *I* is shown in lowercase *i* to indicate that *I* is likely to be non-prominent. The numbers following twenty of the clusters indicate their position on Carter and McCarthy's (2006: 829) table of frequency. Those without numbers are from my own collection.

Three-word clusters

Below is a list of examples of three-word clusters of function words and other frequent forms which are commonly squeezed together into short bursts of spontaneous speech.

a couple of	18	i don't know	1	that you can	
a lot of	2	i don't think	4	that's where it	
a bit of	14	i got a		the sort of	
a piece of		i had a		them in a	
an awful to		i mean i	3	to do that	
and also in		i mean it's		to get the	
and at the		i think it's	15	to have a	
and i was		i want to		to have done	
and it was	17	if i was		to look at	
and so it		it had a		what you do	20
and so on		it was a	9	which are just	
because i was		it was just		which is a	
but i mean	16	more or less		which was called	
but it was		much about that		which you probably	
but you couldn't		not in that		who is the	
by the time		of the very		you have to	8
do you know	13	one of the	7	you know i	10
do you think	5	seems to make		you know the	19
do you want	6	so i did		you know what	12
does it actually		so i was		you may have	
end of the		so they had		you want to	11

The first person pronoun *I* shown in lowercase *i* to indicate that *I* is likely to be non-prominent. The numbers following twenty of the clusters indicate their position on Carter and McCarthy's (2006: 829) table of frequency. Those without numbers are from my own collection.

Four-word clusters

Below is a list of examples of four-word clusters of function words and other frequent forms which are commonly squeezed together into short bursts of spontaneous speech.

a bit of a	7	i don't know if	6	sort of being at	
a great deal of		i don't know what	3	so that you can	
a sort of a		i don't know whether	9	that sort of thing	14
a whole lot of		i don't want to	12	that there's er erm	
an awful lot of		i don't think people		there were no more	
and he had this		i have to say		to get to the	
and that was the		i think it was	8	was it that you	
and were you there		i thought it was	11	well i don't know	17
and so they were		i was at university		well I was doing	
as you can see		i was going to	18	what do you think	10
back in with my		i was very involved		what it's all about	
because i was still		i'm going to be		what to do with	
but then it really		if you want to	16	when i was there	
did you have a		in a bit more		where i was a	
do you know what	5	is supposed to be		while i was in	
do you want to	4	it was the ability		you don't have to	20
for that has been		it was you know		you got to the	
have a look at	19	it's on the way		you know i mean	13
i am in my		know what i mean	2	you know what i	1
i don't know how	15	quite a bit of			

The first person pronoun *I* is shown in lowercase *i* to indicate that *I* is likely to be non-prominent. The numbers following twenty of the clusters indicate their position on Carter and McCarthy's (2006: 829) table of frequency. Those without numbers are from my own collection.

Glossary

acoustic blur The continuous stream of speech which is difficult, if not impossible, to transcribe as a sequence of separate phonemic or phonetic symbols.

activity An observable behaviour – a doing. For example an observer sitting at the back of the class might say *they are doing a listening activity*.

alternative hearing A term used to describe a hearing of one word as another (e.g. *working there* as *working air*) or a group of words as another group of words. The hearing may make no sense in the context, but is allowable because the indeterminate nature of the sound substance may contain evidence for the 'nonsense' decoding.

-blur A general term, following a 't' or 'd' thus 't-blur' or 'd-blur' to signify that the sound is blurred compared to the Greenhouse/citation form. The |t| in the word *little* may undergo 't-blur' so that *little* becomes *liddle* or *lirrul*.

-drop A general term, following a 't' or 'd' thus 't-drop' or 'd-drop' to signify that the sound is dropped (elided). The 't' in *little* may undergo 't-drop' giving us *lil*.

blur gap The gap between the L1 speaker's belief that full words (e.g. *where there were*) were spoken and the acoustic fact that only very small traces (e.g. *weatherwuh* |weðəwə|) were actually present in the sound substance.

botanic metaphor This term refers to the metaphor of the Greenhouse, the Garden and the Jungle, which are used to represent, respectively, citation forms, connected speech and the wildness of spontaneous speech.

botanic walk A classroom drilling technique in which the teacher leads students from the Greenhouse and through the Garden to the Jungle forms of words.

bottom-up An adjective used to describe a route to understanding which starts with sounds then proceeds to words and larger units of meaning.

buzz effect A voiced version of the hiss effect, where the strident buzzing of |z| drowns neighbouring sounds.

careful speech model (CSM) A model of speech based on the guidelines for pronunciation and clear careful speech that appear in most language teaching materials. It is based on standard accents, the citation form and rules about speaking isolated sentences. These rules include *the main stress goes on the last lexical item in a sentence* and *the intonation of yes-no questions rises*. Such rules are inappropriate for teaching listening/decoding.

citation form The maximally-clear pronunciation of a word in isolation in which its segments, syllables and stress patterns are clearly heard.

consonant death A general term used to describe the dropping of consonants.

contours The sound substance equivalent of mountain peaks (high and not so high), valleys (deep and not so deep), and slopes (steep and shallow).

conventional listening lesson A lesson which includes a listening comprehension exercise with pre-, while- and post-listening activities. Activities include: activating schemata, pre-teaching vocabulary, encouraging prediction and reviewing students' answers to items.

creak A rasping slow vibration which accompanies the speech of some people. It is becoming common in the speech of younger people.

crush zone The area of the word-crusher where non-prominent syllables are subjected to extreme streamlining processes (also known as a squeeze zone).

D.R.Y. (Don't Repeat Yourself) A streamlining process where one sound or syllable stands for two (*my application* becomes *mypplication*), the principle being that speakers tend not to repeat two similar sounds in close succession.

d'eth-drop A streamlining process where the consonant |ð| at the beginning of *this*, *the* and *them* is dropped. The symbol is known as 'eth'.

decoding The process of being able to decipher and recognise words in the mush of the sound substance.

decoding gap The gap which occurs in the classroom between what an L1 or expert listener believes they hear, and what the learners actually encounter.

disfluencies A pejorative term used to refer to *ums*, *ahs* and pauses (in the 'wrong' place) as well as re-starts (cf. drafting phenomena).

drafting phenomena The *ums*, *ahs* and pauses in speech, together with re-starts and references to speaker and hearer status, such as *you know*, and *I mean*. These are real-time edits of spontaneous speech, not disfluencies.

duty-blend A label for when words like *due* or *duty* begin not with the sound |d| and |j| but with |dʒ|.

expert listener A term to characterise someone, often (but not necessarily) an L1 listener, who understands the meanings of, and can – if given the opportunity of another listening – accurately report what words were said. Anyone can become an expert listener for a short period of time, when they hold the transcript of a recording.

flexiforms A term, short for 'flexible forms', which refers to the property that all words have of being flexible.

Garden A domain – part of the botanic metaphor – where words come together in polite contact, in accordance with the rules of connected speech.

gleep A term coined by Sue Sullivan to refer to very short stretches of speech which are neither understood nor decoded.

Greenhouse A domain – part of the botanic metaphor – where words occur in isolation, like separately potted plants, with all their segments carefully enunciated. The domain of citation forms.

head-clip A label for when a word loses its initial syllable, e.g. *because* as *'cos* or *Australia* as *'Stralia*.

hiss effect A label for when the strident hissing noise of |s| drowns out neighbouring sounds, e.g. *it's wonderful* as *'swonderful*.

in-between A label for circumstances when the sound substance can be heard to be very approximate and imprecise, or indeterminate.

Jungle A domain – part of the botanic metaphor – where words are messed up in an unruly way; the domain of everyday spontaneous speech.

mid-clip A label for when syllables are omitted from the middle of words, e.g. *everyone* as *evun*.

mondegreen A label for when one set of words e.g. *kiss the sky* can reasonably be heard as *kiss this guy*. Often referred to as a 'mishearing' but is best thought of as a 'reasonable hearing'.

mondegreenland The area of indeterminacy or in-between-ness or uncertainty that exists in the mush of the sound substance and which makes alternative reasonable hearings possible.

mush A technical term for the messy areas of the sound substance where it is difficult to determine where words begin and end, or indeed whether they have occurred at all.

plausible hearing An alternative hearing of the sound substance which results in a hearing of words which was not intended by the speaker, but which more or less fits the context: e.g. *I've not been there for eight years*, heard as *I've not been there for ages*.

polarisk A label to refer to occasions when the sound substance is such that it is difficult to determine whether a positive or negative word form was intended by the speaker.

prominence A property assigned to a word by speakers at the moment of speaking, in contrast with word stress which is a property of a word in the Greenhouse (cf. Appendix 1). Speakers highlight a word by making it more noticeable than the other words around it, and as a consequence other words may become less noticeable. If a speaker chooses to highlight a word, they make the word-stressed syllable prominent; if they choose not to highlight a word, they make it non-prominent.

pronunciation The oral production of a word by a speaker. In some books, authors may write of a word having 'different pronunciations', but the word 'pronunciation' is so laden with connotations of correctness, that in *A Syllabus for Listening: Decoding* it is a term we don't use. We refer to words as having 'soundshapes' rather than alternative pronunciations.

reasonable hearing A term used (in the same sense as 'alternative hearing') to describe an alternative hearing of one word as another (e.g. *working there* as *working air*) or one group of words as another group of words. The hearing may make no sense in the context, but it is reasonable because the nature of the sound substance itself warrants the 'nonsense' decoding.

rough hints A term from Palmer (1936: 82, cited in Brown, 1990: 100) 'Speech is nothing more than a series of rough hints which the hearer must interpret in order to arrive at the meaning which the speaker wishes to convey.'

savouring A metaphor which uses the vocabulary of the sense of taste to help teachers and learners think of ways in which the sense of taste can be enlisted so that learners enjoy the feel of the sound substance as they vocalise it.

sight substance A term to refer to the written language – the visible form of language that sits on the page, or screen, or poster etc. and remains in view, available for inspection at the reader's own pace.

smoothing A label to refer to a streamlining process whereby a diphthong or long vowel is simplified to a single or short vowel, e.g. *south* as *saath*.

soft-focus listening A technique where you stop listening for meaning and instead direct your attention to the sound substance of speech: its rhythms, its different levels of volume, its different speeds, its different contours and its different levels of clarity.

soundshape The acoustic shape of a word. Many people use the term 'pronunciation', but this term (pronunciation) is best avoided in the teaching of listening/decoding.

sound substance A term used to refer to the spoken language – the invisible form of language that passes by very quickly and is gone. It is not available for the listeners inspection – it has to be processed by the listener at speeds which are not under his or her control.

soundscape The aural equivalent to a landscape, the term refers to a distant view of the lay of the land and its shape – whether it consists of rolling hills, a flat plain, or mountains and valleys. I use the term to mean something larger than a speech unit.

speech unit A speaker-defined rhythmic chunk of speech consisting of an alternation of prominent and non-prominent syllables.

speechstream A term used by Sue Sullivan as a label for her listening activities which start off with, and stay with, stretches of speech which her students (initially) do not understand.

spontaneous speech Unscripted, unprepared and unrehearsed speech which is constructed moment-by-moment in real time.

squeeze zone The area of the word-crusher where non-prominent syllables are subjected to extreme streamlining processes (also known as a crush zone).

stepping stones Words which speakers lengthen (usually with a level tone) in order to buy themselves time to plan what to say next.

syllablend A label for the process by which two syllables blend or merge together resulting in a single syllable which shares characteristics of the two original ones, e.g. *so I'll* becomes *swall*.

tail-clip A label for when a word loses its final syllable, e.g. *interested* becomes *interest*

teeny A label for occasions when -teen numbers (thirteen–nineteen) are heard as -ty numbers (thirty–ninety).

Tuesday-blend The process by which the first two consonants of Tuesday – |t| and |j| (yod) become a single consonant like the |tʃ| in *church*, resulting in Tuesday becoming *chewsday*. This is known as 'yod coalescence'.

vocal gymnastics A term used to refer to activities in pursuit of a listening goal which use learners' voices. They look and sound like 'pronunciation' activities going terribly wrong, but we do not use the term 'pronunciation' because of its negative connotations in terms of listening/decoding.

word-crusher A label for a classroom tool which uses the structure of a double-prominence speech unit, allowing learners to practise handling streamlining processes.

zone 1 The area in the speaker's vocal mechanisms where speech is created. This area is studied in articulatory phonetics

zone 2 The space through which speech travels on its way from speaker to hearer. This area is studied in acoustic phonetics.

zone 3 The space where speech arrives and is processed by the hearer. This area is studied in auditory phonetics.

References

Abercrombie, D. (1967). *Elements of general phonetics*. Edinburgh: Edinburgh University Press.

Alameen, G., & Levis, J. (2015). Connected speech. In M. Reed & J. Levis, *The Handbook of English Pronunciation*, 159–174. Chichester: Wiley Blackwell.

Bard, E. G., Anderson, A.H., Sotillo, C., Aylett, M., Doherty-Sneddon, G., & Newlands, A. (2000). Controlling the intelligibility of referring expressions in dialogue. *Journal of Memory and Language*, 42/1, 1–22.

Brazil, D. (1994). *Pronunciation for advanced learners of English*. Cambridge: Cambridge University Press.

Brinton, L.J. & Brinton, D.M. (2010), *The Linguistic Structure of Modern English*. Amsterdam: John Benjamins Publishing Company.

Bruckheimer, J. (Producer), J. Ronning & E. Sandberg (Directors). (2017). *Pirates of the Caribbean: Dead men tell no tales*. Walt Disney Studios.

Bolinger, D. (1986). The English beat: Some notes on rhythm. *Studies in Descriptive Linguistics*, 15, 36–49.

Brown, G. (1990). *Listening to spoken English*. 2nd Edition. London: Longman.

Buck, G. (1995). How to become a good listening teacher. In D.J. Mendelsohn, and J. Rubin (Eds) *A Guide for the teacher of second language listening*, 113–131. San Diego, CA: Dominie Press.

Carter, R., & McCarthy, M. J. (2006). *Cambridge grammar of English: A comprehensive guide to spoken and written grammar and usage*. Cambridge: Cambridge University Press.

Cauldwell, R. (2000). The Functional irrhythmicality of spontaneous speech: A Discourse View of Speech Rhythms. *Apples*, 2/1, 1–24.

Cauldwell, R. (2002). Grasping the nettle: the importance of perception work in listening comprehension. http://www.developingteachers.com

Cauldwell, R. (2015, February 16). Exploring recordings with mp3cut. [Blog post]. Retrieved from www.speechinaction.com/listening-cherrypick-01/

Cauldwell, R. (2016). *Jungle listening: Survival tips for fast speech*. [Draft materials available at www.speechinaction.com] Birmingham: Speech in Action.

Cauldwell, R. (2017). Pronunciation and listening: The case for separation. In O. Kang, R.I. Thomson, & J.M. Murphy, (Eds) *The Routledge handbook of contemporary English pronunciation* (pp. 352–369). Abingdon: Routledge.

Celce-Murcia, M., Brinton, D. M., & Goodwin, J. M. (2010). *Teaching pronunciation: A course book and reference guide*. Cambridge University Press.

Chinn, R. & Willoughby, M. (2016). 'The gap' - training teachers to develop learners' listening skills. Conference paper. IATEFL 2016.

Collins, B. & Mees, I.M. (2013). *Practical phonetics and phonology*. Abingdon: Routledge.

Cruttenden, A. (2014). *Gimson's pronunciation of English*. 8th Edition. Abingdon: Routledge.

Cunningham, S. & Moor, P. (2005). *New cutting edge: Upper intermediate*. Students' Book. Harlow: Pearson Education.

Cutler, A., & Carter, D. M. (1987). The predominance of strong initial syllables in the English vocabulary. *Computer Speech & Language*, 2/3, 133–142.

Dauer, R. M. (1983). Stress-timing and syllable-timing reanalyzed. *Journal of phonetics*, 11, 51–62.

Dellar, H. & Walkley, A. (2010) *Outcomes upper intermediate*. Andover, UK: Heinle Cengage Learning.

Dummet, P., Stephenson, H. & Lansford, L. (2017). *Keynote proficient*. Andover, UK: National Geographic Learning, Cengage Learning.

Ernestus, M. (2014). Acoustic reduction and the roles of abstractions and exemplars in speech processing. *Lingua*, 142, 27–41.

Field, J. (1997). Notes on listening: Authenticity. *Modern English Teacher*, 6, 49–52

Field, J. (1998a). Promoting perception: The Role of phonetics in diagnosing & rectifying breakdowns of understanding. *Journal of the English Language Centre, King's College London, 1*, 23–28.

Field, J. (1998b). The changing face of listening. *English Teaching Professional, 6*, 12–14.

Field, J. (2003). Promoting perception: Lexical segmentation in L2 listening. *ELT Journal, 57/4*, 325–334

Field, J. (2008a). Bricks or mortar: which parts of the input does a second language listener rely on? *TESOL quarterly, 42/3*, 411–432.

Field, J. (2008b). *Listening in the language classroom.* Cambridge: Cambridge University Press.

Field, J. (2009). More listening or better listeners? *English Teaching Professional, 61*, 12–111.

Field, J. (2015). The effects of single and double play upon listening test outcomes and cognitive processing. (AR-G/2015/003). London: British Council English Language Assessment Research Group.

Fraser, H. (2014). When teaching phonology isn't enough: Insights from mondegreens. *Speak Out! IATEFL PronSIG Newsletter, 50*, 42–45.

Fraser, H. (2017) Rethink speech. [Website] Retrieved from https://rethinkspeech.com.au/

Greenberg, S., & Fosler-Lussier, E. (2000, May). The uninvited guest: Information's role in guiding the production of spontaneous speech. In *Proceedings of the Crest Workshop on Models of Speech Production: Motor Planning and Articulatory Modelling* (pp. 129–132).

Grinberg, M. (2017). Catch the sound: Training auditory acuity for language learning. [Video file]. Retrieved from: https://tinyurl.com/yd5t8gua

Haga, Hellen. (2017). [Comment in online seminar on listening].EVO, 30Jan2017

Hancock, M. (2017). *PronPack 3: Pronunciation pairworks.* Chester: Hancock McDonald ELT.

Hancock, M. & McDonald, J. (2104) *Authentic listening resource pack.* DELTA Publishing: Peaslake.

Hasebe, Yoichiro. (2015) Design and implementation of an online corpus of presentation transcripts of TED Talks. Procedia: Social and Behavioral Sciences 198(24), 174–182.

Johns, T. (2002). Data-driven learning: The perpetual challenge. *Language and Computers, 42/1*, 107–117.

Johnson, K. (2004). Massive reduction in conversational American English. In *Spontaneous speech: Data and analysis. Proceedings of the 1st session of the 10th international symposium* (pp. 29–54). Tokyo, Japan: The National International Institute for Japanese Language.

Kjellin, O. (2017). Teaching and learning pronunciation with quality representation. Conference presentation. The 5ᵗʰ English Pronunciation: Issues & Practices Conference, Caen, France.

Laver, J. (1994). *Principles of phonetics.* Cambridge University Press.

Lindsey, G. (2012, January 22) Smoothing then and now [Blog post]. Retrieved from http://englishspeechservices.com/blog/smoothing-then-and-now/

Magnuson, J. S., Mirman, D., & Myers, E. (2013). Spoken word recognition. *The Oxford Handbook of Cognitive Psychology.* (pp. 412–441). Oxford: Oxford University Press.

Mankowska, A, Nowacka, M. & Kloczowska (2009). *"How much wood would a woodchuck chuck": English pronunciation practice book.* Krakow: Konsorcjum Akademiickie.

Mazzoni, D., & Dannenberg, R. (2000). Audacity [software]. Pittsburg. http://www.audacityteam.org/.

Nolan, F., & Kerswill, P. E. (1990). The description of connected speech processes. In S. Ramsaran, (Ed), *Studies in the pronunciation of English: A commemorative volume in honour of A.C. Gimson* pp. 295–316. London: Routledge.

Ogden, R. (2017). *An Introduction to English phonetics.* [2nd Edition]. Edinburgh: Edinburgh University Press.

Pinard, E. (2014). Autonomous listening skill development: activity 1. How do I help a learner get beyond 'just' listening? [Blog post] Retrieved from https://reflectiveteachingreflectivelearning.com/2014/05/22/autonomous-listening-skill-development-activity-1/

Port, R. F. (2007). The graphical basis of phones and phonemes, in O. S. Bohn, & M. J. Munro (Eds.). Language experience in second language speech learning: In honor of James Emil Flege, 349–365.

Flege, J. E. (2007). *Language experience in second language speech learning: In honor of James Emil Flege (Vol. 17).* John Benjamins Publishing.

Redston, C. & Cunningham, G. (2012). *face2face: Pre-intermediate: Students' book.* Cambridge: Cambridge University Press.

Ridgway, T. (2000). Listening strategies – I beg your pardon? *ELT Journal* 54/2, 179–185

Roach, P.J. (1982). 'On the distinction between "stress-timed" and "syllable-timed" languages', pp. 73–79, in D. Crystal (ed.) *Linguistic controversies,* London: Edward Arnold.

Roach, P.J. (2009). *English phonetics and phonology: A practical course.* 4th Edition. Cambridge: Cambridge University Press.

Roach, P.J., Setter, J., & Esling, J. (2011). *Cambridge English pronouncing dictionary.* [Originally edited by Daniel Jones]. [18th Edition] Cambridge: Cambridge University Press.

Robinson, K. (2006, February). Do schools kill creativity? [Video file]. Retrieved from https://www.ted.com/talks/ken_robinson_says_schools_kill_creativity

Rodero, E. (2012). A Comparative analysis of speech rate and perception in radio bulletins. *Text & Talk, 32*(3), 391–411.

Sergeeva, O. & Sukhomlin, K. (2017). TubeQuizard. [Website]. Retrieved from http://tubequizard.com

Shockey, L. (2003). *Sound patterns of spoken English. Oxford: Blackwell.*

Sullivan, S. (2017). Speechstream – helping adults to hear. *Speak Out! IATEFL Pronunciation Special Interest Group Journal,* 56, pp. 8–19.

Sweeney, S. (2016). Developing listening skills: Lessons from learning. Paper presented at the 50th annual conference of the International Association of Teachers of English as a Foreign Language. Birmingham, UK.

Sweeney, S. (2017). Grasping the nettle of fast speech: Developing listening skills. [Blog post]. Retrieved from https://teacherdevelopmentlab.wordpress.com/2017/04/18/ grasping-the-nettle/

Thorn, S. (2009). Mining listening texts. *Modern English Teacher,* 18/2, pp. 5–13.

Thorn, S. (2013). *Real lives, real listening.* [Series] Elementary, A2; Intermediate, B1–B2; Advanced, B2–C1. London Collins.

Tsui, A. B., & Fullilove, J. (1998). Bottom-up or top-down processing as a discriminator of L2 listening performance. *Applied linguistics, 19/4,* 432–451.

Vandergrift, L. & Goh, C.C.M. (2012). *Teaching and learning second language listening: Metacognition in action.* New York: Routledge

Vaughan-Rees, M. (2010). *Rhymes and rhythm.* Reading: Garnet Publishing Ltd.

Walker, R. (2010). *Teaching the pronunciation of English as a lingua franca.* Oxford: Oxford University Press.

Walker, R. (2015, November 22). Illegible accents. [Blog post]. Retrieved from https://englishglobalcom.wordpress.com/2015/11/22/illegible-accents/

Wells, J. C. (2006). *English intonation: An introduction.* Cambridge University Press.

Wells, J.C. (2008). *Longman pronunciation dictionary.* Harlow: Pearson Education.

Willis, J. (1981). *Teaching English through English.* Harlow: Longman.

Wilson, M. (2003). Discovery listening—improving perceptual processing. *ELT Journal, 57/4,* 335–343.

46332108R00145

Printed in Poland
by Amazon Fulfillment
Poland Sp. z o.o., Wrocław